PC Beginners
– First Steps –
Insider Guide

The absolute beginners book for those who haven't used a computer before

Bruce Smith
Stephen Copestake

Bruce Smith Books

PC Beginners
First Steps

© Bruce Smith and Stephen Copestake 1995
ISBN: 1-873308-45-0
First Edition: January1995

Typesetting:
Bruce Smith Books Ltd

All Trademarks and Registered Trademarks used are hereby acknowledged.

All rights reserved. No part of this publication may be reproduced or translated in any form, by any means, mechanical, electronic or otherwise, without the prior written consent of the copyright holder(s).

Disclaimer: While every effort has been made to ensure that the information in this publication (and any programs and software) is correct and accurate, the Publisher can accept no liability for any consequential loss or damage, however caused, arising as a result of using the information printed in this book.

E&OE

The rights of Bruce Smith and Stephen Copestake to be identified as the Authors of the Work has been asserted by them in accordance with the *Copyright, Design and Patents Act, 1988*

Bruce Smith Books is an imprint of Bruce Smith Books Limited.

Published by:
Bruce Smith Books Limited,
PO Box 382, St. Albans,
Herts, AL2 3JD.

Telephone: (01923) 894355
Fax: (01923) 894366.

Registered in England No. 2695164.
Registered Office: Worplesdon Chase, Worplesdon, Guildford, Surrey, GU1 3LA.

Repro by Ford Graphics Limited, Fordingbridge, Hants.

Printed and bound in the UK by Bell & Bain Ltd, Glasgow.

This book is one of many in the *Insider Guide* series from Bruce Smith Books. The *Insider Guide* series takes its name from the unique graphical panels which provide instant step-by-step guidance to performing essential tasks on your computer. These instant guides are complemented by a jargon-free tutorial to using the computer software with no assumptions made.

The *Insider Guide* concept has already proved itself, helping tens of thousands of beginners successfully use their computers, application software and programming languages.

PC Beginners First Steps

Contents

1 Welcome Home 13
Your Computer 15
Basic Terms 16
The Software 19

2 First Time Out 21

3 Starting Windows 25
The Pointer and Mouse 26
Mouse Matters 27
Screen Savers 28
Windows and Icons 28
Little and Large 34
Size is Everything 34
Just Scrolling 35

4 Menus and Icons 39
Control Menus 39
The Kyboard 42
Window Keys 45
Closing Windows 45
Icon Types 47
Windows Hang-Up 48

5 Files 'n Stuff 49
Saving Grace 52
Filing Cabinets 53
Back to Writes 56

6 File Manager 61
FM Selections 64
Making Directories 65
Navigating Directories 67
Renaming 68
Copy and Delete 69

7 Floppy Disks 71
More on Size 73
Formatting 74
Copying Across Disks 77
Multiple Copy or Move 78

8 Desktop Design 81
The Time 82
...The Place 83
Desktop 85
Wallpapering 86
Screen Savers 86
Bits 88
A Touch of Colour 88
Mouse and Keyboard 90
On Hold 92

9 Online Help 93
The Help Menu 94
The Search 96
Keyboard Revisited 97

10 PC Hardware 99
Powerful Stuff 99
Memory 101
Boards and Cards 104
Disk Drives 106

11 Program Manager 109
Program Groups 110
Switching 114
Cascade and Tile 116
More Tiles 119

12 Accessories 121
Clock 121
Calculator 122
Calendar 127

Printing Appointments 130

13 DOS Prompt 131
MS-DOS 131
Changing Times 134
File Format Functions 137
Wildcards 140
Next Time 141
WinDOS 141

14 Notepad 143
Working Notepad 144
Text Selection 145
Word Wrap 146
Inserting the Date/Time 148
Text Searches 148
Opening Files 149
Saving Your Work 150
Printing Your Work 150

15 Printer Choice 151
Types of Printer 152
Printing Types 154
PostScript Printing 157
Printing from Programs 158
Paper Chase 158
Background and Buffers 159
Inking Up 159

16 Print Manager 161
Connecting Up 161
Inner Workings 163
Working with PM 164
Job Priorities 168
Print Emphasis 168
Notepad 169

17 Write 171
   The Letter 172
   Working with Text 174
   Write Moves 175
   Saving Write 176
   Opening Write Files 177

18 Write On 179
   Face and Size 180
   Tabbing Text 182
   Aligning Text 184
   Line Spacings 185
   Using the Ruler 186
   Find and Replace 188
   Cut and Paste 190
   Headers and Footers 190
   Printing Write Documents 191

19 Fonts 193
   Window Fonts 194
   Fonts CP 196
   Charachter Map 197

20 The Clipboard 199
   Cut and Paste 200
   Transfering Text 200
   Transfering Graphics 202
   In the Family 203
   Viewing Clipboard Contents 203
   Load and Save 204
   Clipping DOS Data 204
   DOS-Windows Text Transfers 205
   Windows-DOS Text Transfers 206

21 Games 207
   Solitaire 208
   Scoring and Options 210
   Minesweeper 211

Staring to Play 212

22 Cardfile 213

Launching Cardfile 214
Completing a Card 214
Adding a New Card 215
Saving Your Database 216
Editing and Deleting 217
Card and List View 219
Adding Pictures 219
Merging Databases 220

23 Paintbrush 221

The Palettes 222
Keyboard Routes 224
Using Paintbrush 224
Curves and Polygons 226
Freehand Lines 227
Undo 227
Saving Your Work 227

24 More Paint 229

Pick and Scissors 230
The Airbrush Tools 232
The Roller 233
Pixel Editing 233
The Erasers 234
The Text Tool 236
Wallpaper 237

25 This and That 239

Desktop Housekeeping 239
Icon Tact 240
Automation 240
Recorder 243
Software Versions 246
AUTOEXEC 248
Goodbye 248

26 Free Software 249

Definitions 250
How to Get Shareware 251
Demos and Free Applications 253
Using It 253
Registration 254

27 New Software 255

Planning 256
Installation Options 258
Starting Installation 258
Duration 259
What if it Goes Wrong? 260
Installing DOS Programs 261
Removing Software 262

28 The Home Office 265

The Big Three 266
Wordprocessing 266
What's in a Word? 267
Editing and Checking 268
Presentation 269
Databases 269
What Do You Need? 270
Searching and Reporting 271
Relationships 272
Collecting Data 273
Spreadsheets 273
Manipulating Numbers 274
Text Labels and Reports 275
Integrated Software 275
Desktop Publishing 276
More Figure Work 276

29 Virus Menace 279

What Is It? 280
Viral Types 281
Prevention 282
Finally 283

30 Multimedia **285**
Books on CD 287
PhotoCD 287
Movies on CD 287
Authoring Programs 288
More! 288

A Bruce Smith Books **289**

Index **295**

PC Beginners First Steps

Insider Guides

- #1: Your computer's hardware ...17
- #2: Identifying Windows and Prompts ...23
- #3: The Windows desktop ...29
- #4: Opening Main Accessories ...31
- #5: Minimizing and Maximizing ...33
- #6: Resizing a window ...36
- #7: Multiple Maximized windows ...41
- #8: Starting Write ...50
- #9: The Write Window ...51
- #10: A hierarchical filing system ...57
- #11: Save and Open in Write ...59
- #12: File Manager Anatomy ...63
- #13: Creating a directory ...67
- #14: Floppy disk anatomy ...73
- #15: Filenames ...79
- #16: Creating a Write Disk ...80
- #17: International Settings ...84
- #18: Editing Desktop patterns ...87
- #19: Password Set ...89
- #20: Colour Anatomy ...91
- #21: Contents Help – Write ...95
- #22: Inside the case ...103
- #23: Selecting the tile order ...117
- #24: Number base conversion ...125
- #25: Customising a calendar ...129
- #26: Anatomy of a DIR listing ...135
- #27: Cut and Paste ...147
- #28: Wonderful world of printers ...155
- #29: Print Manager anatomy ...163
- #30: Print Manager Setup ...165
- #31: Adding new printers ...167
- #32: Write anatomy ...173
- #33: Using the Ruler ...187
- #34: Header and Footers ...189
- #35: Font types and font sizes ...195
- #36: Text Cut and Paste ...201
- #37: Scoring at Solitaire ...209
- #38: Using Find ...217
- #39: Paintbrush anatomy ...223
- #40: Icon tidy ...241
- #41: Making a Canary System disk ...282

1 Welcome Home

It cost a lot of money but do you really understand what you have let yourself in for?

Be positive – there's a great time ahead!

Technology is daunting isn't it? A year after I purchased a new all-singing, all-dancing video recorder I'm still struggling to set the time and date let alone make it sing and dance. Yes, I know what you're saying or at least thinking. This guy can't use his video recorder but he is supposed to be showing me how to use my computer. Fair comment, but hear me out here as there is an underlying moral to this tale which will give you hope.

Fifteen years ago, I didn't know a thing about computers either, but like you probably are now, I was fascinated by their potential and what they held for the future. Of course, they were very much more basic then they are now and to be capable of the sort of tasks your PC performs would have required a house full of computers, but that's by-the-by.

With no books available then and little in the way of magazines I set about teaching myself the hard way – using the manuals and experimenting. It worked and even today I get a real kick out of experimenting with all the bits. I was keen to learn how to use the computer, I was motivated to do it and I provided the requisite amount of time and effort to do so. I can't really get excited about putting the same sort of hard work into sorting out that VCR and so recordings are done on the fly or the machine is used to replay hired movies.

The point is simple – if you really want to learn how to use your computer, you will need to apply yourself and be prepared to make mistakes and think a bit about what you are going to do and what you have done. What this book provides, I hope, is some real down-to-earth tuition drawing on my memories of what I found difficult to comprehend and also the things that all those around me took for granted. It was so simple to them, that they did not provide an explanation – they just assumed I knew it.

One of the biggest hindrances is the *jargon* – the words and terms that seem to have come from a degree course on computers which are used and applied to computers and all their associated bits and pieces, and seem to bar the way ahead. Unfortunately these items of jargon grow with every new topic and I've already used a few instances of it in these opening paragraphs when referring to video recorders. But terms such as VCR are now an everyday occurrence. It's getting that way with computers as well which makes learning from scratch a bit harder simply because of that assumption factor. So, the intention in this book is to keep it simple with a motto of *'Don't use one word when three will do'*. That's not to pad the book out but simply to keep it easy to read – the last thing you want is to be working out the meaning of some nine letter word while trying to learn a new concept.

We'll also try to avoid the chicken and egg syndrome as much as possible – to that end there may be the occasional white lie. Well, not so much of a lie as an over-simplification or slight stretching of the truth but necessary when you need to know two new concepts in one go to understand one other. But we'll own up with apologies at the relevant points – honest!

What you will need to do is to read through the chapters as they happen. Don't skip from one to another as you will almost certainly miss out on some building block material. The main thrust of the first part of the book is to move you through the familiarity minefield, getting you used to using and occasionally abusing your computer. From there we'll look into what you can do with it and, most importantly, just how to use it. And, providing you join in and try the examples we give and then create a few of your own, by the time you reach the last page, you'll be wondering what all the fuss was about.

PC Beginners First Steps

So long as you follow this plan of action, I guarantee you'll have no problems and that you will break the computer barrier – you will need to put the effort in though.

Your Computer

PC stands for *Personal Computer* – other terms that you might hear associated with this are IBM PC or *compatible*. IBM are a major American company that produced the first PC which proved to be very popular. However, the IBM PC was generally a business machine and was produced as such which made it very expensive. At around this time the electronics revolution was taking place in the Far East where everything was being made smaller and cheaper. So much so that some companies were so successful that had to move into smaller premises! But seriously, what happened was that these companies produced cheaper versions of the same PCs – clones if you like – and to identify that they were identical in every aspect to the IBM PC they were called *Compatibles*.

Since then things have come a long way and generally this distinction is not made so much because it is taken as read, but there has been an absolute flood of numerous types of PC into the shops. It would be impossible to name every make but some of the more popular ones are Compaq, Packard Bell, Amstrad, Viglen, and Olivetti. You may have one of these or another make – it doesn't matter which because they all offer essentially the same basic functions. Look out of your front window and you will probably see a street full of cars – chances are there will be Fords, BMWs, Rovers, Renaults and so on. All different makes but all are cars.

The car scenario is useful to continue with, because there are cars and there are cars! All work in the same way but the models can differ drastically in what they offer. A BMW 7 series has seats, doors, engine, four wheels and so forth. So does a Renault Clio, but the BMW will have a bigger more powerful engine, alloy wheels, leather interior and many additional extras. Then again the Clio does have Nicole! PCs are much the same, there are many makes and models. More expensive models have extra facilities and like cars are more powerful in that they can operate faster. Obviously I haven't got any idea what type of PC you have but I do know what parts it has because these are standard and as such everything in this book is 100% applicable.

Although the PC is the most popular computer in the world it isn't the only mode of computing. Let's go back to the car scenario for a moment. As we have established there are many different types of cars. However, they are not the only form of motor transport. In addition to travelling by car you can also travel by motorbike and bus to name two.

In a similar fashion there are many different types of computer – the PC is one type (which itself has many different makes and models). Other popular types that you might have seen advertised include the Apple Macintosh and Commodore Amiga. These other types of computer are not generally compatible with PCs in that they achieve the end results in different ways. I'll come back to this in due course, but if it helps think of this by relating to a bus which runs on diesel and a car which runs on petrol. They both go from A to B but use different types of fuel to get there and the fuels are not interchangeable. You wouldn't put diesel in a car that only accepted normal petrol as they are *incompatible*.

Basic Terms

When you get or got your PC home you shouldn't have had too much trouble fitting it together. Most of the plugs are not interchangeable and can only be fitted into the socket made for them. A basic PC system will comprise four main components:

- The main computer
- The screen
- The keyboard
- The mouse

You may also have a fifth item:

- The printer

These physical items are called the *hardware*. The computer is contained within the main *box*. In some instances this may also be part of the screen, but this is the exception rather than the rule. If you were to look inside this box (please don't or you will invalidate your guarantee and may give yourself a shock) you would find that most of it was empty space. This is because the various bits can generate quite a lot of heat and this needs to be removed. Many computers therefore have

Insider Guide #1 – Your computer's hardware

The PC system consists of five basic components. The central point is the main PC box itself. This comes either as a desktop system or as a tower (upright) system which is pictured right. The difference between the two is aesthetic – the tower system is free-floor standing and therefore provides more desktop space; however it is not always practical to access if you are using items such as floppy disks a lot.

All other components plug into the main PC box – generally at the rear.

This includes the screen (monitor or VDU) pictured right. These are available in a large number of makes but all offer the same basic features.

The keyboard allows you to enter information into your PC. Most keyboards have a numeric keypad on the right – this allows quick number entry.

The final component is the mouse (right); this is a relatively easy-to-use device which you move across the desk. This movement is mirrored by a pointer on screen which can be used to select items on the screen. Although sounding complicated it is very intuitive.

NOTE: If you are using a portable PC then the keyboard will be integrated within the main box itself and the screen will be built into the lid that flips up. The screen in this case may be either colour or black and white.

an internal fan which is used to cool it down by moving air through it and for this reason you should *never* cover the venting slots that you will find either on the side or at the back of your PC. The fan may also be responsible for the whirring noise that you hear while your PC is turned on.

The actual part of the computer which does all the hard computing work is quite small. In fact it and all the various supporting parts are held on a small *board* that is normally no larger than a magazine! However, there are a number of other boards that contain the electronics that allow your PC to work with all the various bits you attach to it. In addition there is the power supply – this is where the mains lead goes into and which takes the mains electricity and converts it into the type of electricity that the computer uses. You wouldn't see this as it is fitted inside the main box. The main box will also play home for the *hard* and *floppy* disk drives which we'll explain in due course.

One important point to make here is that you should never move this main computer box when it is switched on – again I'll explain why later.

The three other components on the list, and also the printer if you have one, all plug directly into the main box although on occasions the small *mouse* plugs into the keyboard. The mouse and keyboard are the means by which you will make selections and enter information into your computer.

The keyboard shouldn't present you with too many difficulties. Think of it as a typewriter; certainly if you having any typing skills these will be invaluable. If you don't then the two-fingers approach is fine and you will gain speed with experience. The mouse that I have referred to is called such because the lead that connects it to the computer is supposed to represent its tail. (In some cases you might have a *cordless* mouse. This is a mouse that operates by infra-red in a similar fashion to your TV or VCR remote control.) When your PC is turned on you will use this to pick off selections by an amazingly simple process.

The final base component is the screen. This is often referred to as the *video unit* or the *monitor*. As a rule this is not a television because it doesn't have the TV receiver fitted to it. It is normally a dedicated item of hardware that is designed solely for use with your PC. When you are setting up your PC try to install it somewhere where it will not be in the line of direct sunlight, otherwise you might find trying to view the monitor screen difficult. You probably took that into consideration with the placement of your TV – for similar reasons.

The final item that you might have supplied as standard is a printer. This is not a vital item for the operation of the PC in the way that the other bits of hardware are. For this reason it is often referred to as a *peripheral*.

Almost certainly your computer will have been supplied with a variety of manuals, cards and forms. As a matter of course you should locate your registration card which is used to register your PC with the maker. If you have bought your PC from one of the major stores then your receipt will normally form the guarantee with them and shouldn't affect your normal statutory rights in anyway. However, it is still a good idea to send off the card.

The Software

We have used the term *hardware* to describe the physical components of your PC. The other major aspect of computing is the *software*. The software is the programs that you use on your computer to enable you to work with it. Bear with me for a while as this is one of those chicken and egg situations.

You probably have some form of hi-fi in your home. This is likely to include a cassette tape player or perhaps even a CD player. Well think of the CD player as being the hardware and the music on the CD itself as being the software. You can't physically *see* or *feel* it but you are well aware that it is there.

All computers need software. Without it they're as much use as a CD player without a CD to play on it. The software is supplied in the form of diskettes or disks (sometimes also spelt disc) which are inserted into the disk drive in the front of the main computer box. The disk contains the information that makes the computer work and operate in a particular way. For example, you will have certainly seen adverts for computer games. In many cases these are supplied on disk which can be played on the computer. A very popular reason for purchasing a PC is to have a wordprocessor in the home or office. A wordprocessor is effectively a very modern typewriter. The information to make your PC act as a wordprocessor is supplied on a disk.

The collective name for games and items such as wordprocessors is *programs*. Note that the American spelling is used, ie not programme.

Quite often you might hear someone say that they have purchased a new program for their PC. Another distinction is also made in that when you purchase a program to perform a very specific task – such as wordprocessing or maybe accounting – it is normally referred to as an *application*.

You will probably find a number of disks supplied with your computer; some of these might be for special applications and programs that have been supplied with your computer. For example, popular additions are Windows, Microsoft Works and Microsoft Office. Keep these in a safe place for now. Chances are that when you purchased your computer they were put *on* the computer for you so that they are available to use right away.

A word of warning. You must remember that with almost all commercial software you have normally only bought a right to license the product. You do *not* own it. The terms of such a license is such that you can only use it on one PC – if you use it on a second PC or *give* a copy to a friend (or indeed they give you a copy) you are effectively participating in software theft – also known as software piracy – and this is punishable by law. However, not all software is sold in this way and there are other types that you can get on a try-and-buy (if you like it) basis. This is a subject I'll deal with in Chapter 26.

For now though, let's look at what happens when you take the plunge and switch it on!

2 First Time Out

You need to know what you have in order to be sure where you are going.

Turning on for the first time can reveal an awful lot if you watch out!

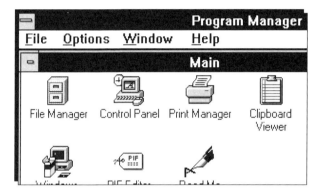

When you're happy that you've plugged everything in correctly (there's no harm in double checking) you can turn on at the plug. When you have done this, flick the switch on your PC – you might also need to turn the monitor on as well. Some PCs have these two integrated together, some as separate items. All being well your PC should now start to come to life. This is normally signified by a series of sounds. The first may be a bell followed by a whirring. If there is a loudish thump this could well be the monitor bursting into life!

A quick look at the monitor screen should show you that things are indeed happening in that various messages – many of which will mean absolutely nothing to you – are displayed one after the other. If nothing happens then do the obvious and check all the connections and that you have indeed turned everything on before starting again.

Assuming that all is well your PC is now *booting-up*. This great term simply means that it is going through an initialisation process that does a number of things including checking what hardware it has attached and setting the software into motion. (If you like, think that when you turn the switch on the electricity gives your PC a boot up the backside to get it going!) This software forms part of the software that has already been put on the computer for you – as mentioned earlier. Much of this software is of a technical nature that is there to make your PC work – but it is worthwhile just sitting and watching this process a few times so that you get familiar with it. This can be a help in future should anything ever go wrong with your PC – you might be able to identify the problem.

Just how long this process takes will depend on your particular PC. But generally you should allow a minute or so. You will normally know when this moment arrives because it will go comparatively quiet and if you have a flashing light at the front of your main PC box this will cease to flash rapidly. What you are presented with on your monitor screen at the end of all this activity will depend on what comes as part of your computer package. There are generally three options:

- Windows
- Prompt
- Custom

Windows is the most popular software to use to control PCs. If you watched your computer going through its start-up process you will know if you have Windows because a large logo identifying the fact will have been displayed. If you didn't see it have a look at your screen now – if it contains a large rectangle with the title 'Program Manager' displayed at the top of it, you have Windows.

If your screen displays as a black background with a small amount of writing similar to this:

```
C:>_
```

with a small flashing line after it, then you have a *prompt* display.

If you have anything else – such as several large squares with words or pictures in – then you almost certainly have a custom display which has been provided by the manufacturer of your PC.

For the purpose of this book you need to be running the Windows software. If you are already 'in' Windows then you can go straight onto the next chapter of this book. If you have the prompt display then carefully press the following three keys on the keyboard: W, I and N. The screen will show:

PC Beginners First Steps

Insider Guide #2 – Identifying Windows & Prompt

Windows is becoming the most popular software to use on the PC. If you want to determine if you already have Windows working on your PC simply look at your screen.

Pictured right is the famous Windows logo – if you see this while your computer is turning itself on then you have Windows. At the end of the booting-up period you should be presented with a 'window' that is titled Program Manager.

This is illustrated – note that your particular version of the Program Manager display might be a little different as for reasons that you will gradually become aware of, no two displays are ever exactly the same. The key is the title Program Manager.

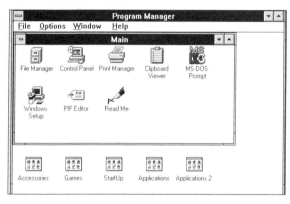

This final screen picture (right) shows how the prompt display looks. If you have this you might still have Windows available to you. The best way to try this is to type:

WIN

at the keyboard and press the big back-to-front L-shaped key.

or:

```
        C:>WIN_
```

```
        C>:win_
```

Now press the large key on the keyboard that is shaped like a back-to-front L. This may have the words 'Enter' or 'Return' on it. In either case you will find it located immediately at the end of the two middle rows of keys. At this your PC will respond with some activity that should result in Windows being activated.

If you think you have a custom display then examine it to see if it allows you to select Windows. If this is signified on the screen (or if it isn't) you will need to consult the booklet that was supplied to you with your computer which provides details on how to use your custom display.

If neither of the above methods work then check the documentation with your PC and in particular the sales literature. It is possible, though unlikely, that Windows was not part of the package that you purchased. Or it might also be possible that the Windows software has been supplied but not yet put onto the computer.

The Windows software is quite complex and is supplied on a number of disks. It is not something you should undertake right now unless you have a bit more knowledge of what you are doing. Unless you know someone who has the experience to put the software on the computer for you I would strongly suggest you read the next few chapters of this book until you do.

3

Starting Windows

Windows is one of the most popular pieces of PC software. But what is it and how does it work?

Read on...

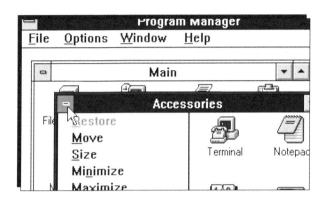

With a bit of luck, and no mean skill on your behalf, you should at this point be in Windows. Just to recap remember that Windows is the software that is currently being run by your PC. Although it doesn't look like it at the moment, your PC is performing thousands of actions every second and is now waiting for you to do something. But hold on a second – there is one question that hasn't been answered that you may have been asking. What is Windows and what is it for?

Okay that's two questions but the answer is essentially the same. Put simply Windows is the software that allows you to control and manage your PC. From it you can do just about anything in computer terms, from putting other programs on your computer to running them once they are in place. What's more it allows you to do this and other housekeeping chores in a very logical and visual manner. This interaction with the PC is often termed interfacing and because Windows does this in a very graphical nature it is often termed a graphical user interface – GUI for short.

GUI is one term for Windows but another more common term is WIMP. This stands for:

Windows
Icons
Menus
Pointer

These are effectively the four main areas that you will work in. This may seem a bit contrived but once you have mastered these four areas of Windows you will be able to use virtually every program you run from it. Windows and other Windows-based programs have been produced so that they all look and feel much the same just to ensure that this is the case. Although what the program may produce as an end result, (a wordprocessor a text document, an accounting program a set of profit and loss reports) how you go about achieving that end result is largely identical. It really is very clever.

But moving on, let's take last things first!

The Pointer and Mouse

If you look at the Windows display on your monitor you should be able to locate an arrow head or more correctly the outline of an arrow head. This is the *pointer* and this is controlled through the mouse. The mouse should be sitting next to your keyboard or by the computer so that the buttons are at the top. Just give it a nudge and notice how the pointer moves a bit as well. Try resting your hand on top of the mouse and gently move it left, right, away from you (up) and towards you (back). The pointer should follow suit.

By moving the mouse in the appropriate direction you can make the pointer traverse every point on the screen. Your reaction to this might be that you're going to need a hellishly big desk to be able to reach every part of the screen. Not so, because you can use a technique called *lift and move* (Actually I like to call it Mouse Droppings but my wife said I couldn't say that in a book.). In fact you can reach every part of the screen comfortably by using an area of the desk no more than six inches square. You see Windows only knows that the mouse is moving when the little ball in its base rotates and sends a signal back down its lead to the computer. So when you get to the edge of the area it is comfortable for you to move in, simply lift the mouse up and move it in the air, back to the other side of the space available and put it back on the desk. You can then carry on moving.

For example, to move the pointer to the right, push the mouse a few inches to the right and watch the pointer move. Then lift the mouse and move it back to where you started from and, with the mouse back on the desk, move to the right again. A few moments of practice is worthwhile so have a go – you'll soon get the hang of it.

Mouse Matters

If you find that your mouse is moving but the pointer isn't (or is labouring to do so) it may be that the desk you are using doesn't have a suitable surface to create the friction needed to grip and turn the ball in the base of the mouse.

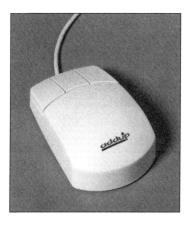

For this reason the purchase of a *mouse mat* is an excellent idea. You may already have one, but if you don't this is simply a small square of rubber-like material that is ideal for the mouse to move on. They generally only cost a few pounds and are worthwhile investments. In addition to providing a platform for your mouse to waltz around on they also reduce the amount of dust and fluff that can accumulate inside your mouse and detract from its performance.

If you need a short-term solution then try using the cover of this or a similar book – or at least experiment with other surfaces until you find one that is easy to use with the mouse.

Screen Savers

No, this isn't an organisation for the rescue of drowning monitors but a special bit of software built into Windows. If you leave Windows running for a minute or so without making any attempts at using the mouse or the keyboard, Windows goes to sleep. Visually what happens is that the *normal* display is replaced by a dark one that has moving objects on it – and almost certainly these will look like different size versions of the Windows logo.

Don't Panic! This is normal. Move the mouse an inch or so and see how the Windows display comes back. The software that automatically runs when you don't use your computer is called a *screen saver*. The inside of your monitor is covered with a phosphorescent chemical that is used to create the image you see. If the same image is left on the screen for a long period then the image can become *burnt-in* – in other words etched onto the inside of the screen. This normally takes a long time to happen but the accumulative periods soon add up. The screen saver prevents this from happening.

Note that this screen saver is only in operation when Windows is running.

Windows and Icons

Windows gets its name because it uses a series of boxes called *windows* to display information. For the most part this information is represented as small pictures or icons. These picture icons are normally fairly unique in the way they look and they also have a name which, along with the image, allows you to readily identify exactly what they are.

The screen that has the title Program Manager within it is a window and from an operational point of view it is the most important one because it will normally contain everything else. Within its bounds will be other windows and icons.

Now I have a small problem in that I cannot be entirely sure what is shown on your screen, because this will depend on how Windows has been loaded and if anything has been done with it prior to this point. So take a look at your screen and see if you can see another window called Main that contains numerous small icons. If you can, fine – if not look to see if you can see a small icon called Main. You will have one or the other. If it is the small icon called Main you will need to

Insider Guide #3 – The Windows desktop

No two desktops are the same – that said they all do exhibit the same features. So while your desktop may look a little different from the one illustrated here all the requisite bits and pieces are there.

The main feature of the desktop is the Program Manager and this is (normally) a window. This window may have other windows inside it – such as the one called Main in the illustration. Windows are like boxes into which you can place and organise other items of your desktop.

Windows have names which are displayed in the Title Bar across the top of the window. They can also be made larger and smaller both vertically and horizontally.

Windows also have menus contained in a menu bar – these are given names and can be used to gain access to functions listed on the menus that can be displayed using the mouse.

The items inside windows are small pictures called icons. These represent things that you can do or things that you have created using Windows.

Icons can also exist outside of the windows and these are special icons which can be expanded into full sized windows such as Main. Equally, windows such as Main can be made smaller into an iconised form.

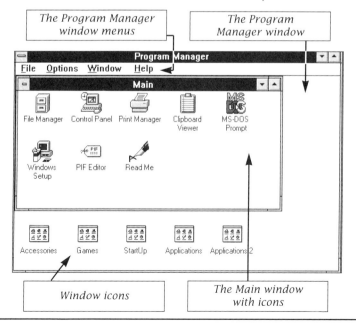

open it to display the Main window. To do this move the mouse so that the pointer is positioned over the small square displayed above the heading.

Now look at the mouse and you will see that there are two buttons within it at the front. This are called the left and right mouse buttons for obvious reasons. With one finger press the left mouse button twice but very quickly. Just imagine you were playing a game with a stopwatch and wanted to see how long it took you to start and then stop it. If you do it right then the Main icon will magically transform into a window called Main that itself contains icons. If this didn't happen try that double mouse click again, making sure that the tip of the pointer is itself over the icon. This double-click process using the left mouse button is called *double-clicking*. Thus if a book or manual says double click on such-and-such you move the mouse so that the pointer is over the icon in question and then press the left mouse button very quickly twice.

The Main window is a typical window as far as Windows is concerned in that it exhibits all the normal characteristics – let's examine each of these in turn.

Windows such as Main can be moved around the screen and re-positioned by dragging them. Dragging is achieved using the mouse and the left mouse button again. The first thing you must do is to select the Main window – in this instance *select* means make it the *active* window. You do this by moving the Pointer so that it is positioned over the window – it can be anywhere over it – and then pressing the left mouse button once. You should instantly notice that the bar running across the window (and containing its title) becomes highlighted. This bar is called the *title bar*. To drag the Main window (or any other window), first select it and then move the pointer so that its tip is within the title bar. It doesn't matter where but positioning it centrally over the window title is sensible. Now press the left mouse button down and keep it pressed down. With the left mouse button depressed move the mouse – as you do so the Main window should move with it like some large pointer.

You can move the window to any position within the Program Manager window, at which point if you release the left mouse button the window will be fixed in that position, or at least until you move it again. Pick the Main window up again and move it randomly around the screen – notice how you can move it over anything that may be on the screen. For example, you can move it over other windows and

PC Beginners First Steps

Insider Guide #4 – Opening Main Accessories

Opening windows is easy-peasy. The two main windows you will use in your formative period are Main and Accessories. If your Windows set up already has these open then you are a step ahead.

The first thing to do is to locate the small windows icon bearing the name of the window you are seeking.

Then move the mouse so that the arrow pointer is sitting over the top of the icon. To open the icon into a window you need to double-click on the left mouse button. Do this very quickly – if the window doesn't open, try again until it does.

If you can't get the window open, then check your pointer position and double-click really quickly.

---

icons. If you move it over any of these and release the mouse button then the window will be left where it is, positioned on the window or icon below it.

This window-moving is a fundamental Windows technique so do try it a few times until you are comfortable with it.

All windows can display a menu and this is displayed using the mouse, pointer and left mouse button again. The menu is located in the windows Control menu box which occupies the top left hand corner of the Main window immediately to the left of the title bar. Move the pointer so its tip is sitting over the small square in the middle and then press and keep pressed the left mouse button. A menu will pop down looking like the one shown overleaf. Keep the mouse button depressed for a moment.

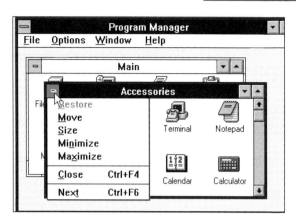

This menu is a standard window item and you will find it and its contents on every window you open in Windows. There are seven items listed down the menu – these are:

>Restore
>Move
>Size
>Minimize
>Maximize
>Close
>Next

We'll come back to these before the end of the chapter – so for now let go of the mouse button and the menu will disappear. (If it doesn't, try depressing the left mouse button again. That should do the trick.)

While this menu appears on every window that you open, there are also a set of general menus that apply to Windows itself – these are all encompassing. If you look at the Program Manager title bar you should be able to see another bar located under this which contains a number of headings within it.

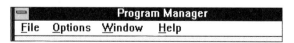

These are the Windows menus and as a matter of course these should be labelled:

>File   Options   Window   Help

PC Beginners First Steps

Insider Guide #5 – Minimizing and Maximizing

Windows are a way of life in Windows. They can be made to dominate the screen or hidden away for later use. These processes are called Maximizing and Minimizing.

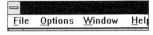

The tools to control this process are located in the extreme top right hand corner of any window.

To Maximize a window – move the pointer so that it sits over the up-arrow and click on the left mouse button once. The window will zoom to the full size of the desktop.

To minimize a window locate the pointer over the down-arrow in the top right hand corner of the window and click once.

The window will be reduced to a minimized icon form. If you minimize the Program Manager then the screen will clear. To restore a minimized window move the pointer over the icon and double-click the left mouse button quickly.

These names refer to the names of the menus that pop down from them. You can look at these menus in much the same way as described on the previous page. Move the mouse so that the pointer tip is located within the word *File*. Press the left mouse button to display the File menu. Note that the menu will displayed even if you release the left mouse button. You can look at what the other menus contain simply by pointing at them and pressing the left mouse as you have just done. To get out of a menu either click the mouse button again (with the pointer the menu name) or move the mouse pointer to a clear area of the Program Manager and press the left mouse button once.

Little and Large

If you examine the top right corner of the Program Manager window you will notice a couple more gadgets that you can use. There should be two small boxes which contain small arrow-heads, one pointing up and the other pointing down. These are in fact *buttons* which can be used to make the Program Manager window either little or large.

The little button is the one that has the arrow head pointing down and this is used to turn the window into an icon. It does this by shrinking it – or in Windows parlance, minimizing it. Try clicking on this button.

NB: Clicking is a new term I have just introduced. You should now be familiar with this process – move the pointer so that its tip is over the required item and then press the left mouse button once.

When you do this, the world in front of you will disappear. The screen will probably go white and all that remains in (probably) the bottom left hand corner is a small icon with the label Program Manager under it. You have minimized the Program Manager. To get it back to its previous state we need to maximize the Program Manager icon. This can be done by double-clicking on the Program Manager icon.

NB: Remember to double click – move the pointer so the tip is placed over the icon itself and then press the left mouse button twice very quickly.

If you don't do this quickly enough you may find that the Program Manager's Control menu appears. If this happens, simply double click again.

The other *up-arrow* button on the Program Manager window converts the window into a full-sized window that will occupy the whole of the screen area. Try clicking on it to see the effect. You will notice that the yellow Program Manager window border has gone and also that the up-arrow button has been replaced by a double-headed arrow. This simply indicated that the window is at its full extent. If you now click on this button, Program Manager will revert to its window state.

Size is Everything

This minimizing and maximizing of windows is useful for a number of reasons, not least because it can make you more space on the desktop. Oos – another new word. *Desktop* in this context refers to your screen – it's the area in which you can do all your work. Just like your desk at home, office or school you can place, move and reposition items to work with. The Windows desktop is no different in this respect as you have already seen.

But this changing of size is quite drastic and more often a subtle increase or decrease in size is all that is required. This, like most things in Windows, is possible. Making a window bigger or smaller is called *resizing* and as with everything else requires the use of the mouse, pointer and left mouse button (of course!).

Locate the window called Main. If you cannot see it, then it might be in the form of an icon in which case you can open it by double clicking on it. If you look carefully at the window you should see that a thin yellow line runs all around its perimeter. This is the sizing line. Carefully move the mouse so that the tip of the pointer is sitting over this line bounding the bottom edge of the window. Magic – notice that the pointer has changed from an arrow head to a two-pronged arrow head. Now press the left mouse button down and keep it depressed as you move the mouse down (or up) to make the window larger or smaller. In fact as you move the mouse you'll notice that an outline of the box's current *new size* appears. When you have reached the required size you can release the left mouse button and the box will re-draw itself to the new size.

In addition to making the box deeper you can also make it wider in an identical fashion by dragging out one of the edges on either side of the window. You do this exactly as described above. If you want to make the window both deeper and wider you could simply do both of the above. However, if you move the pointer into one of the corners of the window you'll see that the double arrow head is a slanted one. If you drag this you'll see that it automatically pulls both edges with it. Try it!

Just Scrolling

The final aspect of a window that we have yet to look at is the scroll bars. If you look at the Main window you might notice that it has a thinnish bar running down its right edge with a different type of arrow button at the top and bottom. If this isn't the case then make the height of the window smaller using the sizing method just outlined. This should make them appear.

Scroll bars allow you to move over items that are held within a window, when the window isn't big enough to show all its contents. It's a bit like looking through a telescope or view finder of a camera – you

PC Beginners First Steps

Insider Guide #6 – Resizing a window

Windows are a bit like credit cards – not that you can use them as an aide spendoire but because they are your flexible friends. You can resize them using a point and drag technique. To enlarge a window either in height or width:

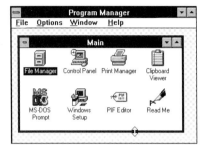

1. Click in the window you require to make it active and bring it to the front of the desktop.

2. Move the pointer to the appropriate edge of the window. As the pointer reaches the yellow border line it will change into a two-way arrow.

3. Press and hold down the left mouse button.

4. Drag the pointer in the direction required to make the window larger (or smaller).

5. When you reach the desired point release the mouse button.

You can resize in both directions at once by dragging from one of the window's corners. When you move the pointer into a corner it turns into a diagonal double-headed arrow as shown left.

see just a small part of the universe and have to move the telescope or camera around to be able to piece it together.

Windows are much the same – there is no real practical limit to what they may contain and they may often contain more than you can see through the open area displayed. Even maximizing the size of the window may not be good enough. To enable you to look through the window at all areas, scroll bars are provided. If you think of the area of the window displayed as a view-finder you can nudge this up and down the length of the total size of the window by clicking on the scroll-up or scroll-down arrows. In between the two scroll arrows is the scroll bar – and within this you should be able to find the scroll box. Whereas the scroll arrows nudge the window view in the relative direction, you can drag the scroll box to move directly to a point within the window. This is done by placing the pointer over the scroll box, pressing down the left mouse button (and keeping it depressed) before *dragging* the box up or down the bar as required. As always a bit of practice here is worth a thousand words from me so experiment!

4

Menus and Icons

Choice can be a difficult thing so simple menus make the process a simple matter.

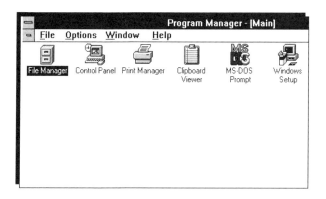

At this point you are hopefully feeling a little bit more at ease with your PC and starting to feel happy with your use of Windows. In fact you have already learnt and hopefully mastered many of the basic techniques that you will need through the rest of your working time with the PC. However, there are two more areas that we need to look at more fully to complete that information base – both of which we touched on briefly in the last chapter – menus and icons. We'll start off first with the use of menus.

Control Menus

The Control menu is a window menu – every window has its own Control menu and they are all the same. All menus, be they Control or general in nature provide a list of items – menu choices if you like – from which you can select items. Making a selection is done by moving the pointer to the item on the menu you require and clicking on it.

Once you have selected an item normally one of two things happens. The most straightforward is that the item that you selected is actioned – carried out. Or, alternatively a new window appears from which you have to either make further selections or type information into. The second option is a special window known as a *dialogue box* and will be discussed in a later chapter.

To see a Control menu ensure that the Main window is displayed and move the pointer to the Control menu box and press the left mouse button. As suggested in the last chapter you don't have to keep the button depressed as the menu should stay visible.

A typical Control menu is illustrated above and if you refer back to what was discussed in the last chapter you might realise that these actions are pretty much the same as the various actions we performed using various buttons and arrows. They are! For example, let's select the Minimize option. To do this move the pointer over the option and click the left mouse button. The Main window shuts and reverts to a small icon. To revive the Main window you can either double click on its icon or – click on the icon once to reveal the Control menu and select Maximize.

If you have done the last step you will get a fully maximized window – one that occupies the whole screen. It does not restore the window to its previous state. To do this select the Restore option on the Control menu. But beware now, because the maximized Main window is held within the Program Manager window. The Main control menu (and that of any other windows that you might subsequently maximize) is immediately below that of the Program Manager's Control menu box and to the right of the File menu in the menu bar. In a like fashion the Minimize and Maximize icons are combined into one at the opposite end of the Window menu bar. This can be a bit confusing at the start but as you can easily change the effect of clicking the wrong button you'll soon learn by your mistakes (and there's no better way to learn!).

PC Beginners First Steps

Insider Guide #7 – Multiple Maximized windows

With maximized windows the Program manager window is always the dominant window. As such its sizing controls are always the upper most.

Things can become confusing if you then maximize a second window. The second window's sizing controls sit under the Program Manager's controls. In the illustration below the Main window is maximised and its sizing controls are contained as a double arrow inside one box below those of the Program Managers.

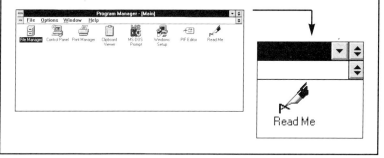

Back to options – the Control menu. The Close option has much the same effect as Minimize and both Move and Size start the process of allowing you to move the position of a window or alter its size. When you select either of these two the pointer changes into a cross-hairs arrowhead. With Move selected you can pick up the title bar and drag the window around the desktop. With Size selected you can pick-up move this to near the window edges and drag out in the direction you wish to enlarge the window. Note that when you select Size from the Control menu the resizing border around the window goes fuzzy or greyed. This renders it un-usable which is why you can only resize the window from within that particular outer border. If you try to pick the border up you will simply lose the cross-hair pointer in favour of the vanilla flavour version.

As you can see, most of the actions we carried out in the previous chapter by using the mouse and pointer have similar entry routes through the window Control menu. This is fairly typical for most

Windows functions, and, believe it or not, there is most often a third entry route which we'll examine later in this chapter. The menu route is one most flouted at beginners because it offers a positive way of seeing first what you select, and then what you have selected – a reinforcement factor if you like. However, direct use of the pointer on the window, for instance, is a lot quicker and often easier to grasp.

However, there are often options on menus that have no direct (or at least obvious) implementation via the mouse and pointer. The final option on the Control menu is one such option – Next. If you select this then Windows will select another window – or if there is no other window open, it will select one of the closed window icons. This can be useful – however, clearly it would be much easier simply to select another by moving the mouse pointer to it and clicking within the window. This is true but this route is only easy if there are only a few windows open. Imagine a situation where the desktop contains many windows stacked over one another. Looking for a specific one within a pile would be difficult – using the Next option allows you to re-order a stack of windows if you like, until the window you are seeking is at the top.

Even so, continually selecting Next from every emerging window can be laborious. There is another alternative called a *hot-key* selection. This involves pressing, normally, two keys simultaneously to get the desired effect. If you select the Main window Control menu again and look at the last option for Next you will see alongside it on the right the words:

CTRL+F6

This is the hot-key combination to implement Next direct from the keyboard. However, at present this is probably just gobbledygook. Let's look at the keyboard.

The Keyboard

If you ever watch Star Trek then you'll know how they get their computer to do things – they talk to it. Well you could try talking to your PC but everyone will just assume it's got to you. But when things get tough in Star Trek they forget about talking to the walls and start pressing buttons on futuristic keyboards. Well unfortunately, even though there are some computers around that do recognise speech and can act on it (even PCs), I'm afraid you're almost certainly going to have to get used to using the keyboard.

PC Beginners First Steps

If you have any typing experience at all you'll have no problems using the standard QWERTY keyboard (so called after the six alphabetical keys, top left, on the keyboard). If you have no typing experience then you will find it slow going at first but you will gradually get more proficient – take it from a 100 words a minute two-finger typist!

PC keyboards have some basic ingredients but like PCs themselves they can also have some extra bells and whistles. The basic difference between keyboards is some have a numeric keypad (like a telephone keypad) on the right and some don't. That's it. The photo below shows a keyboard with a numeric keypad. For now we'll concentrate on the main keyboard and ignore any additional keypads.

If you look at the keyboard you should find that it contains six rows of keys in all. Briefly, the top row of keys are the function keys, while the remaining five rows are the normal *typewriter* keys. Intermingled with these normal typewriter keys are a number of special action keys.

The function keys are quite often a different colour to the rest of the keys on the keyboard. Each of the keys has a legend on them. The one on the top left is normally called ESC. This stands for Escape and as such their key is normally called the Escape key. The keys to the right of the Escape key will be labelled F1 through to F10 which stands for Function key 1, Function key 2 and so forth. Some keyboards have extra function keys and these are normally numbered in the same sequence, ie, F11, F12 etc. This top line of function keys are normally assigned specific tasks and normally they are 'taken over' by the software you have running. For instance, pressing a particular key might send the contents of your screen to the printer, pressing another might display the number of words you have typed into a wordprocessor and so on.

Now it's not my intention to provide you with a typing tutorial – I'm no expert and there are plenty of other books to do that. So here I'm going to limit myself to details of what the other special keys do within the block of normal keys and how to use them.

The normal typewriter style keys produce their normal characters. The numeric keys, like a standard typewriter, also include a second set of characters. For example the key 5 also has the % sign on it. Normally if you press the 5 key a 5 is produced, if you hold down the SHIFT key (to the left of the Z key) you will get the other character – for this reason this keypress is often called SHIFT 5. Equally the standard letter keys will produced the lower case versions of the keys, for instance, q,w,e,r,t,y. If you press the SHIFT key and then press the same keys you will get the uppercase (capital versions) – Q,W,E,R,T,Y. If you want to produce upper case letters all the time press the CAPS LOCK key (this should have an associated light somewhere on the keyboard that lights up when you have pressed it). Now all keypresses produce their uppercase versions and if you hold down the SHIFT key you get the lower case versions.

OK now this is all fine, but of course whatever you type at the keyboard at the moment has absolutely no affect on the screen because there is nothing to type into. Well, again this is one of those chicken and egg situations and you will need some of these skills soon to get text into those dialogue boxes I mentioned a bit earlier.

Other keys on your keyboard will be the ones labelled CTRL and ALT. These keys have special roles and are pronounced Control and Alt (as in Alternative). Two other important keys are the RETURN key and the ANY key.

The RETURN key is also often called the ENTER key, although if you have an extended keyboard (that's one with a numeric keypad) then this has a special key that is the ENTER key. The RETURN key is the equivalent of the carriage return on a typewriter. You use it to start a new line of typing. In computer terms this means that you are telling the computer that you have finished your line of typing and that it should now take action on what you have typed in. The ANY key is a very popular one and is often referred to in computer books and magazines – and quite often in messages displayed by the computer to you. The trouble is that as hard as you look you won't find any key called ANY on the keyboard. That's because the ANY key is *any* key on the keyboard. Often you will encounter a message or an instruction that says:

Press any key on the keyboard

And that's what you do. For safety though it's a good idea to get into the habit of using the big RETURN key to be the ANY key.

In the text above I have used capital letters to spell out key names and this is a standard for the book – this will help you avoid confusion when keypresses are written about within the text.

Window Keys

So much for a quick look at the keyboard – but now let's get active by using the keys to carry out some of the things that we have been using the mouse for. First let's try out that Next function. You will recall from our discussion above that the hot-key combination to perform the Control menu function was:

CTRL+F6

This means that you must press the control key (CTRL) and function key 6 (F6) simultaneously. In fact what you do is to press the key labelled CTRL down and hold it down and then press the key labelled F6 before releasing them both together. The selected window will change. If you press CTRL+F6 again the next window (or iconised window) will be selected and so on. In fact you don't have to release the CTRL key – you can quickly run around all the windows by keeping CTRL pressed down and simply pressing F6 several times.

The hot-key combination can be used to close windows. If you pop up the window Control menu then you see that the combination to do this is:

CTRL+F4

Try selecting this.

Closing Windows

If you close all the open windows in this way you will notice that the Program Manager window stays open. If you look at its Control menu you will see that it has a different hot-key combination:

ALT+F4

If you close the Program Menu you will also shut down or exit Windows. This is why I made the point earlier that Close and

Minimize are in fact different. You should learn now how to shut down your PC so try this.

First select Close from the Program Manager Control menu or press ALT+F4.

The pointer will change into an hourglass. This hourglass icon is displayed whenever the computer is thinking – doing something. What is happening now is that Windows is making sure everything is tidy before it gets ready to say goodnight. Within a few seconds a special window called an alert box will be displayed.

This Exit Windows box will contain two buttons inside it – one labelled OK, the other labelled Cancel. The message inside the box will be short and to the point:

This will end your Windows session.

This alert box is also a *safety net*. If you decide that you don't want to quit Windows you can cancel the operation by clicking on the Cancel button. To proceed with the shut-down click on the OK button. (Remember to click, you move the pointer onto the button and press the left mouse button.)

If you have clicked OK then you will probably end up at the prompt display which will look like this on screen:

C:>_

You can now turn off your PC by flicking the switch and disconnecting the mains. If you want to resurrect Windows type:

WIN

at the keyboard and press Return as described in Chapter Two.

There are various schools of thought about computers. Some say you shouldn't turn them off but leave them running – perhaps just switching off the monitor. The thinking goes that the power surge that takes place inside your PC when you turn it on and off is damaging. For my part I tend to leave the PC on during the day if I am using it and only turn it off when I am going to see the Sandman. I feel it's safer that way all round.

PC Beginners First Steps

Icon Types

I've mentioned before that there are different types of icons that are used by Windows. Take note that I say 'types' – this is not the same as different pictures. If you haven't done so already close the Main window by choosing the Close option from the windows Control menu. Look carefully at the icon you are left with a square with a bar across the top and six small 'items' inside the rest of the box. This icon type is a window icon. This is the picture which Windows uses to tell you the user that if you open the icon then you will be opening a window.

If you now open the Main window and enlarge it (or maximize it) you will see that it contains a number of other icons. These are called application icons (also known as program icons and sometimes file icons!) – if you try to open one of these then you will actually not normally open a window but run a program – a piece of software.

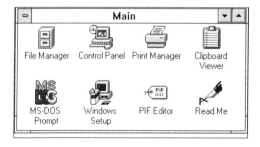

Try double clicking on the icon called MS-DOS Prompt. When you do this, after a brief pause, the Windows screen will disappear and leave you facing the prompt that we discussed in Chapter Two and also in the section above about closing down your machine. If you look at the top of the screen you will see a few messages to you. You can escape back to Windows by typing:

    EXIT

at the keyboard. In fact this isn't actually true – you must type EXIT but then press the RETURN key to finish the job. A lot of magazines and books don't tell you this so be aware of it.

PC Beginners First Steps

You can try opening some of the other icons in the Main window if you want to have a look. Remember to use the Control menu to Close each one after you. For the moment avoid the File Manager icon though.

Windows Hang-up

If you get a little carried away in your experimenting and find that you are somehow somewhere where you can't escape from and you feel lost then you can always resort to the Windows File menu. The last item on this will normally be Exit. This will get you out of Windows. If all else fails then you can simply turn off the PC itself. Use this as a last resort and always wait a good half minute before turning on again.

5
Files 'n Stuff

You can use your PC to create things – but what do you do with your creations and how can you get them back at a later date?

So far we haven't really done too much in the way of actually using the PC. That fact isn't going to change too much in this chapter – but once you have mastered what lays ahead in the run-up to Chapter Six you can start to get to grips with Windows in its entirety. The reason is that this chapter deals with files, disks and finding your way around the 'inside' of your computer.

But first let's have a dabble with the wordprocessor that you get free with Windows – this is called Write. You will find this located in the Accessories window which will be located within the Program Manager window. You run Write by double clicking on its icon. When you have done this, Write will open its own operating window. This window will be very similar to the others you have encountered – in the title bar will be:

```
Write - [Untitled]
```

and there will be seven named menus in its menu bar. You should also notice that in addition to there being a vertical scroll bar there is also a horizontal scroll bar. The text 'Page 1' should appear to the left of the horizontal scroll bar and in the

PC Beginners First Steps

Insider Guide #8 – Starting Write

Write is located in the Accessories window. To start it running you must locate its icon. To do this:

1. Open the Accessories window (if it isn't already open).

2. Move the pointer so that it sits over the Write icon (this is normally located in the top left hand corner of the Accessories window).

3. Double click on the Write icon to launch Write. The Write screen should then appear.

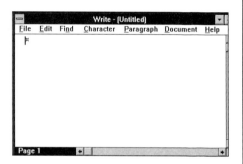

---

blank area immediately below the File menu name you will see a blinking vertical line and a small star-like character.

The large blank area is the typing area which you can liken to a large sheet of white paper and the flashing line is the Write cursor – this determines the position of an imaginary pen tip. If you type text at the keyboard then it will appear at the point where the cursor is which will move to the right (towards the end of the line) to accommodate it. Now, it's not my intention to give you a tutorial on Write at present – that will start in Chapter 17 – so I'm only going to outline a couple of things that will serve us here.

Type a few words in at the keyboard. Try entering your name using the SHIFT key to produce the capital letters of your names:

    Bruce Smith

Notice how the cursor moves to the right. If nothing is happening when you type it might be because the Write window is not selected. Try clicking the pointer in the Write window.

PC Beginners First Steps

Insider Guide #9 – The Write Window

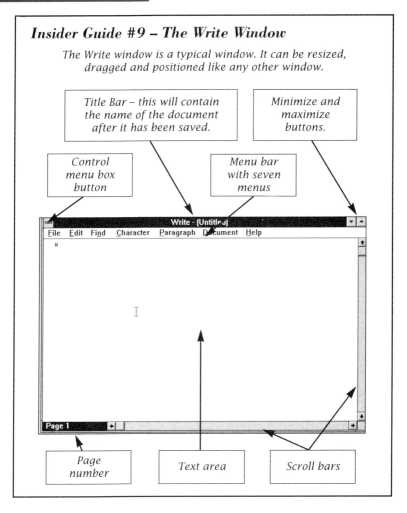

The big wide bar in the bottom row of keys is the space bar that allows you to insert spaces. If you make a mistake you can delete letters to the left of the cursor by pressing the Back Space key (Which is above the ENTER key often with an arrow sign on it) to remove the erroneous letter or letters before you type again.

When you have entered your name start a new line by pressing the RETURN key. The cursor will drop down onto a new line immediately below where it was originally placed. You can enter a few more lines of text – perhaps completing your address – to get used to using the keyboard.

What you have done may not look overly spectacular but it is special in its own way because you have put it there and created it from scratch. This of course might be the start of a letter to a friend, a report for the office or perhaps the opening page in a novel. Where you take it from here is up to you – but before you set about that blockbuster how do you preserve what you have done? If you were to turn your PC off at this point, everything you have done will be lost. Gone. Gone forever and a day.

The answer is that you can *save* what you have done. Then you can recall it at anytime in the future, add to it or change it, and then re-save it. This is what makes PCs and other computers so useful and such productive items when you learn how to use them.

Saving Grace

Every application in Windows allows you to save your work. It does this by creating converting what you have done into a special format that it can handle. This format is called a *file*. What you do then is to create a file of your work – and to distinguish files from one another we give them names. On PCs these names are generally limited to eight letters. So, for example, you could save what you have typed into Write as a file called ADDRESS as ADDRESS has exactly just seven letters. You don't have to use all eight letters, for example you could call the file ADRS or ARESS – all are acceptable – you must use one letter and the maximum is eight. Not surprisingly this naming of a file is generally refereed to as the *filename*. Thus the *filename* of the file just created is ADDRESS.

In addition to their eight letters, filenames may also have three additional letters as part of their name (bringing the total to 11). The additional letters are distinguished by the fact that they are separated from the filename by a full stop. Examples therefore are:

> MINUTES.DOC
> HELLO.YOU
> THIS.TXT

These three extra letters are referred to as the *filename extension* and they are used most of the time to signify the type of file they represent. Look at those three names. Can you tell me which ones were created using Write, or for that matter which files were created by which software? This last point is important. Different software creates different types of information. For example, you couldn't load a file into Write that was created using accounting software and vice versa. The formats are incompatible and the end result would be unpredictable and quite likely to confuse you and your software. You wouldn't (normally) try and play your favourite CD on a record deck. You wouldn't do either any good – equally you wouldn't get a long playing record and try to play it on a CD player – even if you could get it to fit – the two are *incompatible*.

There are a couple of way to ensure you avoid this type of file confusion. Firstly, group all your like files together – which is a matter of good housekeeping anyway and which I'll be discussing in a later chapter – and the second is to use the filename extension to signify the file type. This is a standard convention and files have standard file extensions which you should always use. For example, the standard recognised file extension for files created by Write is:

WRI

Thus when you see a list of files names such as these:

MINUTE.DOC
HELLO.TXT
ADDRESS.WRI

You can immediately know that the last file in the list was created by Write because it has the file extension WRI.

For the time being we're going to ignore what you have typed because what we do need to do is to understand quite clearly just how your PC and in particular, how Windows, organises its files. This is most important because unless you do grasp the concepts here you will have a torrid time. But, and there's always a but, this is easy to learn. The theory is simple and you almost certainly know about it, but have never associated it with computers before.

If you want to close the Write application select Close from Write's Control menu. A small window – a dialogue box – will be displayed which you should click on the No button.

Filing Cabinets

You will know what a filing cabinet is (I can't believe you won't!). Imagine a filing cabinet that has three draws labelled:

    Home
    Office
    Personal

Inside each of these three drawers are hanging files which you slip your letters and forms into. Your birth certificate and NHS medical card you would put into folders in the Personal drawer. Details of mortgage or loans would be placed in folders in the drawer labelled Home. Work that you might bring home would be kept in the drawer labelled Office. You have a small and hopefully reasonably well-organised Filing System.

You PC has its own filing system which works in an identical way and you can place your files into folders which are stored in drawers. The only slight difference in terminology is that when dealing with drawers and folders on computers we tend to refer to them as *directories*. So in the earlier example of the ADDRESS.WRI file we could store this in the Home drawer/directory or even the Personal directory.

The filing cabinet to hold this information is already fitted within your PC – it's called a *hard disk*. Think of it as a massive music cassette onto which you can almost instantly store your file and then retrieve them. Your hard disk will offer you a lot of storage space but it is not an unlimited amount of space. But that's a subject we will come back to when we examine the use of another type of disk which you will probably have heard of – the floppy disk.

The hard disk is fitted inside you computer and is always available to you whenever your PC is switched on. It also has a name. Unfortunately this name isn't memorable. Your hard disk isn't called Jack or Bill, neither is it called Madeline or Clare. It's called C. Yes the letter C is what your hard disk is known as. Again this is one of those standard computer naming conventions.

Go back to the Windows desktop and have a look again at the window called Main. Main is nothing more than a directory within Windows and it contains files – although these files are in fact programs. Equally, all those other windows that can be opened within the Program Manager are directories and they all hold their own groups of files. However, it doesn't stop there because directories may themselves create directories which they themselves also contain directories and so on – a process called *nesting*.

For example, take the Home drawer from the filing cabinet. In actual fact it is unlikely that you would just place individual letters or documents straight into the hanging files. You are much more likely to want to sub-divide them and group them together. Thus in the Home drawer you will probably have folders that have names such as:

House
Services
Banking
Credit Cards

And if you have a lot of paper you might further sub-divide these folders. For example the Service folder might have folders within it called:

Electricity
Gas
Telephone
Water

Now let's call this three-drawer filing cabinet 'C'. If you wanted to tell someone to get your latest letter to the Gas company you might say to them:

'Go to filing cabinet C, look in the Home draw, locate the folder Services and this has a folder in it called Gas. The letter is called PAYMENT'

The PAYMENT file could be stored on your PC in the same way. And you could provide the route to the file in a much simpler way just by listing the folders in order:

`C - Home - Services - Gas - Payment`

By tradition, in computer terms the first thing you always specify is the disk drive name (because you can have more than one) and the last is always the filename. If the payment file was produced in Write then the correct 'address' or location of the file would be written as:

`C:/Home/Services/Gas/Payment.Wri`

The colon after the C is used to signify that we are referring to a disk. The backslash characters '/' are used to separate each of the directories. This address or file location is normally called the *path*.

The fact that we have stored these directories inside one another makes them subordinate to the previous one and they are therefore often called sub-directories. The the Service directory is a sub-directory of Home. This type of filling system is called a hierarchical filing system which means that it can have multiple levels.

Because of its arrangement it is sometimes called a tree or tree directory. You can imagine the various sub-directories being the roots of a tree, or if you turn the lot upside down, the branches of a tree. The very top of the tree structure, ie the top directory (this is the one that is displayed when you open a disk icon) is normally referred to as the *root directory* for this reason.

If you look down the root structure of the Home directory (see *Insider Guide #10*) you will notice that several directories are on the same level but they are not connected directly. For instance, the directories Banking and Services are both sub-directories of Home but there is no direct connection between them other than via the Home directory itself. This is a very important concept and one that you should fully understand.

Imagine you are working on a file stored in the Services directory. This is called the *current* directory. To go to the Banking directory you must first go *up* to Home (ie up the directory tree) and then down to Banking (ie down the directory tree).

The directory from which all other files and directories are accessed is often referred to as the root directory. All the directories that radiate from it are known as branches of the root directory.

Another analogy that is often used is that of parent and sibling directories. The starting directory is called the parent directory and any directories created here are child directories (or sibling directories). Obviously directories created in the child directory will become its child directories whilst it becomes their parent directory! If you are struggling to understand this terminology then simply apply your family tree to it. Your father is your parent and you are the child. You father is the child of your grandfather while your father is your grandfather's child!

Back to Writes

Let's go back and finish this chapter where we started it – by using Write. Open the application again by double clicking on its icon in the Accessories window. Enter your name and address, exactly as before. Now, let's save your work as a file. To do this go to the File menu within the Write window and select the Save or Save As option from it. This will display the Save As dialogue window.

This window, like so many others that you will use in Windows, is divided into two main areas. On the immediate left of the File area and on the centre right is the Directory area. Both these areas are dominated by scroll boxes – these are small windows within a dialogue

Insider Guide #10: A hierarchical filing system.

The tree-like nature of a hierarchical filing system is shown below. Each drawer or directory is represented by a named box – the first two of these, Home and Personal, are in the root directory.

Home has two sibling drawers (sub-directories) called Banking and Services. If you are in Banking you cannot go directly to Services – you must go via Home. Home is the parent of Banking and Services.

Services also has siblings which are Electricity and Gas. Files can have similar names provided they are stored in different drawers.

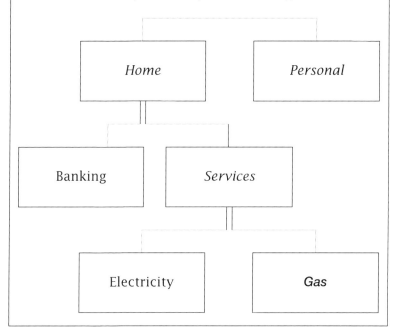

box which list information through which you can scroll – typically to choose an item – which are only 'active' if the list is longer than can fit in the window.

If you examine the Directory area you will see items which are very similar to what we have discussed. The directories it has listed inside it are represented by small icons which themselves look like folders. Chances are the directory will be shown as:

    `c:\windows`

Above the file scroll area will be a small box which will have a flashing cursor inside it. Above this will be the legend:

File Name:

If you now type the name that you wish to save your file as it will appear in here. Type:

ADDRESS.WRI

You can use the Back Space key to erase any errors. When you have done this click on the button marked OK. The hourglass will reappear to show you that the file is being saved.

Quit Write as you did earlier. Now start it again as we are going to reload the file called ADDRESS.WRI. When Write has opened and presented a blank window go to the File menu and select Open. This time an Open dialogue box will be displayed – and you will be amazed just how similar it is to the Save As dialogue box. If you look in the File scroll box you should see your file there ADDRESS.WRI. Move the pointer to it and click on its name once. When you do this the filename will appear in the small text box you had entered it into a few moments ago when saving it. The file name will also be highlighted in the File list box. You have selected the file, now click on OK and after a few moments your original work will appear in the Write window.

Note also that the title bar of Write now contains the name of your file:

Write - ADDRESS.WRI

That is how easy it is to save and re-load files that you create, or anyone else creates for that matter. As you may have realised there were a few 'other' areas in both those dialogue boxes that I didn't remark on. We'll put that right in due course.

Insider Guide #11 – Save and Open in Write

To save any work you have created in Write use the Save option.

1. Select Save from the File menu.

2. Locate the directory where you want to save your file using the directory scroll box.

3. Enter the name for the file in the filename box. You do not have to add the WRI extension – Write will do this automatically if you don't enter it.

4. Click on OK.

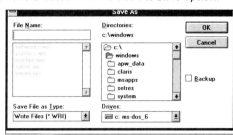

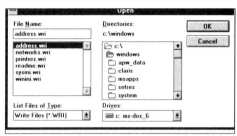

To open a previously saved Write file:

1. Select Open from the File menu.

2. If required, locate the directory containing the Write file.

3. Double-click on the file name in the list of WRI files.

The Save and Open windows are very similar. The Save window provides a text entry box for a file name to be added. The Open window provides a window in which files are listed.

> File names and the files list are detailed on the left hand side of the window.

> Directory details are listed on the right hand side of the window.

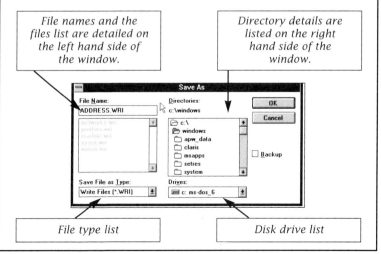

| File type list | Disk drive list |

6

File Manager

Files rule your life as far as computers are concerned – so Windows provides a program that allows you to manage them with the minimum of fuss. Not surprisingly it's called File Manager.

```
                    C:\WINDOWS\*.*
  [=] a [= ] c                     C: [MS-DOS_6]
    ├─ 📁 temp                  ↑ │ 📁..
    ├─ 📁 tfw                     │ 📁 apw_data
    ├─ 📁 trident                 │ 📁 claris
    ├─ 📁 tvgautil                │ 📁 msapps
    ├─ 📁 vidplay                 │ 📁 setres
    ├─ 📁 wcup                    │ 📁 system
    ├─ 📁 windows                 │ 📁 wgpo
         ├─ 📁 apw_data           │ 📄 _default.pif
         ├─ 📁 claris             │ 📄 256color.bmp
```

*T*he last chapter introduced the basics of directories and files and if you are sure you have understood how they work and mastered that simple Save and Open from within Write you shouldn't have too many problems with this chapter. If you are still a bit vague – and there's no reason why you shouldn't be – then have another read. If that doesn't do the trick then still have a go at this chapter as it may just help the penny drop. As I said at the start of the last chapter, these two chapters are very important to grasp, otherwise you will find that looking for a file on your hard disk can be like looking for the proverbial needle in a haystack.

File Manager is an application that allows you to manage files. That much might be obvious, but in addition it also allows you to manage your directories and in turn your hard disk. Or put another way File Manager allows you to perform a wide range of operations on anything that is held on your hard disk (and any other disks your PC might have). These files might be ones that you have yourself created (such as Write files) or that have been supplied to you with Windows (such as Write itself) or on new software that you might purchase in future.

In a nutshell File Manager allows you to select, move, copy, duplicate, delete, create, name, re-name and search for items on your disks. This may sound complicated but once again Windows makes this easy to do by using simple icons and boxes combined with menus and the pointer.

You access File Manager through the Main window. Locate the Main window (remember you can use CTRL+F6 to display windows in turn) and then double click on the File Manager icon. File Manager normally presents as a maximized window and will contain a window within its own borders. The title of this window will almost certainly be:

    `C:/WINDOWS/*.*`

and this is illustrated opposite.

File Manager windows can become quite cluttered therefore *always* use it in the maximized form – in many ways it is best thinking of File Manager as an application that you can only use on its own. Open it, perform your tasks, and then close it – avoid the temptation to use it alongside other windows.

The File Manager window is not too dissimilar from the look of the Program Manager and you must be careful not to get the two confused. Because of its nature and the wide range of things you can do with it, it also has one of the biggest selections of menus – seven in all.

The window displayed inside File Manager provides you with access to your hard drive. The title:

    `C:/WINDOWS/*.*`

shows you exactly where the window is 'looking'. Remember our analogy earlier about a window being like a camera viewfinder in that you can only see part of the world around you through it. This window is absolutely no different and the title tells you that you are currently looking at files and directories held in the Windows directory located on drive C (the hard disk drive). The last bit of the title:

    `*.*`

is a shorthand way of saying all files. This is in fact the filename part of the path and an asterisk '*' is like a wild joker in a game of cards and can stand for anything. This can be very useful and we'll come back to this subject again.

PC Beginners First Steps

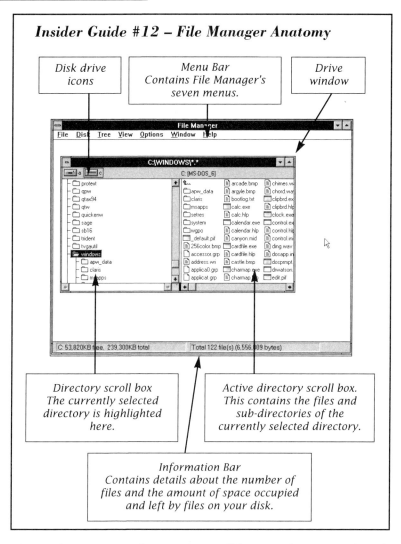

Insider Guide #12 – File Manager Anatomy

The window consists of two main scroll boxes – the one on the left lists the directories on the hard disk. The scroll window on the right lists the directories and files within the currently selected directory. The currently selected directory is Windows itself (as per the title as above). If you look in the directory scroll box you will see that the Windows directory is highlighted and also that the folder it represents is 'open'. This is shown visually by the graphic used and also by the fact that sub-directories in the Windows directory are shown indented from the others.

These same sub-directories can be seen in the right-hand scroll box and these are followed by the files that Windows has already in place. These are all listed alphabetically and you should be able to clearly distinguish from the directories and the files. If you look carefully you should also be able to see the file called ADDRESS.WRI that you created earlier.

Note: In File Manager, directory names and file names are always displayed as lower case (small) letters. This is the opposite to how we display them in this book (to enable you to be able to distinguish them from the text, and the way that Windows displays them in dialogue boxes). Confused? Don't be – you'll get used to it.

You can use the scroll bars in both of the scroll boxes to view the contents of both these sub-windows. Have a play and see if there are any directories and files with familiar names. There may be – don't be concerned if there aren't.

Above the scrolling directory boxes you will see icons representing the disk drives you have connected to your PC. There will be a minimum of two – labelled A and C. The C drive is of course the hard disk and the A is the floppy disk drive which we have yet to investigate (but we will do in the next chapter). It is possible you have another one or two drives connected (for example a CD drive) and these will be shown if you have. The fact that the hard disk drive is the currently selected disk drive is signified by the fact that it has a box around it.

FM Selections

Making selections within File Manager is done in what should now be a familiar fashion – point and click. For example, to select the floppy disk drive move the pointer so that it is over it and click on it. The floppy disk drive in the front of your PC's main box will come to life and make some weird scratching type noises. This is because the mechanics inside are looking for a disk and there isn't one (unless you have put one in previously). After a few seconds an alert box will appear on the screen title 'Error Selecting Drive'. For now click the Cancel button to remove it from the screen.

PC Beginners First Steps

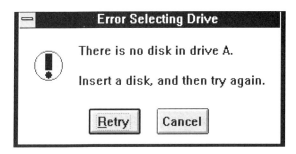

To select a directory or a file you click on it once. Here I stress the once as double clicking on a file or directory can have differing actions. For instance if you double-click on a special type of file you can actually run a program associated with it. Double clicking on a directory has a less drastic effect in that it will normally open the directory concerned and show whatever it contains. Let's look at a few examples.

Locate the ADDRESS.WRI file that you created in the last chapter. (If you didn't follow the example through, shame on you – quit File Manager and go back to the exercise as we'll be using this file a fair bit in this chapter.) Double-click on the small icon. The famous hourglass will be displayed and within several moments Write itself will have appeared and not only that, the ADDRESS.WRI file will have been loaded into it! This self-loading facility is very useful and it is supported by many of the applications you can use with Windows – and even if it doesn't it is still possible for you to create this file *association*. But that's a more advanced topic which we'll ignore for now.

Making Directories

One of the best ways to organise files is to place them into specific directories. You can create new directories through File Manager. For example, you can create a directory to put your Write files in. You can do this at any point on your hard disk – that's up to you – but for now I suggest you keep everything in the Windows directory until you have had time to learn how to navigate your way through drive C comfortably.

Creating the Write directory is simple. First ensure that the Windows directory is the currently selected one. You can do this just by checking that the title of the file window has the same name as we originally started with. It's easy to locate the Window directory in the left-hand scroll window and double click on it. This will leave the Windows icon highlighted and provide a list of the directories and files within Windows.

Next go to the File menu of File Manager and select the tenth item on the File menu list – Create Directory. This will display a simple dialogue box called Create Directory. Into the text box enter the name of the new directory by typing it at the keyboard – Write seems a reasonable name. Once you have done this, click on the OK button and the new directory called Write should appear. Note that two copies of the directory will almost certainly appear – one in the left window and one in the right. Don't get confused – these are the same directories, but the left scroll window also lists files.

All being well you can now transfer any WRI files you have created into it. This is a process called *moving* and is a drag and drop technique similar to the type we have used in earlier examples – the moving of a window for example. Locate the ADDRESS.WRI file and move the pointer to its icon. Click the left mouse button and keep it depressed. Move the pointer so that it moves the file icon (as you move it a '+' sign appears inside the icon). As you start to move over directories you will find that the selected directory is signified by an outline box appearing around it.

When you have reached, and selected, the Write directory, release the mouse button. At this point a 'Confirm Mouse Operation' dialogue box will appear asking if you really want to move the selected file. Again, this is that safety net. Click on the Yes button and it will happen! Notice that the file has gone from its original location – this is because we have moved it from one directory to a sub-directory. In computer path terms we have moved the file called:

    `C:\WINDOWS\ADDRESS.WRI`

to:

    `C:\WINDOWS\WRITE\ADDRESS.WRI`

This drag and drop method can be used to move not just files but also whole directories. The process is the same – locate, select, drag and drop.

Insider Guide #13 – Creating a directory

File Manager simplifies the process of creating a directory.

1. Locate the point where you wish to create the directory. The new directory will be placed in the directory that is named in the File Manager directory window. In this example it will be placed in the Windows directory.

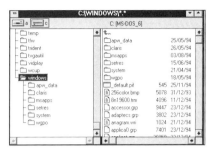

2. Select the File menu and choose the Create Directory option from the list provided.

3. This will display the Create Directory dialogue box into which you can enter the name to be assigned to the directory.

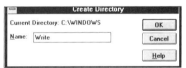

4. The new directory will be created and can be selected by double clicking on its icon in the File Manager window.

Navigating Directories

Moving up and down through what can be a large maze of directories is important to master for reasons that have already been outlined. Because it is such an important task Windows ensures that it is straightforward. Once you have moved your ADDRESS.WRI file into the Write directory you can open the Write directory and see the file simply by double clicking on the folder icon of the Write directory. It doesn't matter if you double click on the icon in the left or right scroll box – the effect is the same. Once you have done this the right-hand scroll box will clearly show just the Write file.

Moving up through the directory tree is just as straightforward. Normally the right-hand scroll box will show your current position, whereas the left hand scroll box shows a nearly complete map of the selected drive with the current directory highlighted. To move to any other point you need to just locate the directory you seek in the left scroll box and double click on it. If you want to move up a single directory you can use this technique or you can double-click on the up-arrow at the top of the right hand scroll box.

Renaming

You can rename files and directories using the File Manager. This is useful if you are trying to re-organise your data and don't want to have to go through the long-winded approach of re-creating files from scratch. For example, you might decide that you don't need the Write directory any more because you wish to re-organise your folders so that you rename it Home.

To do this you select the Write directory (or any directory or file you want to rename) by clicking on the folder icon once and then select the Rename option from the File menu. This produces a Rename dialogue box similar to the one shown below:

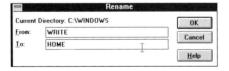

The cursor will be in the To box and you can now type in the new name of the directory:

HOME

After the brief appearance of the hourglass the Home directory will have taken the place of the Write directory. If you open this you will see that the file inside is still intact. Renaming a file is done in the exact same way.

Copy and Delete

You can make instant copies of just about anything using File Manager. The Copy option is in the File menu and this (and for that matter any other similar option) uses the standard Windows technique or select, choose option, name, OK.

The copy is useful in that you can use it to make duplicates of files. For example, your ADDRESS.WRI file can be duplicated and renamed so that you can use it without affecting the original. Typically you might do this before creating a new letter. Perhaps you need to write to the Bank – you can duplicate the ADDRESS.WRI file (which is your template) and then rename it as BANK1.WRI for instance to signify that it is letter one to your bank. You could then open this and add your letter to it.

To copy-duplicate the ADDRESS.WRI file, select the file by clicking on its icon and select the Copy option from the File menu. This will throw up the Copy dialogue box. Type into this the name of the file you want ADDRESS.WRI copied 'into':

BANK1.WRI

and click on OK. If you now examine the directory you'll see that the duplicate copy is there!

Deleting files and directories is just as easy – and that makes it *very* dangerous. This is because once you have deleted something you cannot, repeat, *cannot* get it back. So never, ever delete a file or directory unless you are quite sure you really don't want it!

To delete the BANK1.WRI file (as an example) select the file and then choose Delete from the File menu. This will display the Delete dialogue box at which point you can check the file details and then OK. As Deleting is irreversible a Confirm File Delete window will be displayed – here you can select Yes, or No to cancel the operation.

7

Floppy Disks

Floppy disks are your flexible friends. They allow you to transfer files and programs with relative ease.

[Format Disk dialog box: Disk In: Drive A:, Capacity: 1.44 MB, Options — Label: WRITE, ☐ Make System Disk, ☐ Quick Format, buttons: OK, Cancel, Help]

*F*loppy disks aren't floppy at all! In fact at first sight you could be forgiven for thinking they were hard disks because they have a hard plastic case. But the term has stuck since the days when they were floppy, simply because they are portable and at the present time the most cost-effective way of transferring files and applications from one computer to another. They are also relatively cheap and a useful means of keeping safe copies of your important files called *backups*.

I find it difficult to believe that you haven't yet seen a floppy disk – but if you haven't then there's a picture of one overleaf and have a look through the various packs you got with your PC where they will be located. They take the form of a small square of plastic (which comes in a variety of colours). This is dominated at one edge by a large fold of metal which can slide from side to side. If you slide this back it will reveal inside the disk itself – *don't touch this!* The disk surface is very delicate and the grease and dirt from your fingers can damage its surface rendering it unusable. (So can cigarette smoke so if you partake give up now!) The disk will also have a small hole in one corner – this is the write protection notch and the slider (on one side of the disk) should be drawn back to expose the hole (this is the normal situation).

A floppy disk is a smaller version of a hard disk. This is not just physically but also in terms of storage. Typically a hard disk can hold over 100 to 1000 times more information than a floppy disk. The other obvious point that is still worth making is that your hard disk is permanently connected to your PC whereas floppy disks have to be changed as and when you require information from them. For this reason it is very important to label your disks with what they contain by using the sticky adhesive labels that are normally supplied when you purchase them.

The most common type of floppy disk nowadays is the high density disk and the letters HD can normally be found embossed in the plastic casing near the metal slider. This disk normally has a storage capacity of 1.44Mb when formatted. The other common type of disk is the double density disk (DD) which has a storage capacity of 720k when formatted. OK, there are a few jargonistic terms there which need examining – namely formatted, 1.44Mb and 720k.

Before any type of disk can be used, be it a hard disk or floppy disk – it has to be *formatted*. This is a process that the PC carries out that lays down a form of electronic street map. This allows the PC to quickly locate files already on the disk and also allows it to create an index of the disk contents similar to the one displayed by File Manager. The location of each file on the disk is given an *address* which the software such as File Manager can read. Addresses are very important – imagine a situation where no-one in the British Isles had a street or house number – sending a letter to someone would be nigh on impossible. The difference between a disk-based address and the Post Office version is that we as users don't need to know the address – all that is handled by the computer and so it is 'invisible' to us the user and we can rely on standard naming conventions.

You *format* a disk using File Manager – however you should remember that when you format a disk it will *totally* erase everything on it. Therefore any files that you might have had on it will be lost *forever*. This is not normally a problem as you will normally only format disks when they are new, ie, once. However, there are times when a disk can become damaged slightly so you might want to re-format to see if this cures the problem.

PC Beginners First Steps

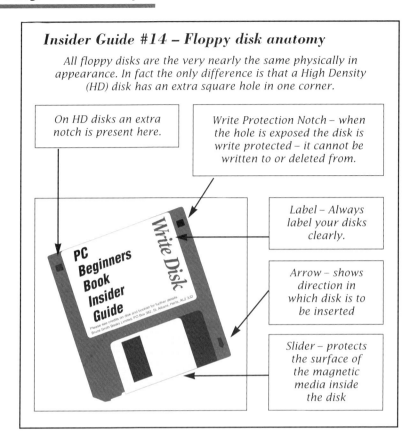

One other very important point. Only format *floppy* disks – you should *never* format a hard disk unless you are quite sure you know what you are doing. If you do and are not sure what you are doing you may render your PC useless and need to employ professional help to get your software working again.

More on Size

Before we actually have a go at formatting a disk – perhaps now we should examine this aspect of storage space and the size of things. It's a little bit technical but something you should try to understand because it will help you understand very much more as we progress.

Let's pose a question to get us started. "How much can a floppy disk hold?" How much what? If we are talking about Write files we might possibly answer about 300 pages of typing. But this isn't really an answer because it's a bit like asking "How long is a bit of string?" and answering "About three books". It means nothing because it assumes that all books are standard and that isn't the case – nor is it with files.

Information is stored on a disk electronically and for ease of understanding let's say that the smallest storage space is a single character. Thus each letter of this page would take a single unit of storage space on the disk. This single unit is called a *byte*. However, the byte is a very small item in computer terms and it is an impractical unit to work with. So to keep things manageable we tend to think in terms of thousands of bytes which are called *kilobytes*. A simple analogy here is that the kilometre is an easier unit to handle than the metre when taking of distances around the UK. You would say that the distance between London and Birmingham is 200 kilometres – 200km – rather than 2,000,000 metres. Like kilometres, kilobytes is abbreviated to k or kb, which is pronounced 'kay', ie, 720kay.

On a double density disk the storage space is 720k – 720 kilobytes. The term Mb is used to represent Megabytes, or 1000k units. Thus the storage space on a high density disk is 1.44Mb which is 1440k – or twice as much space as the double density disk. The term Mb is normally pronounced as 'Meg' – thus a HD disk is a 1.44Meg disk.

To go back to where we started, it isn't really true to say that a byte is effectively the space taken by a character, because the software used to write the file to a disk is so sophisticated nowadays that it can sometimes compact much more information in. Equally, if you were to look at a file's size you couldn't take this as a true gauge to the number of characters in the file because other information is also stored in the file.

In some respects then storage is a bit of an abstract term but it is one that you will become very familiar with as you use your PC more and more. The one thing that you can be sure of is that as applications become more and more sophisticated they need more and more storage space both for themselves and their files.

Formatting

Let's look at how to format a floppy disk. Now I am assuming that you have some unformatted (new) disks. If you haven't then you should definitely buy a box of ten because you will want them. The first step is to identify what type of disk you have (DD or HD) and to make sure that it is all right to use on your PC. This is because it is only since mid to late 1993 that the HD disk drives have been commonplace. You will need to check the specification of your PC to ensure that you purchase the correct disks.

You insert the floppy disk into the floppy disk drive taking care to insert it in the correct way (arrow on front side of disk up and to the front so that the metal edge goes in first). Then run File Manager – the display will be as it was in the earlier examples with a window showing the directory of the hard disk.

Go to the Disk menu and select the Format Disk option – this will display the Format Disk dialogue box similar to that illustrated below:

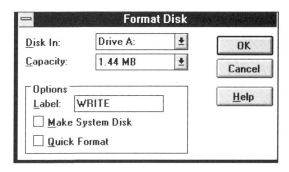

Your floppy disk drive will be called drive A and this will be selected in the Disk In box. Below this is the Capacity option and this will have either 1.44Mb or 720k selected. If you wish to change this, click on the down arrow to the side of the box to display the other options and select the one you require. At this point you can set about formatting the disk – however before you do that you should really name your disk by entering a title in the Label box. This label can be up to 12 characters long. Once you are happy, click on the OK button. This will in turn throw up a Confirm dialogue box and again select Yes to start formatting.

As formatting proceeds, the Formatting Disk dialogue box will display just how much of the formatting has been completed. You can cancel formatting at any point by clicking on the Cancel button – although there is nothing much to be achieved by doing this other than freeing the computer for immediate use. When the format is complete you have the option of formatting another disk. If the answer is No you will be dropped back onto the File Manager window.

To view the contents of the floppy disk click just once on the floppy disk icon of drive A. If you do this correctly then the window for drive

C will be replaced by one for drive A. The composition of this window is exactly the same – but as there are no files and directories then the two scroll boxes are devoid of files.

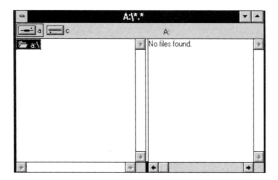

Being windows you can display more than one at a time, so it is possible to display windows onto more than one drive at the same time. The way to do this is to double click on the drive you want to display. This creates the new drive window but does so without removing the one you already have on the screen. So if you have the A drive shown on the screen, double click on the C icon and the drive window for this will appear.

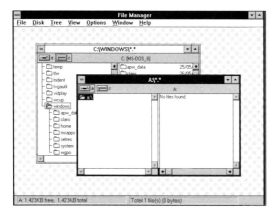

Being windows you can drag and re-size them in the normal Windows fashion – however unlike Program Manager you cannot drag directory windows outside of the File Manager.

Copying Across Disks

The process of copying files across disks is almost identical to moving files from one directory to another. The only difference here is that you move the file or directory from one window to another. Locate the ADDRESS.WRI file in the C directory window and then drag this across onto the A directory window. For this purpose you may want to re-position the two windows to enable you to do this comfortably. After the normal confirmation has taken place the file will be copied from drive C to drive A – remember your original copy is *not* affected by this process.

Unless you really need to you don't actually have to display the drive A directory window to copy a file onto a floppy disk – all you need to do is to drag the file icon you want to copy onto the icon of drive A – this is good enough and will copy the file into the root directory of the floppy disk. If you want to copy into a specific directory then you will need to use the windows display.

Have a go at what I have just described – when you have dragged the ADDRESS.WRI icon onto the drive A icon you will get a new dialogue box. This is the Confirm File Replace one.

This has come to life because before you copy a file anywhere File Manager checks the destination. On checking the floppy disk it has 'seen' that there is a file with the same name located there (the one copied just before). If it goes ahead and copies the latest file this will over write the existing one. You see each filename must be unique – you cannot have two files with the same name. No, that's not entirely true – you cannot have two files with the same name in the same directory. In other words you could have a million files called ADDRESS.WRI on a disk provided they were held in a million different directories – and these directories may be sub-directories of these directories.

If you want to copy – and therefore replace – the original file, then click on the Yes button. Alternatively you can select Cancel or No to abort the operation.

Multiple Copy or Move

If you have more than one file or directory to copy, it can be a very time consuming process to select, drag and drop individual files. One of the features of File Manager is that it allows you to select a set of files and then drag and drop these as a collective item. Selecting more than one file can be done in a couple of ways. First though, ensure you have at least two files to copy – the best way to do this to recreate the BANK1.WRI file that we deleted earlier.

The first thing is to ensure that the files you want to copy are all easily accessible. Thus you should limit yourself to copying groups of files that are in the same directory. The easiest way is to use a combination of pointer and keyboard to select the files to copy. This is done by using the point and click technique but while holding the CTRL key down. So, hold down the CTRL key and then click on each of the files you want to copy. As you do this each selected file will be highlighted. When you have clicked on the last file, drag the lot to where you want to copy them and then the process is the same as for copying a single file.

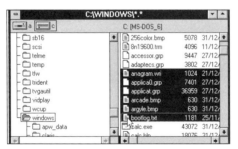

The above method is great if the files are scattered throughout the directory. If the files you want to copy are all located in a continuous block (see illustration above) you can select these using the SHIFT key. In this case you depress the SHIFT key and then click on the first and last file you want to copy – then every file between these two and including them will be selected. Copying then just needs them dragging to the destination.

A couple of points to bear in mind here. First remember that if you select files and copy them to another part of the directory structure on the same disk you are in fact *moving* the files. If you are using another disk drive then the files are copied leaving the originals intact where they are. If one or several of the files in the group you are copying has

Insider Guide #15 – Filenames

If you try to use a filename or directory name that already exists within the currently selected directory then you will get either a warning that the name already exists or you will be asked if you want to replace the file. Filenames and directory names must be unique to the directory where they will be placed.

However, you can use the same name as many times as you want provided it is in a different directory. Look at the diagram below. The filename ADDRESS.WRI has been used three times. This is perfectly permissible because each occurrence of it is in a different directory.

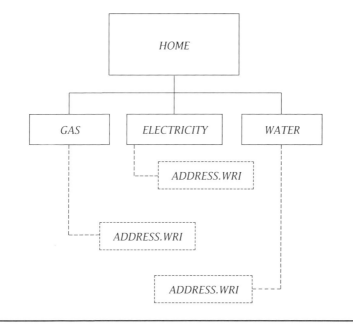

a name clash with their destination then File Manager will throw up a dialogue box to this effect. You may have noticed before that one of the buttons on the Confirm File Replace box was called 'Yes to All'. Clicking this will automatically copy *all* files over existing ones.

The other thing to beware of is space. If you are coping several files and already have some in place then it might be that there isn't enough space to copy all. File Manager will copy as many of them as it can before alerting you that there is no more room. At this point you need to either delete some of the unwanted files or use another disk for the remaining files.

PC Beginners First Steps

Insider Guide #16 – Creating a Write Disk

The most important use of floppy disks is to transfer files from one PC to another. You may have a PC at home and one in the office. You can use a floppy disk to transfer the files you create on one PC to another. Even if you are not transferring files you should still keep backup copies on floppy disk for safety's sake.

You could keep copies of files simply by copying them onto floppy disks in no particular order. However, disks can become cluttered very quickly, so a useful habit to get into is to create a series of specialist disks. This may be a little wasteful but as floppy disks are so cheap these days it is worthwhile because the time saved in looking through disks for a particular file can be so great.

Thus you could create a disk specifically to hold your Write files. Then if you need a copy of, say the ADDRESS.WRI file, you know immediately where to look for it.

1. Format a new floppy disk – or take a blank disk that you have previously formatted. Name the disk 'Write'.

2. Stick to this a disk label that you have previously annotated with the name of the disk, ie Write.

3. If your original files are already in specific Write directories then drag-copy these across. If not create the directories on the floppy disk by first selecting the disk and then the Create Directory option.

4. Drag-copy the files into their relative directories.

5. Safely store the Write disk away in a disk box or a disk wallet and don't forget to copy newly created or updated files across as you do them!

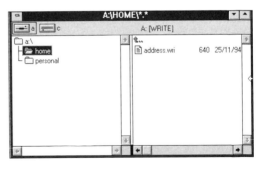

8

Desktop Design

Time to make your mark!

Stamp your own personality on your Windows environment and make it suit your own little ways...

*ime off for good behaviour now! Lots to take in already so this chapter looks at some of the more playful aspects of Windows and in particular shows you how you can set about giving your desktop not so much a face-lift but a personal touch. A bit like decorating a new house or flat to your own tastes really. This chapter then is going to concentrate on some of the smaller applications that come with Windows that are quite often referred to as applets. By this stage you should also be familiar with the basic terminology (clicking, select, double clicking and so forth) so from this point on there are no reminders as to how you carry out each one. Equally, I'm also going to start to assume that you can work your way through the Windows files and directories without too many problems. If you need to refer back at any point then there is no harm in doing so.

The various applets that help you re-vamp your desktop are located in the Accessories window. If you go to Program Manager and locate this you will find that it has a file called Control Panel. In fact the file isn't one but a further directory. If you double click on the Control Panel icon a window will

PC Beginners First Steps

open and display further icons. The Control Panel is the means by which you control the functionality of Windows – the small icons displayed in the Control Panel are a form of preset file in which you can define how particular aspects of Windows work, look and feel to use. It uses a combination of menus and selections which Windows looks at when it starts or after a change to them. What you specify as your preference in the Control Panel is what Windows is guided by – for this reason these are sometimes called Preference files on other computers and in other applications. For the most part you will find using the Control Panel files as simple as manipulating a dialogue box – that's the beauty of Windows – you do virtually everything in the same way!

When you make any changes in the control panels they will take immediate effect; however they will not be permanent unless the 'Save Settings on Exit' option from the Options menu in Program Manager is set. To see if this option is active, display the Options menu – if this choice on the menu has a tick next to it then it is set. If it doesn't then you can activate it by selecting it – this will place the tick next to it. In a like fashion if it is set it can be turned off by selecting it. This option is a bit like a toggle switch which can have only two settings – on or off.

The Time...

Your PC will have a built-in clock. It's a bit like a digital watch really, utilising the microchip within it to count out the seconds. However, you may need to set the correct date and time, especially if we've gone from BST to GMT. One of the control panels in the Control Panel window is Date/Time. Double click on this and a very simple Date & Time window is presented. You can change any segment of either of these func-

PC Beginners First Steps

tions by selecting the component and then using the adjacent up and down arrows to change the setting of either.

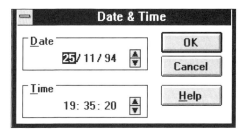

When you select the OK button the PC's internal clock will be updated and keep good time from thereon.

...The Place

Having set the date and time you can set or rather fine-tune the details about where you are and how you want things displayed. Windows selects a standard set of information but, being an American engineered product, there are points (like date display) that you will probably want to change. To do this double click on the International control panel which will reveal a more substantial dialogue box.

The first four options here allow you to change the Country, Language, Keyboard Layout and Measurement system. A basic set is already set up for you but by clicking on the down arrow at the right of the boxes you will be able to produce a menu of other settings which you can select in the normal fashion.

The List Separator is the character that Windows uses to separate items of information – this is a more advanced topic and as the comma is the best item to use anyway ignore it for now. The final four settings relate to the format of how Dates, Currency, Time and Numbers are displayed. Each of these sections has change buttons which you can click on to bring up further dialogue boxes to make finer selections. These are useful to experiment with so do so – if you make a change you don't like just select the Cancel button to ignore what you have done. Some of these selections are the subject of an insider guide in this chapter.

Insider Guide #17 – International Settings

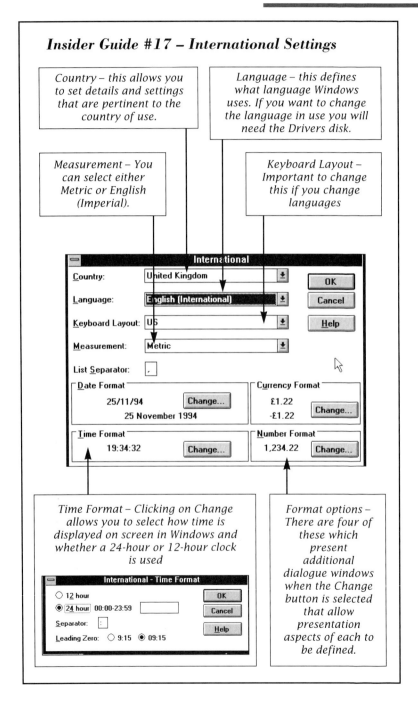

Country – this allows you to set details and settings that are pertinent to the country of use.

Language – this defines what language Windows uses. If you want to change the language in use you will need the Drivers disk.

Measurement – You can select either Metric or English (Imperial).

Keyboard Layout – Important to change this if you change languages

Time Format – Clicking on Change allows you to select how time is displayed on screen in Windows and whether a 24-hour or 12-hour clock is used

Format options – There are four of these which present additional dialogue windows when the Change button is selected that allow presentation aspects of each to be defined.

PC Beginners First Steps

Desktop

The Desktop control panel is probably the one that provides the most fun because it allows you to add that personal touch to your working environment. In all there are seven areas on the Desktop control panel which are clearly displayed once you have displayed the control panel itself.

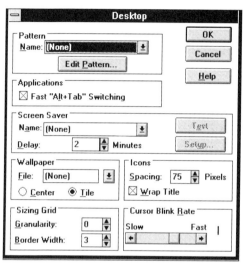

The Pattern control allows you to define what the background screen of your PC looks like. The background screen is the area on which all your windows sit. If you minimize the Program Manager you'll get a much clearer view of it – in fact apart from the Program Manager icon that's all you'll see!

Each of the patterns is given a name and these are listed in the drop-down menu to the right of the Pattern name. You can select any of these in the usual fashion. For instance scroll down and select the pattern called Weave. To see how this looks you need to quit the Desktop control panel. So, with Weave now selected in the Pattern box, click on the OK button. As the control panel disappears from the screen the background will change. If it doesn't then check to see that you aren't using Program Manager – or any other program – in its maximized form. With everything being displayed in Windows you'll see the change. To reset the pattern or choose another you'll need to go back to the Desktop control panel. The default setting is (None).

Wallpapering

One of the most common and popular ways to personalise your desktop is to wallpaper it! This is, in many respects, identical to using the Pattern option, but instead of placing a simple dot pattern behind it you use a picture. The format of this picture is important – it has to be what is called a bitmap. These can be created using many different applications, one of which is supplied with Windows. It's called Paint and this is discussed in a forthcoming chapter.

However, in traditional Blue Peter fashion some wallpapers have already been pre-created and you can try these examples for yourself. If you select the drop-down menu in the Wallpaper area of the Desktop control panel a list will be presented. Select the one called:

```
marble.bmp
```

Again you will need to quit the Desktop control panel to see it take effect by clicking on OK. The Wallpaper section also has a couple of what are called check buttons. These are called Center and Tile. These type of buttons are what is known as mutually exclusive. What that fancy term means is that selecting one automatically excludes the other. You select one by clicking in it. The Tile option is normally best set because it will repeat (or tile) the wallpaper to completely cover your screen. The Center option only displays the image used for the wallpaper once and positions it centrally in the screen. Therefore, if the image is not big enough to cover the entire screen area you probably won't see it unless you minimize everything.

Screen Savers

We have already encountered the screen saver and it is from within the Desktop control panel that you determine just how this works. A variety of different images are available for you to show and you can select these from the drop-down menu. Once you have selected the saver of your choice you can see how it looks by clicking on the Test button. Clicking again will drop you back to the desktop.

The Delay buttons allow you to increase or decrease the number of minutes that your PC is left idle before the screen save comes into effect. There is also another button – this is the Setup button. This produces a dialogue box that allows you to set specifics about the way the screen saver is displayed. For example, if you have chosen the Flying Windows saver then you can move a slide to determine how

Insider Guide #18 – Editing Desktop patterns

You can make or edit your own Desktop patterns by using the Edit Pattern option. To do this select the Desktop control panel and then click on the Edit Pattern button which will display the Edit Pattern window.

To see a particular pattern select it from the drop-down menu. For example select the Boxes pattern. A sample of the pattern – as it would appear on your desktop – appears in the larger window on the left. The window in the centre shows a zoomed view of the individual element that makes up the whole pattern. We can edit this, or any other pattern, to change them or create new ones.

Using the Boxes pattern we can create a new one called Panes. To do this click the pointer in the Name box and edit the title to say Panes. Now click on the Add button to add this new pattern to the

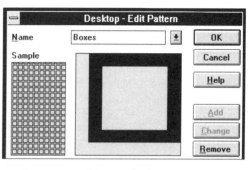

list – this effectively makes a copy of Boxes which remains intact.

Now you can use the pointer to set elements within the main view – these elements of the picture are called pixels. Move the pointer so that it is sitting inside the large square – press the left mouse button once. A black square appears at the point – you have set this point. If you click again at the same point the black square will go (if has been replaced by a white one) – you have cleared the point. Using this technique you can add a cross in the centre of the box. Notice how as you set or clear a point it is reflected in the Sample view.

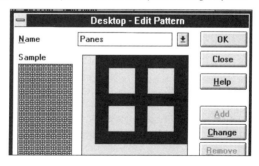

When you are happy click on the Change button, and then OK to quit the Desktop Edit Pattern window. You should now be able to select the new panes pattern from the Pattern drop-down menu and apply it to the screen.

If you dislike what you have done you can remove it by selecting the Remove button from the Edit pattern window.

fast they fly and the number of windows that are displayed. These dialogue boxes are all different so a specific example is of little use – however, you can't do any harm by experimenting with them so do have a go.

You can also set a password. If you have set a password then once the screen saver has become active you will have to enter your password before you can return to your normal screen. This is a security procedure that is implemented once you have moved the mouse or selected a key and is done via a dialogue box.

Bits

The Desktop control panel includes four other items that can be set. Three of these we'll ignore for now but the Cursor Blink Rate allows you to set the speed at which the line cursor blinks. You can make this faster or slower by dragging the scroll box in the appropriate direction. The cursor to the right of this gives an indication as to the actual blink rate.

A Touch of Colour

While the Pattern and Wallpaper options in the Desktop control panel affect what is displayed in the Windows background, the Color control panel allows you to select the way windows look by changing their colours. Invariably this is much more aesthetically pleasing than some of the garish backdrop patterns in use!

When you run the Color (American spelling) control panel a somewhat crammed-looking window appears which is divided into three basic regions. The top part of this defines the colour scheme to be used in the windows. A number of these are available to you already supplied. Selecting one is a matter of using the pop-down menu.

The middle region shows all the elements of a window – active and inactive – and when you choose a colour scheme from the list the colours are displayed in the sample windows. The two buttons allow you to Remove Schemes (the currently selected one) and also to Save Schemes. The latter applies to new colour schemes you create and these are created by first selecting the large Color Palette button near the bottom of the dialogue box. When you do this the dialogue box doubles in size to provide an editing area.

PC Beginners First Steps

Insider Guide #19 – Password Set

Many of the screen savers have a password protection facility. This is easy to use provided you remember your password! To set a password first locate the password protection box. This is located within the Setup dialogue box of the screen saver you are using. Click in the square to set it at which time the Set Password button will become active.

Click on the Set Password button and this will display the Change Password dialogue box. Click in the New Password box and now type in your password. For each letter you type, an asterisk will appear on the screen.

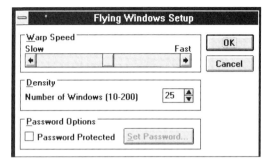

Next click in the Retype New Password box and now retype the password exactly as before. This is a safety check.

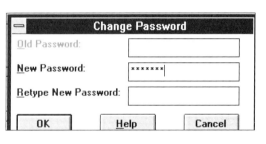

Now click on OK. If your two entries match then the Change Password dialogue box will disappear and be active. If your entries do not match then you will be asked to start over again.

Assuming all is well, if you now leave the password Test dialogue when you click to restore the screen the screen saver dialogue box will appear asking you to enter the password. Once you do this and press OK you will be back at the desktop. If you type an incorrect password then you will be invited to try again!

If you want to change the password at anytime then you can only do this by first typing the current password into the Old Password box in the Password Setup dialogue box.

Creating a new scheme is performed in a near identical fashion to that for creating a new pattern for the desktop. First define a name for the new scheme by clicking the Save Scheme button. An appropriate dialogue box will appear and you can enter the name here before clicking

Save. It is worthwhile saving a new named scheme even before you start to prevent you accidentally overwriting an existing one.

Once done you can set about selecting the colours for the various windows parts. This is done by selecting the named windows elements in turn. You can do this by clicking on the elements or by selecting them in turn from the Window Element menu. It might surprise you to see that there are 21 elements to be defined bearing in mind that you must cater for both the active and inactive windows. Of course you don't have to change them all – you may want to base your new colour scheme on an existing one with a few elements changed.

Having selected the element to be altered click on one of the colour boxes displayed in the Basic Color grid. As you do this the selected element will change in the preview area for you to see the effect. At this point you can re-select, or if happy, move onto the next element to be changed.

If you are not happy with the basic range of colours available, you can custom design some of your own. To do this click on the Define Custom Color box to display the Custom Color Selector window. Here you can click in the colour palette window to select a colour from the large vignette of them, or you can construct one by selecting its various elements from the other boxes. The best way here is to play and fiddle for yourself. To be frank the colours on offer through this route aren't that effective and I personally feel, apart from the fun factor, there isn't a great deal to be gained from defining more. But if you find a combination you are happy with you can add it to the basic colour by clicking the Add Color button which will copy it into the next free colour box. You can add up to 16 custom colours in this way.

Once you are happy with your final scheme you should save it again by using the Save Scheme button again and save using your previously chosen name of course.

The Remove Scheme button does the opposite – select a scheme in the drop-down menu and then select the button in the normal fashion.

Mouse and Keyboard

The Mouse control panel defines how your favourite friend performs under your control; equally the Keyboard control panel depicts how the keys interact with the user. Looking at the Mouse control panel first you can change how quickly the mouse

Insider Guide #20 – Color Anatomy

Using the Color control panel you can define how various aspects of your desktop look in terms of colour. Not only can you change the colour scheme to one of many that have been predefined you can also dream up your own from the colours supplied or by mixing your own custom colours!

Colour Schemes – this menu drops down to reveal 23 pre-defined screens. New definitions are added here.

Desktop Elements – a drop down menu listing the 21 aspects which go to make a screen display.

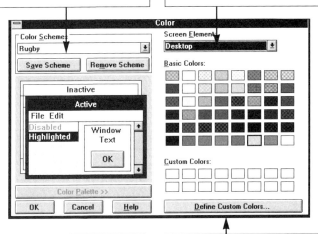

Color Refiner Box – select colour from here

Click on Define Custom Colors to display Color Selector window.

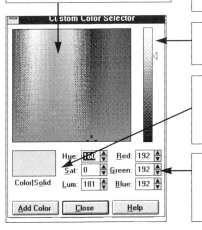

Luminosity Bar – select the brightness of the colour.

Color/Solid – the left side of box reflects current colour while the right shows the nearest solid colour.

Use the nudge buttons to select values between 0-255 for each colour component.

PC Beginners First Steps

moves across the screen by sliding the Mouse Tracking speed control in the appropriate direction.

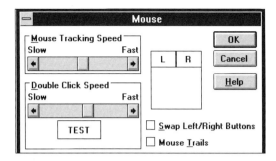

The Double Click Speed slider determines how quickly you need to do the two-button classic to make a selection. Again this requires you to drag the slider in the relevant direction and the Test button gives you a place to double click to determine if you are happy with the setting. If you have successfully double-clicked then the Test button is selected. If it remains white you can't match the setting!

The simple diagram of the mouse shows the position of the L(eft) and R(ight) keys. You can swap these if you want by selecting the Swap Left/Right Buttons. Finally selecting the Mouse Trail button simply creates an irritating pointer trail.

The Keyboard control panel allows you to use sliders to change two aspects of the keyboard. This is the delay before the first repeat and then the repeat rate. If you run Write and then hold down any key on the keyboard it will repeat. Not right away but after a small delay – these is the Delay Before First Repeat; how quickly it then repeats is the Repeat Rate.

The Test box allows you to test the above out. Play with the settings and then see the differences by holding down a key on the keyboard.

On Hold

There are plenty of other panels in the Control Panel but these require a bit more knowledge before you can get to grips with them.

9 Online Help

The first rule of Windows is "Don't Panic!"

The reason for this is that every Windows application and applet comes with its own Help system. This not only provides some basic details on how to use it or them but also some interesting titbits.

*T*his far into using Windows you will for sure have noticed that virtually everywhere you go and whatever window or dialogue box you call up there is a button called Help. I have avoided introducing this before now because although you can get a lot of information about what you are actively doing in Windows by clicking on the Help button, you also need to have some basic grounding in how Windows works to be able to use Help effectively and without getting frustrated.

The type of Help offered by Windows is known as *Online Context Sensitive Help* – a bit of a mouthful to say the least. Let's break it down into manageable parts. Online means that it is available to you all the time you are using Windows – it is online to you. Context Sensitive means that when you click the Help button the Help you will receive is relevant to what you are doing. For example, if you are using the Desktop control panel and click on the Help button then you will receive help on the Desktop control panel – nothing more, nothing less.

The next question is just what is Help and what format does it take? Windows help is provided in a window and takes the form of text – a sort of small book of informative points and memory joggers with examples where relevant.

But Help isn't limited to dialogue box buttons – applications and applets normally have help associated with them but you will use these most of the time without a dialogue box or access to a Help button. In these cases a Help menu is often available – some also use the F1 key (Function one key) as a way of accessing Help. In fact just about every single application and accessory you receive with Windows and any extra ones that you buy and install yourself, will have Help available with it.

Help that is implemented in this fashion is also often referred to as an Online Manual. That is and isn't entirely true because in many respects it assumes that you already know about the topic you are dealing with and in most cases doesn't supply worked or illustrated examples. What it definitely is, is an Online Reference which makes it invaluable in its own way.

The Help Menu

Applications such as Write normally provide a Help menu as the last item in their menu bar. If you display these menus there will normally be four items listed. The illustration below is of a typical Help menu:

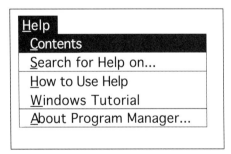

The Contents option provides an alphabetical list of topics that you can get Help on. The Search option allows you to enter the name of an item you want to search for Help on and the How to Use option provides details on how to use Help itself – yes, there's even help on Help!

The last item – About – provides version information on your current topic. Versions are something that we have yet to discuss.

Insider Guide #21 – Contents Help – Write

Help is provided on all Windows applications including Write. When you select the Contents option from the Help menu a scrolling list of topics (which are highlighted in green) is displayed.

When the topic required is found move the pointer over it – at this point it will transform from an arrow to a hand.

You can grab details of what you are after at this time by double-clicking the mouse button.

The Contents list will then be taken over by the details of the topic you have selected Help on. Any text that is highlighted in green can

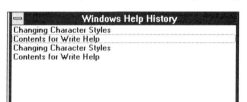

also be expanded upon simply by clicking on the green word.

You can return to the Contents list at any time just by clicking on the Contents button – you can also go to the previous topic by selecting the Back button.

If you click on the History button a list of all Help topics you have used in the current session is listed and you can move directly to one of these by clicking on its name in the list.

If, at any point, you need to remind yourself of a particular aspect of Windows you can do so by clicking on the Glossary button. This displays a totally separate window which has a complete A-Z of most topics. Just scroll and select as required.

Remember to treat Help as an individual application – one that you can leave open on the screen as long as you want!

PC Beginners First Steps

To use Contents Help select it from the Help menu and then scroll down the list of topic headings until you find the one that is relevant to what you are looking for and then click on it. (You can also scroll down the topic list by pressing the TAB key and then the RETURN key to select the topic.) This will then display the help file that is available for the selected topic.

The Search

When you know specifically what you are looking for help on then you can cut out the long-winded approach by going straight to it. From the applications Help menu select the Search for Help On... option. This displays the Search dialogue box.

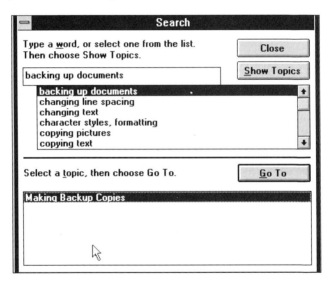

Here you can either scroll through the list of topics and select the one required, or enter the name of the topic you seek. This will display a list (if found) in the box from which you can make your selection.

All this said, the best way to use Help is to experiment with it. There's nothing you can do that will harm your computer or your software so go for it! You'll also learn a lot more about the subject because there is a large number of useful hints and tips within the Help files.

Keyboard Revisited

Up to now we have concentrated on using the pointer and mouse to make all the selections we require. For the most part this is the best and most efficient way – not least because you have the mouse in your hand most of the time. However, you can access most Windows functions through the keyboard. This can be more effective if you are already using the keyboard, or a life saver, if your mouse has packed up working.

You may have noticed that most of the options you select (such as menus or options on menus) have a letter in their title underlined. For example, in Program Manager the File menu has the letter F underlined. This is the hot-key letter. If you press this along with the ALT key then the File menu will drop down. Equally if you press ALT+H (this is shorthand way of writing press ALT and H together although it is also sometimes written as ALT-H) the Help menu will be displayed. In either case you can select any items on the menus by pressing ALT and the underlined character.

Remember that these hot-key combinations are context sensitive. ALT+F will normally always select the File menu from a window – but it selects the File menu from the currently selected window – to move to the next window remember you need to press CTRL+F6. Another way to access a menu is to activate the menu bar by pressing F10 – this will highlight the first menu at which point you can use the left or right arrow keys to highlight menus. Once the menu you require has been activated you can select it by using the Return key. You can then use the up-arrow and down-arrow keys to highlight options on the selected menu. Again pressing Return selects the menu that has been highlighted.

10 PC Hardware

Time for another journey back to the nuts and bolts of your computer.

Learn about speed, memory and disk drives to name but a few.

*W*e had a very basic look at the hardware, or more correctly the components that constitute the hardware of your PC. This chapter follows on from that by having a more detailed look at exactly what you have and the terminology that goes with it. Because the following chapters are not dependent on this chapter you can choose to skip over it if you wish. But if you are still worried by terms such as RAM, video card, 486 and so forth then you might find it informative. And as they say – there's no time like the present!

Powerful Stuff

One term that you will hear an awful lot is the word powerful. This can be applied to both hardware and software. The normal phraseology is *'My PC is very powerful'* or *'It's the most powerful software around'*. What does powerful mean? Well, I'm afraid I don't really know – it's one of those terms I absolutely hate and people tend to use it because they have a limited vocabulary and can't fully describe what they mean. A bit like the reasons why some people swear a lot really.

PC Beginners First Steps

In the broadest sense it can boil down to meaning that whatever it is you're talking about is both very fast and very good at whatever it is doing. In hardware terms it is most often taken to mean that the PC you have is very fast – that is it operates quickly.

The speed at which a PC runs is defined mainly by the type of chip or chips it uses, although the amount of memory you have fitted can also play a factor. Chip is the microprocessor or microchip that forms the anatomical heart of your PC – it is the bit that has the silicon chip inside. It regulates its pulse – the faster the pulse the faster it can pump instructions around inside. The *processor*, as it is more commonly called, is distinguished from others by its name – and like most computer names it is in fact a number. At the time of writing the most popular type of processor is the 486 (Four-eight-six). Prior to this we had the 386 (Three-eight-six) and the 286 (Two-eight-six) processors. As you can see successive processors were distinguished by changing the first number and the higher the number the better the processor. Thus the 486 is a more recent and more efficient processor than the 386. The reasons for this are manifold and ones that I'm not going to get involved in here.

For best results to run Windows 3.1 you should use a 486 machine. It will run on a 386 PC (not as efficiently though). Now there are 486 processors and 486 processors. The difference between individual types of processors is their clock speed. This speed effectively regulates how fast the pulse of the computer beats – how quickly it can work on information coming in and going out – how quickly it can process. Processor speeds are measured in megahertz or Mhz. Typical speeds are 33Mhz, 50Mhz, 66Mhz and 100Mhz. Again these speeds are a little abstract because just by looking at a PC running Windows you wouldn't be able to immediately tie down what sort of processor it had unless you had lots of experience.

You might therefore have a 486 66Mhz PC. Unfortunately it doesn't stop there because 486 processors can be further sub divided into types – the most common two are DX and SX. Therefore you might read a PC's specifications as being:

        486DX 66Mhz

or:

        486SX 66Mhz

The DX specification is a better one than the SX one.

PC Beginners First Steps

If all this is confusing you don't worry – it's confusing to all but the real experts. If you are looking through adverts at machines then the best guide is the price. Many dealers now list the systems by processor – only the named brands tend to be boxed separately – so you can see what are the better PCs by their price. The fast, better processor they have the more expensive they are. Like everything in life – it's a good guide. After the 486 should come the 586 but no. The chip after the 486 is called the Pentium.

The other specification used is whether the PC is a Desktop or Tower system. You'll be glad to know this has nothing to do with processor speeds – it's just the type of box it comes in! A Desktop system is one that can sit on the desktop and you would normally place the monitor on it. The Tower system is one that is free standing and normally sits on the floor next to or under the desk. It resembles a Desktop box placed on one side!

Memory

With all this information coming in, going out and doing who knows what else – your PC needs somewhere to store it all, work on it and then retrieve it. This area is called the memory. In some respects you can liken memory to a brain. But the computers 'brain' has two distinct regions – one region for remembering and one for thinking. The reason I say this is because there are two types of memory – ROM and RAM.

ROM and RAM are acronyms which stand for Read Only Memory and Random Access Memory. The Read Only Memory is the memory that holds the software that is pre-supplied with the computer. This normally contains all the basic material that your PC needs to operate. Your PC's ROM is normally fixed – you do not need to add to it or worry about getting more. From a users point of view you never need to know about it – much more important to you as a computer user is RAM.

Random Access Memory is used by your PC to store information that is forever changing or that needs to be accessed very quickly – this is normally when a program or application is running. The most popular misconception that many people have when discussing RAM (memory) is that it determines how much information your computer can hold. This isn't true. In fact this is determined by the size of your hard disk (detailed later). RAM determines the limits within which a program can operate. This will become clearer in due course.

Typically when you run a program Windows will copy the program, or at least part of it, into memory where it will start executing. Equally any files that the program creates and therefore the information it is working on, sits alongside it in this memory. The memory in your PC has a finite size. When this limit is reached the software running it has two options. Firstly it says – 'Oh, I'm full-up – reached my limit – I'm afraid you can't do any more'– this is normally displayed by an 'Out of memory' alert. Secondly it saves what it has and moves the first or last bit onto your hard disk using this as extra memory space (this is normally called virtual memory). The problem now is that each time you need to move from one part of a file to another, the software has to read and write to and from the disk and this slows its operation down. And suppose you now wanted to run another program – this too has to be swapped in and out of disk. The whole effect is a slowing down in the operation of your software (not the computer). The bottom line then is the more memory (RAM) you have the more efficient your computer will be.

Memory size is measured in megabytes (Mb) which was introduced when we looked at floppy disks. To run Windows 3.1 effectively you should consider 4Mb as the minimum. This will allow it to work effectively although you will find that 8Mb and more would be even better. Certainly if you are running any major applications (such as Microsoft Office) you would notice a big difference in operation between a 4Mb PC and one with 8Mb. If you are running graphics packages then 16Mb would be a practical amount. However, having set those figures, Windows will run in less but not as efficiently and you will probably spend your time getting friendly with the hourglass!

That's memory in abstract terms but what is it in physical terms? Well, like most things inside your computer it comes in little black slices (rather like after dinner mints with legs!) called memory chips.

There are two major differences that exist between ROM and RAM that I have not yet made clear. Firstly, as is implied by its name, ROM can only be read *from*. You cannot store information in it. Because this information is pre-stored when the ROM is manufactured it is always there and cannot, under normal circumstances, be erased. RAM can be read from and written to and unlike ROM it is *volatile*. This means that the information it contains is only there while the

Insider Guide #22 – Inside the case

The picture above shows a tower PC system without its case. The motherboard can be seen at the back of the box. Note the mass of ribbon cable used to tie the motherboard to its other essential components. The metal box at the top left is the power supply. The metal racking at the top right houses the disk drives.

The picture below shows a close-up of the main printed circuit board. Towards the right you can see the large Intel microprocessor chip with the legend i486SX clearly on it. Below this there is room for a second chip to be added.

To the left of the picture there are a number of slots into which extra boards can be plugged. These can be seen in position in the picture above.

computer is turned on or at least has power applied to it. When the power is turned off the contents of the RAM are lost – lost forever.

Because memory is so important it is increasingly being built into processors. This type of memory is called cache memory. The amount of cache built into processors such as the 486 is quite small – normally just 8k – but it can vastly improve the efficiency, and therefore the speed, of your PC. The function of this is relatively straightforward. The processor tries to guess what information it is going to need next while it is waiting for something to happen, and so gets the information and loads it into the cache. This means that if it has guessed right, the information is instantly available to it. Of course this is only a time saving if the processor has guessed correctly – and the more efficient the processor becomes, the more advantageous this is. Thankfully processors are now very good guessers and so there is an overall noticeable speed improvement. Although a bigger cache size does not necessarily offer a corresponding increase in speed, it is worth getting the biggest cache memory size your budget allows. 256k is well worthwhile especially if you are using a DX 486 processor.

Board and Cards

The *motherboard* is the main item of importance inside the PC case. It is where all the processor and chips that make up the various types of memory, plus support memory and other electronics are mounted. The motherboard is a printed circuit board (PCB) made from a green plastic material onto which electronic tracks have been etched. Mounted on this is a variety of sockets into which the chips are inserted, although it is now normally more common for the chips to be mounted directly onto the board.

The motherboard also contains sockets that can house other boards. These boards or cards can be very specialist in nature but two are very essential – these are the Display Adaptor and the I/O card. The Display Adaptor is also often known as the Video Card – this contains the necessary components that turn your computer's signals into a form that can be displayed on the screen of your monitor. Physically, if you look at the back of your PC's main box then the point where the cable attaches the monitor and the PC together is where the video card is located.

This particular item of the computer's hardware isn't built in as standard. This is because there are many different types of monitors with

PC Beginners First Steps

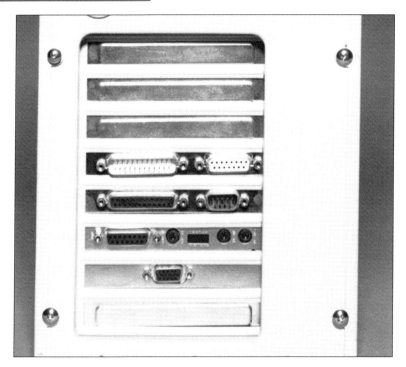

Additional boards can be added to a PC. One of these boards is an I/O board – which is fitted as standard – and this provides D-shaped sockets into which printers and mice can be plugged.

new more sophisticated ones being produced each year. Each has a very specific requirement and therefore needs to have the PC's video signals produced in a particular format. For this reason, when you buy a monitor you tend also to buy the video card at the same time. The video card also has some memory mounted on it. This RAM is normally called video RAM because it is used to store the image that it then sends to the monitor.

The other type of card that is already installed in your PC is called an I/O card. I/O standing for Input/Output. This normally has at least two sockets that project out of the back of your PCs main box. The two sockets (and there may be four) are very different in shape and size as shown in the picture above. The first of these is used to plug the other end of the mouse into. It is normally a 9-pin D-shaped socket. This is called the serial port and is normally called COM1. However, this isn't always the case because some mice can be of the parallel type (but this is rare).

PC Beginners First Steps

The other, larger, socket is the one where you will normally plug your printer – this is the parallel port and is normally called LPT1. Both of these terms we will come back to when we re-visit the Control Panel in a few chapters' time.

Disk Drives

We have already encountered the two basic types of disk drive: the floppy disk drive and the hard disk drive. Most computers will have one of each – but there is nothing to stop you having more than one and it is very common to have a second hard disk drive fitted. The other increasingly popular disk drive is one to take CDs.

The basic type of floppy disk drive is one that accepts HD – high density – disks. Other than that there is not much to say. They are normally very reliable and you can expect many years of use from them if you look after them. That basically means don't try to take a disk out (eject the disk) while the computer is using it – by reading or writing information to it – and don't try inserting any foreign objects into it (watch out for any small children – this is a favourite pastime of theirs as my kids have proved many times!). But like any mechanical device they can go wrong so beware.

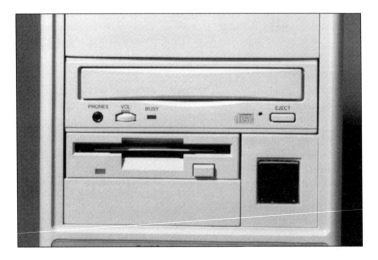

Hard disks are where all your programs and files are stored and in some cases they can be used as extra memory – virtual memory. The prices of hard disks have fallen significantly in recent years so much so that 100Mb disks and above are commonplace and 240Mb are edging towards the norm. You can add additional hard disks – this upgrade to your system is best done by someone qualified to do it – and if you do this it is a good idea to get the largest capacity disk you can afford. If you have no other disk drives then it is likely that an additional hard disk would be called D.

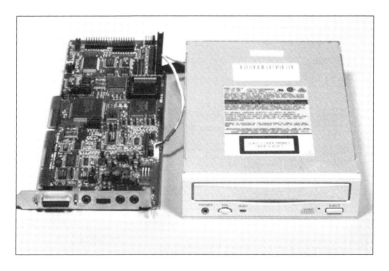

The other type of drive that is becoming commonplace is the CD drive. The photograph above shows a CD drive along with the circuit board that connects it to the PC by plugging it into one of the sockets on the motherboard. The CD drive allows you to load and run software that is supplied on compact disks. Because this type of disk is a read only device, computer CDs are normally referred to as CD-ROMs. They are revolutionising the way PCs are used and if you are looking to improve your system then it should be a prime consideration (if you don't have one). For more details see our sister title – the *PC Multimedia Insider Guide* – which is detailed in an appendix at the rear of this book.

Just to remind you of what I said at the start of this book – the foregoing pages covering this discussion of hardware are somewhat simplified and there are a number of aspects that haven't been discussed because of their more technical nature. For example, other aspects to consider when buying extra RAM or an additional hard disk is access speed. You can have the fastest PC in the world but if you add low rated extras then it will impair performance. The basis of the above is that it should give you a basic understanding of how things work – if you are looking to add to what you have make sure you know the specifications of your PC and discuss the matter fully with your dealer.

"Getting to know you, getting to know all about you". Julie Andrews will never be the same now, but Program Manager will and the more you know about it, the better your computing performance.

We have already had a very good basic look at Program Manager in earlier chapters. In this chapter we'll explore the features we haven't already seen and I'll also show you how you can use it effectively to group your programs and files together which should enable you to keep a relatively clutter-free desktop. We'll also have a look at the *Options* and *Windows* menus that we have so far neglected.

One of the things that Program Manager allows you to do is to run more than one application at once. You could, for example, have all the applets in the Accessories window up and working at the same time. This is called *multitasking*. In fact this running of multiple applications is a bit of an illusion. What actually happens is that Windows runs a bit of each program in succession. But because it does this at such a phenomenally quick speed it gives the impression that they are all working in unison and at the same time – and for practical purposes they are. The limitations as to how many programs you can multitask together are effectively determined by some of the factors we discussed in the last chapter: how fast your PC is and how much memory you have fitted. When you reach the limits of these then the ability to run bits of each very quickly becomes impaired and there is a noticeable slowing, not only the operation of the programs, but also in the ability of you to be able to use the PC. For these reasons it is a good idea to close applications when you are finished with them and only run them when you need them.

Program Groups

Because of this ability to have several and even numerous programs running, being able to move through the windows where you can launch them into action from is important. Although we have used the term windows to refer to the likes of Accessories and Main it isn't the terminology that is generally used. They are more commonly known as *Groups*. Thus rather than saying the Accessories window we should refer to it as the Accessories Group or the Main Group. However they are displayed in windows – thus we have the Accessories Group window and so on.

The icons that you see in these group windows are not the programs themselves. They are links to the program. Imagine the Oval Office – there on Mr President's desk is *the* button. Now if Mr P wants to launch the bomb he presses the button. The button isn't the bomb itself, simply a link to it. Icons in program groups are the same. The button might be one of several scattered around the White House – all linked to the same bomb. In a like fashion you can have several icons all linking to the same application. Using this feature you can create additional program groups that arrange your work in an easy-to-use format.

For example, in the chapter on Floppy Disks we created a Write disk onto which you could put all your Write files. In the same way we can create a Write Group into which all your Write work and files are stored. Indeed we can take this a step further and create a Home Office group where you can group together all the bits you need for producing your home correspondence. Let's try this.

First we need to create the Group window. Go to the File menu and select New. This displays the New Program Object dialogue box. Check the Program Group button and select OK.

PC Beginners First Steps

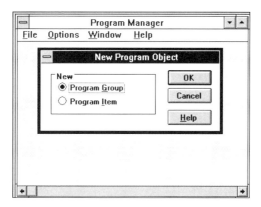

This then in turn displays the Program Group properties box which has two text boxes for you to enter Description and Group File details. In the Description box type:

    Home Office

Then click on the OK button. Don't worry about the Group File box – Windows will sort this out for you.

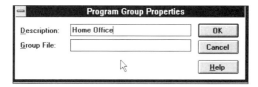

As you click on OK, the new Home Office group window will be created for you and added to the Program Manager. As, this example is based around Write we need to copy this into the Home Office Group – or rather copy its icon into the Group window. Dragging the Write icon from the Accessories Group window to the Home Office Group window doesn't have the desired effect. This is because it will be moved from the Accessories window. What we want to do is to make a copy of it. To do this hold down the CTRL key and then do the drag. This forces a copy operation leaving the original intact.

PC Beginners First Steps

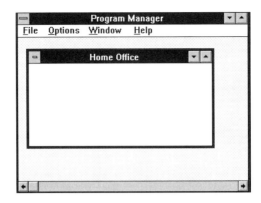

The next step is to make a working directory for Write. This is where Write will look for and store the files it creates. If you have tried the previous examples in this book then this directory will already be in place – it was called Home (see Chapter Six). To make this the working directory select Write (click on it once) and then select the Properties option from the Program Manager File menu. This will throw up the Program Item Properties window.

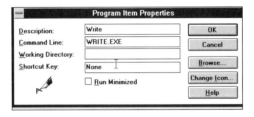

This window allows you to define various aspects of an icon. The Description box details the name that appears below the icon. There is no reason to change this from Write although you could call it Home Write if you wanted. The Command Line is the name of the program that will be run when the icon is double clicked. You should not change this.

The third item is the one we are seeking – Working Directory. In here you type the path of the directory where the files are to be stored. However, to avoid problems it is best to use the Browse button to help you locate it. First click in the Working Directory box and then select Browse.

This will display a dialogue box through which you can locate the Home directory and select this. You should be able to do this now – if not go back to the chapters on File Manager. Once you have located Home make a note of its location which is:

`C:\Windows\Home`

and quit the Browse area by clicking on OK. Next enter the path into the Working Directory box, then select OK.

The working directory has now been set – if you now run this version of Write and select Open from the File menu you will see that you are already in the Home directory and the ADDRESS.WRI file, for example, created earlier is there waiting for you!

You can also use this technique to create an icon within your Group for your frequently used files. Here the ADDRESS.WRI file would be a useful one to have on the desktop as this would probably be used a fair bit. This is done in much the same way. First make sure that the Home Office Group window is the active window. Then select New from the Program Manager File menu. In the dialogue box check the Program Item box, select OK and then in the Description box of the Program Item Properties type:

`Address`

We now have to set the Command Line – this is the location of the ADDRESS.WRI file. This can be set through the Browse button by locating the file. First ensure that the Command Line box is selected, and click on Browse.

In the File Name window of the Browse window delete what is there and enter:

`*.WRI`

As required locate the Home directory and double click on the ADDRESS.WRI file name. Click on OK and the path will be copied for you into the Command Line box. Set the Working Directory as before.

The final thing to do is to set the icon. Do this by clicking on the Change Icon button. This will show the normal Write icon by default which is best to use until you create some of your own (!).

Click on OK and then OK again. The Home Office Group window will show the Address icon in place.

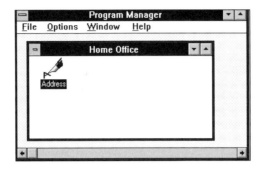

If you double click on the Address icon it will not only run Write for you but also load the ADDRESS.WRI file!

Switching

If you have several Groups open then you can use the CTRL+F6 hot-key combination to trek around each one in turn. The term trek is probably right here because you may have to go through each one in turn to find the Group you are after. And there's some law that says it will be the last one in the list. A much quicker and more efficient way to go straight to the Group window you are after is to select it from the Windows menu offered by Program Manager.

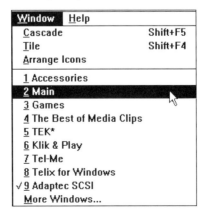

If you click on the Windows menu the lower section of it lists each of the Group windows and from this you can simply click on the name of the one you want. If the Group you select is in its minimized icon format then it will be opened for you.

The only things this doesn't allow you to do is to move quickly between applications that are running. However there are a number of ways that you can do this – and if you want to try some of these out run Write and open the Control Panel.

The first most obvious way is to simply click in the window of one of them – this is the most efficient but it does rely on your being able to see part of the window of the application you are after. Many applications also allow you to have more than one file open at the same time as well. In these cases – provided you can see the file you are after – you just click on part of its window.

Another route is to use the keyboard to switch between each of the running applications. To do this you keep the ALT key pressed down then press the TAB key. With each press of the TAB key the title of the next application currently running is displayed. When the name of the application you want to switch to is displayed you should release the ALT key and the application will be brought to the front.

There is a further method that involves using a list similar to the one produced by the Windows menu in Program Manager. To use this method you must have some of the background showing (in other words you must be able to click outside all the windows therefore there should be no maximized windows displayed). All you do is to double click anywhere on the desktop background – that is totally outside any window including that of Program Manager. If you have already installed some wallpaper or a background pattern using the Desktop control panel, you effectively need to double click on this!

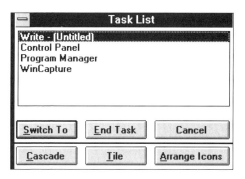

When you have double-clicked on the background the Task List window will be displayed. This will include a list of the applications that are currently running. To switch to the application you want just double click on its name in the list. Windows uses the word *task* to describe a running program.

Cascade and Tile

Windows provides several ways in which you can almost instantly tidy up your desktop by arranging your Program Groups for you. This is handled by a couple of options at the top of the Windows menu in Program Manager. These are Cascade and Tile.

Both are easy to use and fathom. If you select Cascade then each of the open Group windows will be resized into rectangles and then arranged offset from one another – overlapping so that the title bar of each can be seen with any unopened program groups arranged across the bottom of the Program Manager window. This is illustrated below:

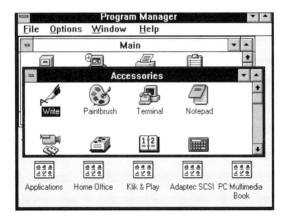

If the number of open program groups exceeds what can be displayed on the screen within the bounds of the Program Manager then after the bottom is reached the windows continue again from the top so that you can still see other parts of the previous windows. The window that was active at the time Cascade was used is always placed at the top of the stack.

The Tile option resizes all your open group windows so that they can sit juxtaposed to one another and all within the Program Manager window – as shown below overleaf.

PC Beginners First Steps

Insider Guide #23 – Selecting the tile order

When you tile, Windows is selective in the way it orders the group windows. It starts with the active window and then moves down the pecking order so that the last tile it creates was the window that was last active. At first sight this looks restrictive because you may want to order your tiles in a particular way to help you work. This is possible but the answer is so blatantly obvious most new users (and even experienced ones) fail to recognise it.

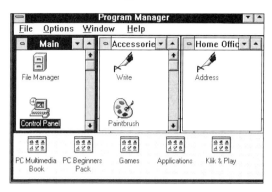

Consider that you want the group windows ordered so that Main is on the left, Accessories is in the centre and Home Write is on the right. The solution is:

1. Click in the Home Write window
2. Click in the Accessories window
3. Click in the Main window
4. Select Tile from the Windows menu

It really is that simple!

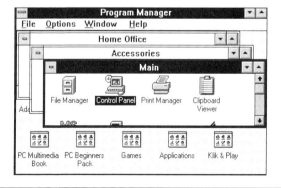

PC Beginners First Steps

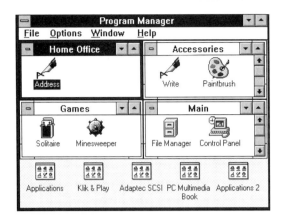

From an operational point of view this is the method I prefer to use because you can see all your groups together, use the scroll bars to get at anything within a particular window and also instantly maximize a window of your choice and then just as quickly re-size it back into its tiled state. A six tiled window is shown below:

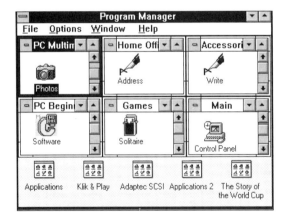

In the examples of tiling the active window at the time of tiling is always placed in the first position which is the top left hand corner window tile. Windows are then arranged across the screen from left to right with the least recently used window at the right. If more than one row of tiles are created then the least recently used window is in the bottom right hand corner.

More Tiles

There are two other places where you can tile from. If you run the Task List and then select the Tile button you can tile all open tasks. Remember that Program Manager is a task and if you have previously titled this it becomes a bit unusable if you then tile it from the Task List! You could then select Tile again from the Windows option but this starts to get a bit silly!

The other place you can tile from is File Manager. This is useful if you have several drive or directory windows open and want to see them all. Just select Tile (or Cascade) from the Windows menu in File Manager.

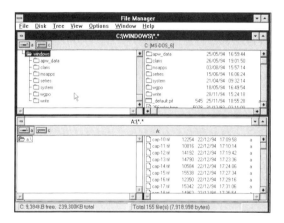

12

Accessories

Any past-time has its accessories – and Windows is no different. Here's a few which are on the computer that can help you organise your computing time better than ever before.

[Calculator window screenshot]

The Accessories group provides a number of useful mini applications – applets – which provide you with a basic set of programs with which to organise yourself a mini-office. The larger of these such as Write, Paintbrush, Cardfile and Notepad we will be looking at in coming chapters. Several of the others are also dealt with at other points in the book. This chapter though, introduces three items which will at least be familiar to you, even if you've never used them on a computer before. They are Clock, Calculator and Calendar.

Clock

Double-clicking the Clock icon launches an on-screen clock on the Windows desktop and in its own window. As with real life you can have either an analogue clock or a digital clock. Examples of both of these are illustrated over the page and as the pictures show the clock can also be used to display the date. As the Clock is in a window it can be re-sized to make it bigger or smaller – the clock fits the available window space.

PC Beginners First Steps

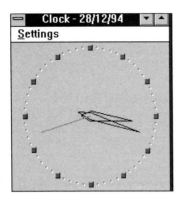

The Clock has a single menu called Setting and from this you can do a variety of things. The two most handy of these are to turn the heading off and to keep the clock as the top window at all times. If you make these two choices the effect is that you have a permanent desktop clock. Position this in the Program Manager window as shown – or even off in the corner of the desktop, and as the illustration shows you have time on you hands all the time!

In a later chapter we'll examine how to make the Clock start automatically every time you turn your PC on.

Calculator

Windows provides you with a real digital Digital calculator! When you first double click on the Calculator icon the applet opens up as a standard calculator.

But by going to the View menu you can select the other setting which adds even more functionality by converting the standard format into a full scientific one:

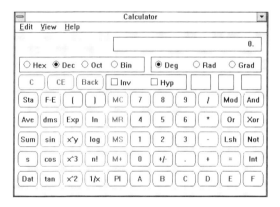

Both formats function in a similar fashion to a standard desktop or pocket calculator – which I am sure you are familiar with. The one thing that most new users to a computer find difficult is in remembering that there is not a normal multiplication sign – instead the asterisk sign '*' is used to signify multiplication. The standard operational keys and their functions are listed in the table on the next page.

To use Calculator select it and then either use the pointer to click on the buttons and functions as required or use the numeric keys on your keyboard.

Button	Key	Action
+	+	Adds the last two numbers.
-	-	Subtracts the last two numbers.
*	*	Multiplies the last two numbers.
/	/	Divides the last two numbers.
+/-	F9	Changes the sign of the number displayed.
.	.	Inserts a decimal point.
sqrt	@	Calculates the square root of the value displayed.
%	%	Calculates percentages.
=	=	Performs any operation on the previous two numbers.
1/x	r	Calculates the reciprocal of the displayed number.
Back	BACKSPACE	Deletes the rightmost digit of the number displayed.
C	ESC	Clears the current calculation.
CE	DEL	Clears the displayed number.
MC	CTRL+L	Clears any value stored in memory.
MR	CTRL+R	Recalls the value stored in memory. The value remains in memory.
MS	CTRL+M	Stores the displayed value in memory.
M+	CTRL+P	Adds the displayed value to any value already in memory.

To enter a calculation first enter (by typing or pointing and clicking) the first number in the calculation. Choose the operator and then enter the next number in the calculation. Continue to enter any remaining numbers and operators in sequence before selecting the equal sign button (=) or press the ENTER key to calculate and display the result.

If you make a mistake at any point you can either select the C button (or press ESC) to clear the entire calculation. If you want to delete a digit or digits press the Back button or select the CE button (or press DEL) to clear the entire number.

PC Beginners First Steps

Insider Guide #24 – Number base conversion

When you start the scientific calculator, it is set to work in the decimal number system. However there are other number bases available including binary and hexadecimal to name but two.

To convert a value by using the scientific calculator:

1. Enter the value you wish to convert either via the pointer or at the keyboard.

2. Select the option for the number system you want to convert to – Bin (binary), Hex (hexadecimal), Dec (decimal), or Oct (octal).

The illustrations above show a decimal number (256) being converted into a binary number (10000000). Note though that if you try to convert a number that has a decimal portion, ie, 256.7 then the Calculator shortens the number to its integer prior to conversion.

We will look at the subject of cut and paste in the next chapter – but suffice to say now that you can transfer the results of your calculations into other applications using this technique. This will become clearer in due course.

The scientific flavoured calculator provides a wide range of operator functions. The most common of these are listed below – this list is not exhaustive and the scientific calculator can perform many more functions. Refer to the online help for more details if you need these. To use any of the functions listed below click on the button or press the designated key on the keyboard.

Button	Key	Action
(	(	Opens a new level of parentheses. A total of 25 levels can be nested and the current number of levels appears below the display.
)	)	Closes the current level of parentheses.
And	&	Calculates bitwise AND.
Int	;	Displays the integer portion of a decimal value. Inv+Int will display the fractional portion of a decimal value.
Lsh	<	Shifts left. Inv+Lsh shifts right. After selecting this button, you must specify (in binary) how many positions to the left or to the right you want to shift the number in the display area. Then press = (to complete the function).
Mod	%	Displays the modulus, or remainder, of x/y.
Not	~	Calculates bitwise inverse.
Or	|	Calculates bitwise OR.
Xor	^	Calculates bitwise exclusive OR.

Calendar

The Windows Calendar is in fact much more than that – it is also an appointments diary and alarm. When you start Calendar it presents as a large window set to the current date and time:

The two scroll arrows sandwiched between the time and date allow you to move through the days on the Calendar by clicking on the left and right arrows to move backwards and forwards respectively through the dates.

The main area of the calendar though is the Appointments area. Once you have selected the date you require you can click in the Appointment area at the desired time and a text cursor will appear. Using the keyboard you can then enter the detail into your Calendar, editing it as required in the normal fashion.

PC Beginners First Steps

If you want to edit or delete a previous entry then you can just locate it, click on it and use the DELETE key to delete the entry in the normal editing fashion. Alternatively you can remove appointments for a single day or a range of days by using the Remove option in the Edit menu. If you select this the Remove dialogue box is displayed.

Enter the date range by typing the start and end dates in the From and To boxes and then select the OK button. To remove entries from one day only, leave the To box blank.

You can also get Calendar to remind you of the appointment by setting the alarm. To do this select the desired appointment time and then, from the Alarm menu, select the Set option – you can also use this exact same technique to remove a previously set alarm. When you set the alarm a small bell icon will be placed in the margin next to the required time.

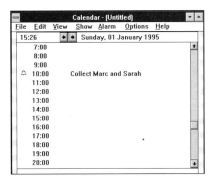

When the time is reached, and provided the PC is turned on and Windows is running, the alarm will be given in one of the following ways: If Calendar is the active window a dialogue box reminds you of the appointment. If it is the inactive window the Calendar title bar and borders flash. If it is not open the calendar icon flashes.

The Calendar has an early ring function that allows you to make the alarm go off early. You might, for example, have a 10 o'clock appointment and want to be warned 10 minutes beforehand to enable you to

Insider Guide #25 – Customising a calendar

You can customise the Day view of your calendar so that it fits in with your working schedule. You can specify the starting time of the appointments list, whether a 12-hour or 24-hour clock is used and the interval between appointments.

To change the day settings:

1. Select Day Settings from the Options menu.

2. Change the appropriate options, and then choose the OK button.

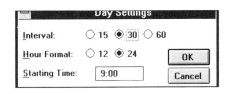

You can also add a specific special time – this is a time that falls between the regular time intervals of 15, 30, or 60 minutes –for example, 10.25. To add a special time:

1. Select Special Time from the Options menu.

2. In the Special Time box, type the time.

3. Select the AM or PM option if you are using a 12-hour clock.

4. Choose the Insert button.

To remove a previously set special time:

1. Move the insertion point to the time.

2. Select Special Time from the Options menu.

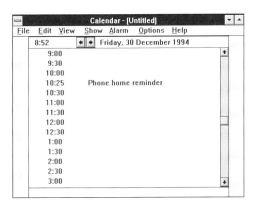

3. Select the Delete button.

The special customised calendar is illustrated above.

get ready for it. To do this select the Controls option from the Alarm menu. This displays the Alarm Controls dialogue box. In here enter a number between 0 and 10 and select OK. To ensure that the Alarm makes an audible sound when it goes off ensure that the Sound box is checked.

The Calendar includes a scratch pad area at its base – if you click into this (or press the TAB key) you can enter up to three lines of text – this is useful for notes and reminders that are non time specific.

In addition to a day by day view, the Calendar has a month view – this effectively shows a month at a time:

By clicking on the left and right arrows in the status line (the line containing the time and date) you can move up or down through the months – alternatively you can use the Show menu to access the Next, Previous and Today options. You can also select Date from this menu and enter a date you want to move to – this can also be used in the day view.

Printing Appointments

You can print a list of your appointments provided you have a printer. We have yet to encounter printers, which can be a complex subject and is dealt with in two chapters a bit later in this book. However, for completeness you select the Print option from the File menu and then enter the start and end date of the appointment you wish to print out.

13

DOS Prompt

'DOS – The Final Frontier'.
Well, actually it's more like the forgotten frontier – but it still has a very important role to play. So why not have a dabble?

```
┌─ ───────── MS-DOS Prompt ─────────
│WINLOGO   BMP         38,518 31/12/93
│WINMINE   EXE         27,776 31/12/93
│WINMINE   HLP         12,754 31/12/93
│WINMINE   INI            176 19/12/94
│WINTUTOR  DAT         57,356 31/12/93
│WINTUTOR  EXE        124,416 31/12/93
│WINVER    EXE          3,904 31/12/93
│WINWORD6  INI          1,511 30/11/94
│WORD      PIF            545 25/11/94
│Press any key to continue . . .
│
│(continuing C:\WINDOWS)
```

*I*f you have followed and worked through the examples thus far and been able to use them yourself in separate circumstances you will have moved out of the novice stage and while not being an accomplished user at least be a relatively confident user. But at this point we're going to leave Windows for a chapter and examine life outside of it. In doing this we're also going to look at the different types of files and examine the file and directory structure of your PC a little more. This will also provide you with some more knowledge that will be beneficial in your use of Windows – you see there are some times when it is simply a lot easier to do things outside of Windows.

MS-DOS

Microsoft DOS or 'DOS' for short is literally a whole new world. Asking what DOS is like is a bit like asking what is beyond the edge of the Universe – you have to experience it for yourself to find out. Er, not that I've experienced life outside the Universe! You see DOS existed long before Windows ever did. It was largely decreed as the thing that held the PC back from everyday users and in many respects that is true. But knowing a bit about DOS is like having a history lesson – knowing where you have come from gives you a better understanding as to where you are going and allows you to appreciate more what you have.

You may have already had some brief experience with DOS if you have had to use it to start Windows – to get into DOS from Windows select the Exit Windows option from the Program Manager File menu and select the OK button from the Exit Windows alert box.

Whoa! Black screen, a few cryptic letters and a flashing white line. Don't Panic! You are at the DOS prompt:

> `C:\>_`

The C:\ portion defines that you are logged onto the C drive and that you are in the root directory. The >_ is the prompt and signifies where any text typed at the keyboard will be displayed. I say text typed in – this is because at this point your mouse is useless – try moving it but don't waste too much time looking for the pointer – it isn't there and ain't coming back here!

Very carefully at the keyboard type the letters D, I, R; the screen will show:

> `C:\>DIR_`

You can use either capital or small letters but as before, for the sake of clarity capital letters will be the order of the day here. Now press the RETURN key.

Some information will flash up on your screen – if you have a hard disk that has a lot of files on it a long list may result scrolling through the screen. What you have done is to produce a directory listing of your hard disk. Nearly the File Manager equivalent of a drive window.

DIR is the DOS command for DIRectory.

If you have a long listing you can format it to provide a more pleasing look (if that is possible in DOS) with the command:

> `DIR /W`

Note that there is a space between the DIR and /W parts of the command. Spaces are normally very important in DOS and you should always be careful to include them. If you press RETURN you will get the same directory listing formatted neatly into five columns across the screen.

If you make a mistake by mistyping a command or by failing to insert a space at the correct point it is not normally disastrous. You'll simply get a terse message to the effect. For example, try entering the last command without the / or space:

DIRW

and you'll get the error message:

Bad command or file name

displayed on the screen.

If you have a very long DIRectory listing you can halt it after each screen page by entering:

DIR /P

Now when the bottom of the page is reached the listing will stop until you press the spacebar at which point the next screenful will be displayed etc. You can also combine these effects:

DIR /W/P

This will produce the five column formatted listing a page at a time!

In this and further examples you will have noticed that I have dropped the prompt bit of the command line. It is still there but now I'm just concentrating on what you need to type in. Equally, I'm not reminding you to press the RETURN key at the end of the line – take this as read unless I say otherwise.

All of these commands have so far acted on the hard disk that you are logged onto – which will almost certainly be drive C. You can also catalogue other disk drives by specifying the drive letter. For example, put a floppy disk into drive A (a disk that you have formatted and used before) and then type:

DIR A:

The floppy drive will burst into life and list the files on the disk. As before you can combine formatting effects to the DIRectory listing:

DIR A: /W/P

as you want.

If you type the DIR /W/P command again and look closely at the screen you'll notice that there are two types of files; files that are inside square brackets and files that aren't. The files inside the square brackets are infact directories! For example:

    [WINDOWS]   is the Windows directory

    AUTOEXEC.BAT   is a file

If you use the normal DIR listing then you can distinguish a directory from a file by the fact that it has:

    `<DIR>`

listed to the right of it. Also, as the example above showed, filenames tend to have a three letter extension to their filename.

Changing Times

Now that you know how to identify a directory let's see how to move into one using DOS. To change to a new directory you use the Change Directory mnemonic CD. So, to change to the WINDOWS directory type:

    `CD WINDOWS`

Again be sure to include the space.

When you have done this the chances are that you will notice a different prompt:

    `C:\WINDOWS>_`

DOS will normally include the path of the directory you are currently in as part of its prompt as a reminder to you.

You might now want to try all those directory commands again and see if there are any filenames that are familiar. If you did the HOME examples in earlier chapters then you can change to this directory by typing:

    `CD HOME`

The prompt will probably then show:

    `C:\WINDOWS\HOME`

and if you now type DIR you should be able to see the ADDRESS.WRI file!

Insider Guide #26 – Anatomy of a DIR listing

DOS listings are not as neatly laid out as those of File Manager. If you type DIR at the DOS prompt you will get a listing of files and directories that can look like your worst nightmare supermarket shopping bill.

Shown right is a shorter listing of the HOME directory. This shows that there are three files.

```
C:\WINDOWS\HOME>dir
 Volume in drive C is MS-DOS_6
 Volume Serial Number is 1B8A-BB87
 Directory of C:\WINDOWS\HOME

.            <DIR>        27/12/94   15:27
..           <DIR>        27/12/94   15:27
ADDRESS  WRI        640   25/11/94   19:29
         3 file(s)         640 bytes
                     8,146,944 bytes free

C:\WINDOWS\HOME>
```

The ADDRESS.WRI file is clear but the other two are in fact special directories called '.' and '..'. The latter allow you to move up to parent directories by typing

CD ..

Directories are signified by the fact that they have the words <DIR> listed after them. Files have their size, in bytes, listed and both have their time and date of creation.

If you are not interested in the latter, but only the files and directories themselves, then typing:

DIR /W

will produce a more regimented listing that is arranged in five columns as shown below.

```
c:\windows>cd ..

c:\>dir /w
 Volume in drive C is MS-DOS_6    Serial number is 1B8A:BB87
 Directory of c:\*.*

[ACCESS]       [AREPLAY]      [BRUCE]        [CASHFLOW]     [CPM]
[CSERVE]       [DOS]          [KNP]          [MARKS]        [MB]
[MOUSE]        [MSOFFICE]     [NU]           [OBPROGS]      [PANA]
[PAY]          [PHAROS]       [PPTEMP]       [PROTEXT]      [QPW]
[QTAX94]       [QTW]          [QUICKENW]     [ROMDEMO]      [SAGE]
[SAGEV7]       [SB16]         [SCSI]         [TELME]        [TEMP]
[TFW]          [TRIDENT]      [TUGAUTIL]     [VIDPLAY]      [WCUP]
[WINDOWS]      arvran.ram     autoexec.bat   autoexec.inb   autoexec.nu0
autoexec.sav   bankline.bat   cashflow.bat   chklist.ms     command.com
config.000     config.001     config.002     config.003     config.b~k
config.inb     config.nu8     config.old     config.sys     con_bak.old
image.bak      image.dat      ini.tmp        instcomp.log   markscli.ex_
marksgws.ex_   marksgws.hl_   marksgws.wr_   marksord.fr_   marksord.wr_
ndos.com       pay.bat        sage.bat       sageu6.bat     wina20.386
    983,052 bytes in 70 file(s)      1,077,248 bytes allocated
 12,378,112 bytes free

c:\>
```

Both types of listings end with a count of the number of files (including directories) listed, the total number of bytes they occupy and the number of bytes free on the disk.

So much for moving down the directory tree; what about moving up it? The simplest way is to leap up a rung at a time. If you type:

CD ..

– that's CD, a space and then two full stops – you'll move up to the next directory. So typing that from the HOME directory would plonk you in the WINDOWS directory. Doing it again would leave you in the root directory – C:.

If you know exactly where you want to move you can do so by typing the full path after the CD command. For example to move from the root directory straight to the HOME directory:

CD C:\WINDOWS\HOME

All this typing can get a little tiresome – unfortunately there's not really anyway around it in DOS other than the fact that the last thing you typed is recorded internally and you can recall this by pressing F3 (Function key 3). Try typing:

DIR

to see it work and then press F3 – you will need to press the RETURN key though after pressing F3 – it doesn't remember this!

By default the C: drive is the one that is set – but just as you can change a directory you can also change a drive. Assuming you have a floppy disk in drive A: you can move from drive C: to the floppy drive just by typing:

A:

Now any commands you care to enter, such as DIR, will work on the floppy drive. This assumes that you have a disk inserted – if you don't you will get an error message telling and asking you:

Not ready reading drive A
Abort, Retry, Fail?

DOS now needs you to select one of these by pressing A, R or F. If you have simply forgotten to put the disk in the drive then do so and press R for retry. Abort is best otherwise, as this should put you back from whence you came!

After experimenting with the A: drive you can move back to the hard disk by typing:

PC Beginners First Steps

```
C:
```

If you have been trying all this but you haven't been getting the directory details displayed as part of your prompt – don't panic! DOS provides a PROMPT command that allows you to customise how your display looks in this respect. Try typing this:

PROMPT T_PG

Now you'll not only get the current directory but also the current time (to one hundredth of a second) before it, thus:

```
11:12:18.07
C:\WINDOWS>_
```

You can set the basic directory only-prompt by typing the command:

PROMPT PG

File Format Functions

What we'll look at now is how to perform some of the actions on files that we did when we were looking at how to use File Manager. Namely copying, moving and deleting files. However we also did a few other things including formatting disks.

Formatting a disk through DOS is, in some respects, a quicker process than using File Manager. Find a blank disk and put it into your floppy disk drive. If you have a HD disk (High Density) you can just:

FORMAT A:

at the DOS prompt. If you have a DD disk (Double Density) then you should type:

FORMAT A: /F:720

The former version will automatically format a 1.44Mb disk, the second will force a 720k disk to be formatted in the drive. In either case when you press RETURN you will get the message:

```
Insert new diskette for drive A:
and press ENTER when ready
```

Press the RETURN key when you have put the disk to be formatted into the floppy drive (if it isn't already there). You may get one or two messages printed on the screen (depending on the version of DOS you are using – more on which in a later chapter) before it starts to format and verify the format. When the format is completed you will be asked to enter a label (title) for the disk. Enter this if you want or press RETURN to continue. Then DOS will display some numbers to show you how much of the disk is available for use and then ask you if you want to format another disk. Answer Y or N accordingly.

Sometimes you get a duff disk – this cannot be formatted as it is damaged in some way. If you get a message to this effect you have a couple of options. If you are trying to format it as a HD disk, try formatting it as a DD disk using the:

FORMAT A: /F:720

option. Otherwise either get a credit on the disk (most are guaranteed) or bin it!

Once you have a formatted floppy disk you can create a new directory (or directories) using the MaKe DIRectory command – MKDIR. To make a directory called TEST proceed as follows:

A:

MKDIR TEST

If you catalogue the floppy disk you should see that the TEST directory is in place.

Copying a file from one disk to another is done with the COPY command and then it is all about getting the filenames correct. If you are already in the directory where the file name is, then you need to specify the full pathname of the file to be copied. This is often fraught with problems so the best way to do this is to get yourself into the directory by using the CD command.

Suppose you want to copy the ADDRESS.WRI file to the floppy disk in drive A. You would proceed as follows. First set the prompt to be in the directory which contains the file in question. This can be performed in one of two ways (assuming you are logged at C:):

CD WINDOWS

CD HOME

or:

CD C:\WINDOWS\HOME

Once this is displayed in your prompt you can use the copy command in which you need to specify the filename, leave a space and then specify where you want it copied:

COPY ADDRESS.WRI A:

This should set the process in motion. If you catalogue the A drive by typing:

DIR A:

you should see the file in place. In fact the file is there but is in the root directory of the floppy disk. Suppose you had wanted to copy the file into the TEST directory. The answer is that you just specify the destination directory as part of the place where you want it copied thus:

COPY ADDRESS.WRI A:\TEST

Try this for yourself and then see that it is indeed there.

Deleting a file is just as (dangerously) simple. Again you must specify the full path details of the file you want to get rid of unless you are logged into the directory that contains it. The DEL command is used to delete files. To remove the ADDRESS.WRI file that is in the root directory on the floppy disk in drive A you would enter:

A:

DEL ADDRESS.WRI

The file would then be deleted. Note that here in the DOS world you don't have the safety net of an 'Are You Sure?' type alert box.

Renaming files is easy and can be done in two ways. Essentially all you have to do is to use the RENAME command and follow this with the old name, a space and then the new name. For example:

RENAME ADDRESS.WRI HOME.WRI

would rename the file called ADDRESS.WRI that is in the current directory to HOME.WRI. The other way to rename a file is to do it when you make a copy of it. If you wanted to move the ADDRESS.WRI file to the TEST directory on the floppy disk and call it HOME.WRI you could use:

COPY ADDRESS.WRI A:\TEST\HOME.WRI

You might like to try this one for yourself.

Wildcards

Just like a game of cards DOS has its very own wildcard character that can be used to represent part of a filename. Used in combination with the above commands it can be a very effective foil. The joker in the pack is *. Yes a good old-fashioned asterisk. You can use this to represent part or all of a filename. Here are a few examples.

Log onto the C drive and get yourself into the Windows directory:

C:

CD WINDOWS

Now type:

DIR *.EXE

The directory listing appears but notice how only the files that have extension EXE are listed. Here the asterisk is taken to mean any filename with the extension EXE. Also notice in the listing how the full stop delimiter does not appear between the filename and its extension – this is normal but you must always include it when using DOS commands.

The * can be used to represent all of the filename or just part of it. Typing this in:

DIR C*.EXE

would list all the files beginning with C that have the extension EXE. If you wanted to list all the files that began with the letters CO that had any extension you could use:

DIR CO*.*

The possibilities are endless and it's fun to experiment with them.

As mentioned at the beginning of this section you can use the * within any DOS commands that deal with files. For instance if you wanted to copy all your WRI files from the current directory to the floppy disk in drive A: you would use:

COPY *.WRI A:

You can use the * both sides of the delimiter. So you could copy all the files in the current directory to drive A by using:

COPY *.* A:

This process can also be used to block-delete files. The same techniques can be used:

DEL *.WRI

deletes all the files with the extension WRI from the current directory.

Next Time

Here I have only just touched on the subject of DOS but really if you can master the above then you have a good working knowledge of it because these are the commands that you will use most of all. If you're eager for more then try ploughing through the pile of manuals that came with your system – you should have one there specifically dealing with DOS – and now you know the basics you should be able to learn a bit from it.

WinDOS

Given that there are times that you will want to use DOS while you are working in Windows it would be a little long-winded to have to quit Windows each time you wanted to run a few DOS commands. For this reason Windows provides the MS-DOS Prompt program which you will find in the Accessories group. If you double click on this the Desktop will disappear and you will be presented with a typical black screen. However, the screen will provide you with a few messages that will tell you how to proceed further. Make sure you read and understand them before doing anything else.

If you don't want to enter an DOS commands, you can return to Windows by typing:

EXIT

when you are finished.

However, if you anticipate needing to switch between DOS and Windows at a regular rate then you can turn the DOS screen into a Windows based window by pressing:

ALT-ENTER

This can then be treated as a normal window and is illustrated overleaf. However, there is no 'close' function available to you from the

Control menu box as with other windows. To exit from the MS-DOS prompt window you need to type EXIT at the DOS prompt.

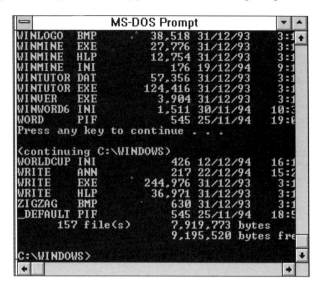

The Control menu offers a number of extra items that you can select from. These are generally for more advanced users but one of the more useful is the Fonts option. With this you can select how the MS-DOS Prompt looks on the screen. This is illustrated below and is worth experimenting with.

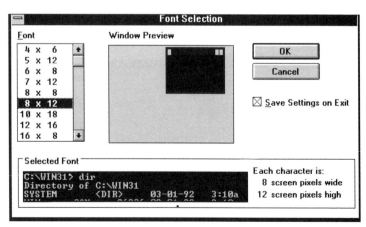

**What it lacks in features, Notepad
makes up for in downright ease of use.**

Preserve trees – keep it on your desktop!

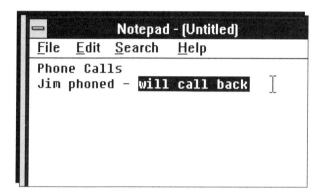

*N*otepad is a simple desktop jotter – a sort of ultra mini wordprocessor – if it were yellow in colour then you might consider it to be the Windows version of Post-It notes and – as the name implies – it is a way and means of making small notes. I stress the small aspect because there is a size limitation imposed on the files it can both create and read. When run it can fit into a corner of the screen and is of great use when you are working on a bigger job and want to make a series of jottings or reminders. It is great to use when you are making notes from phonecalls and isn't that bad for keeping up to date with the shopping list! Do remember that Notepad has its limitations. If you need to work with files which are reasonably large, use Write instead.

The file restriction imposed on Notepad isn't so small that it can't handle some serious jottings. If you want the technical details, 'small' in this context means that it cannot create files that are larger than 52k, and it can only open text files up to 45k. You don't need to worry about what these limits actually mean; however, you should bear in mind that 45k is at best average in terms of file size – and besides if you are creating files of this size Write is a much less clumsy option.

Working Notepad

As with all Windows programs and certainly the Accessories, you can start Notepad by double-clicking on its icon and the end result is a familiar window looking a bit like the one illustrated below.

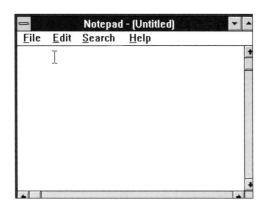

Once up and running you can start typing text into Notepad from the keyboard. If you are using it as a note-taking facility then you can either minimize it when you don't need it, or move it into a corner of the screen out of the way. In either case, do remember that you need to select the Notepad window to start entering text into it again.

Notepad isn't a wordprocessor so all those fancy things you might have seen happening in other people's wordprocessors can't be done here – many of them can be done in Write which is covered in a chapter very shortly. Notepad takes and uses simple text. You enter this by typing and you press the RETURN key when you want to start a new line. If you want to put an indent at the start of the line you press Tab and that's pretty much all there is to it, apart from some refinements detailed below. Anything you type is added to the screen at the point of insertion. This *insertion* point is marked by the flashing line which is the cursor.

This ability to begin work immediately is very useful. You don't need to tell Notepad to create a new file as soon as you've launched it. Of course, you do need to save your information when you've finished – see 'Saving Your Work' later.

PC Beginners First Steps

You can use standard Windows techniques for moving around Notepad. The following table lists some of the keyboard shortcuts you can use.

Key	Action
HOME	Moves the insertion point to the start of the current line
END	Moves the insertion point to the end of the current line
CTRL-HOME	Moves the insertion point to the start of the document
CTRL-END	Moves the insertion point to the end of the document
PAGE UP	Moves the insertion point up by one screen
PAGE DOWN	Moves the insertion point down by one screen
CTRL-PAGE UP	Moves the insertion point to the right by one screen
CTRL-PAGE DOWN	Moves the insertion point to the left by one screen
Right arrow	Moves the insertion point one character to the right
Left arrow	Moves the insertion point one character to the left
Up arrow	Moves the insertion point one line up
Down arrow	Moves the insertion point one line down
CTRL-right arrow	Moves the insertion point one word to the right
CTRL-left arrow	Moves the insertion point one word to the left

Text Selection

Pressing one SHIFT key while you use any of these combinations 'selects' (highlights) the relevant text. For instance, if the insertion point is at the start of a line, pressing SHIFT-END will select the entire line. Naturally, you can also use the mouse to select text. Simply position the insertion point at the beginning of the text. Click and hold down the left mouse button. Drag the cursor over the text. When you release the button, the text is selected.

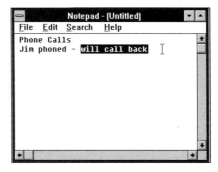

Selection is the key to performing editing operations on text in Notepad. For instance, if you want to delete text, select it and press the DELETE key (or pull down the Edit menu and click on Delete). However, you can be much more constructive than that such as re-ordering your notes into more logical points using a method called Cut and Paste.

Word Wrap

Look at the next illustration. Here, text has been entered in the normal way. Unlike most wordprocessors, Notepad does not recognise when the end of a line has been reached: it simply keeps entering text on the original line.

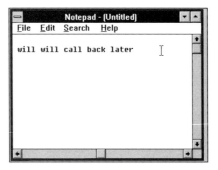

This probably won't be what you want; for one thing, it's hard to follow text which doesn't conform to the bounds of the containing win-

PC Beginners First Steps

Insider Guide #27 – Cut and Paste

Cut and Paste is a very basic Windows technique. Learn it now and you will have a life of relative computing simplicity. It is a simple and straightforward task and just involves you selecting the text you want to move, cutting it from where it is, identifying its new location and then pasting it into place.

The screen shows five lines of text in Notepad. To move line two to in between lines four and five proceed as follows:

1. Move the insertion point to the start of line two.

2. Hold down the SHIFT key and press END to select the entire line.

3. Select Cut from the Edit menu. The highlighted text will disappear.

4. Move the insertion point to the start of line five.

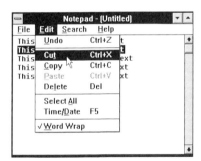

5. Press the RETURN key to move the line down to leave a blank line above it.

6. Move the insertion point onto the blank line.

7. Select Paste from the Edit menu to insert the previous cut text.

The text that was cut has been held in a temporary storage place called the Clipboard which is dealt with in a later chapter. If you want to keep the original text intact then you can do so by selecting Copy from the File menu rather than Cut. Try copying line one to create a new line at the end.

dow. However, you can easily rectify this. Click on Edit to pull down the Edit menu and choose Word Wrap. This is the result:

If you want to turn off word wrap, simply repeat this procedure.

Inserting the Date/Time

If you are making notes, and especially if you are using the phone you may want to keep track of the date and time of the call. You can have Notepad insert the current date and time (it gets this information from your computer's internal clock). To do this, pull down the Edit menu and choose Time/Date. Or simply press the F5 key.

Text Searches

Most wordprocessors allow you to do particular tasks that can be very helpful. Firstly, find specific occurrences of text and secondly, replace these with other text. Notepad, however, because it isn't a fully-fledged wordprocessor, will only let you do the first of these.

To locate a specific occurrence of text within a Notepad document, place the insertion point at the location from which you want the search to begin. Pull down the Search menu and select the Find option.

PC Beginners First Steps

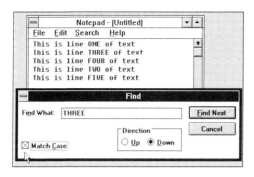

In the Find What field of the Find dialogue, type in the text you want Notepad to search for. Click on Up if you want Notepad to search towards the start of your document, Down if you want it to search towards the end. Click on Match Case if you want the search to be case-specific. In other words, if you want Notepad to find all instances of 'book' but not 'Book', type 'book' in the Find What box and select this. Click on Find Next to have Notepad begin the search. Press the ESC key when you've finished searching.

If you've already instructed Notepad to carry out a search and have then returned to your document, you can begin the search again without launching the Find dialogue by pressing F3. Notepad uses the search parameters you inserted earlier.

Opening Files

You can use Notepad to open – and then amend – existing text files. Notepad will open any text file, irrespective of the suffix. However, convention dictates that text files will often have one of the following suffices:

.TXT
.SYS
.BAT
.ASC
.CFG
.INI

To open a text file into Notepad, pull down the File menu and choose Open. Notepad recognises text files which end in .TXT automatically. If you want to open other text files, click on the arrow next to the List Files of Type field and choose All Files from the drop-down list.

If the file you want to open isn't on the drive shown in the Drive field, click on the arrow to the right and select the correct drive from the list. Select the correct directory in the Directories field. Finally, highlight the appropriate file in the list below the Filename field. Click on OK to open the file. Note that unlike many other Windows applications Notepad will only open one file at a time.

Saving Your Work

When you've finished editing a Notepad document, do the following to save it to disk by using the Save option from the File menu. Notepad writes the file to disk. If, however, your document hasn't been saved before, Notepad produces the Save As dialogue box which we saw earlier with Write.

Choose the drive and directory to which you want the document saved (since the Save As dialogue is functionally identical to the Open dialogue). Type in a name in the File Name box. Choose OK to have Notepad save the file under the name you specified.

Printing Your Work

Notepad has limited print capabilities. However you can print to an attached printer if you want. Now we haven't at this stage discussed printers and how to print from Windows and its applications. However, this is discussed from the start of the next chapter – if you know that your printer is connected and have worked it correctly beforehand then jump to the section called Printing Notepad which can be found at the end of Chapter 16.

15 Printer Choice

An understanding of how your printer works is the first step to controlling the way it prints your documents.

*I*t's a fact of life but even a long time after you have mastered your PC and Windows you will probably still be having problems with your printer. Not that there is likely to be anything wrong with your printer – it's just that unless you have bought a totally integrated hardware package, getting software and printer to work in perfect harmony is fraught with problems. Even if they work perfectly now there's no guarantee they will when you introduce some new software.

This chapter is designed to provide you with details of the various types of printers and how they work. If you have an understanding of that then you will be better equipped to sort out any problems should they occur. The next chapter deals with how to sort out the software side of things.

One point to bear in mind at the very off here is that while solving printer problems may be infuriating, do remember that one of the best ways of solving them is to experiment. By obtaining printed output at each stage (or lack of it) you should be able to see what actions have what effect.

PC Beginners First Steps

While there are quite literally hundreds of printers to choose from, it is important to remember that there are also different types of printers from which you can make your selection. The distinction is important because the type of printer determines the way in which the printer produces its final printed output.

The key to using a printer with the PC and in particular Windows is the availability of a suitable *printer driver* – this being the software interface between your PC, ie Windows and your printer. You need a driver because no two printers are the same and even though the printers manufactured by Epson printers have long been regarded as a *de facto* standard, standards are never quite that!

Most of the time you'll find a suitable driver supplied with your printer or with Windows for use with the Printer Setup which is discussed in the next chapter. Another outlet for printer drivers that cater for less popular printers is the Shareware libraries. Shareware is a subject that is covered in a chapter later in this book. When you buy your printer ensure that you get a printer driver at the time you buy it. And best of all try to see the printer in operation with a PC and ideally being used from Windows. This is the best way to solve all potential problems. If you already have a printer and after these next two chapters are sure you don't have a printer driver that is able to deliver the goods, then go back to where you purchased the printer and demand one!

The main complication is that not all printers are the same. There are different ways of reproducing what you have on the screen to paper – this is called the *hardcopy*. These include hitting the paper with wire pins through an inked ribbon (dot matrix) and spurting drops of ink onto paper (ink and bubblejet) and putting a charge on the surface of the paper only to remove it where the ink must settle (laser). We'll go through the types of printer and then mention how your PC goes about printing and what to look for in printer consumables. As already mentioned earlier actually getting your printer set up is dealt with in the next chapter. First, let's look at the various types of printers.

Types of Printer

There is a wide and varied range of printer types which are classified by the way in which they perform the process of printing. The more popular methods are detailed briefly on the following page.

Daisywheel

The grand old daisywheel is still around with its typewriter action which results in perfectly formed characters if all you need is A to Z and 0 to 9. These are becoming less and less popular and chances are you won't ever come across one. They are not much use for a graphics-based computer but you can still use one from your wordprocessor if daisywheel quality is needed for business letters or form filling.

Inkjet/Bubblejet

The modern inkjet printer was pioneered for micros in this country in the early 80s by Olivetti but lost out to the rise of the dot matrix printer.

The inkjet has been joined by a near relation, the bubblejet. The Canon Bubblejet and the Hewlett Packard Deskjet have proved very popular because they can offer laser-like quality at prices substantially below that of most laser printers. The Canon Bubblejet for example has 48 jets which give a resolution of 360 dots per inch (dpi), a more detailed printout than most laser printers can achieve.

Inkjet printing is also the key to the best colour printing on the PC. The software however is not up to perfectly matching all available screen colours through mixing the printers' inks. Some inkjets improve colour printing greatly by offering a separate black cartridge so that any blacks in the picture do not have to be created by mixing coloured inks which can drown the paper in ink and result in brown black! This does mean you need to swap cartridges – but the end results are worthwhile provided you take good care of the cartridge not in use – many printers of this type provide a special storage box to put cartridges that are not in use into. Use it!

Dot Matrix

Dot matrix printers are the most successful breed of printers, partly because they are cheap to purchase and cheap to run, partly because they reproduce both text and graphics to an acceptable quality. Dot matrix printers fall into the two main categories of 9-pin and 24-pin, the latter offering better quality and speed in most cases. There are some 18-pin and 48-pin printers.

Dot matrix printers come in different carriage (paper) widths, can accommodate sheet feeders (like a photocopier) to automatically feed in single sheets of 'normal' paper for business stationery and can be fitted with a mechanism to print in colour via four different colour ribbons. The versatility of the dot matrix printer is its strong point. Nor have the possibilities been exhausted as new methods of describing graphical displays to the printer mechanism are invented and incorporated into computer software.

The latest dot matrix printers have colour printing mechanisms as standard. These print through a multicolored ribbon under software control. The printer driver detects which colour is being sent and sends the appropriate code to move the ribbon into position. 24-pin dot matrix colour printouts are very impressive, though a little slow and noisy.

Laser

The classic office laser printer is based on the Hewlett Packard Laserjet standard however the PostScript compatible laser offers a higher quality end product albeit at a higher cost. Laser printers which are driven directly from Windows are now common and reproduce Windows documents effectively at near inkjet prices. PC graphics benefit less from mono laser than business documents with text and line drawings. Lasers come with trays which hold single sheets and their print quality – the resolution at which they print – is usually 300 dots per inch or 600 dots per inch. As a basic rule of thumb, the higher the resolution (the dpi) the better the final printed product and the higher the price!

Laser printers range from the very slow to the very fast and again cost is often a factor here. Four pages a minute is often OK for the odd home job but not for everyday office work – especially as four pages per minute doesn't always mean four pages a minute.

A variety of page description languages (see PostScript below) are built into these printers, most not supported by PC/Windows software. Running costs vary greatly and may be too much for home use.

Printing Types

There are a number of methods which software will use to get what is on screen onto the paper that awaits it. The two most common ways are through graphic images or through a special program called PostScript. The simplest way though is straight text printing.

Text printing relates to printing ASCII characters in the font styles which are built into the printer. An ASCII character is simply an

Insider Guide #28 – Wonderful world of printers

The dot-matrix printer is the most common and cheapest to run of the printers currently available. It comes in two forms, 9-pin and 24-pin, the latter providing a higher quality output. Paper can be sheet-fed or more commonly sprocket-fed in a continuous form as illustrated.

The inkjet or bubblejet printers provide a higher quality output but are more expensive to run. They only accept sheet-fed paper but are very quiet in operation compared to the dot-matrix printer. They also require less office space.

The laser printer looks and operates much like a photocopier. The final quality printout is superior but may be slow. It is expensive to run but is quiet. Single sheet paper is placed into trays or bins which may hold in excess of 500 sheets.

alphanumeric character that has, under an international standard, been allocated a particular code. This code is simply a number, normally in the range 0 to 255 – for example the ASCII code of an A is 65. Therefore when a printer receives an ASCII code number 65 it knows it has to print an A. Simple really.

However, fonts and printers have become more sophisticated so that even the basic text printers of the dot-matrix type allow the printing of draft text with bold and italics to Near Letter Quality (NLQ) or LQ (Letter Quality) fonts with portrait or landscape orientations. Both the NLQ and LQ formats endeavour to produce Daisywheel quality print. However, text format printing is becoming less commonplace because programs such as Windows use graphics to produce hardcopy. Many printers are sold on the basis of their ability to take font cartridges and to download fonts from the computer but this is only relevant to printing in character mode or to take advantage of PostScript. Plug-in font cartridges or cards are available for most 24-pin printers, and for the Deskjets and Laserjets.

Windows – as you are well aware by now – is a predominately graphics orientated application and unless you are using PostScript (which I'll discuss in a moment) most of what you print from Windows via the Print Manager will be done as a graphic – even text – in other words it won't be making use of any of the character sets which are built into the printer. Instead the whole page will be created from mixing patterns of dots on the paper. The driver software will create an appropriate dot pattern (called *dithering*) to represent each of the colours or different grey levels which make up a screen picture. Different patterns are needed for the different available resolutions.

Monochrome graphics printing turns off any attempts by the printer driver software to do any dithering so you literally get a black and white version. Depending on the picture, this can result in an attractive print and you can use it for the ultimate draft or proof graphics dump. Avoid this setting if you are printing from a desktop publishing (DTP) program because it will distort the printing of fonts as well as conventional graphics. Fonts in DTP programs are created with grey pixels around the edges to help them keep their curves! Fonts in the DTP context are often called type. Fonts are covered in their own chapter in this book.

The dot matrix machines normally print bidirectionally (during the up and down stroke), for speed, but since in graphics mode slight skew can be seen – especially in text – unidirectional printing may be selected.

PostScript Printing

PostScript is a *page description language* and this is normally used in tandem with a PostScript laser printer. These are more expensive than the classic sort but because of the way PostScript works you normally get a superior output especially if you are using programs that require it – a desktop publishing package for example. This is because PostScript is resolution independent which basically means that you should get a good image that takes full advantage of your printer's resolution.

When you are using a PostScript printer the printer driver sends the file to the printer in the form of a program (a list of instructions) that fully describes the page or pages you want to print. You can think of this program as being a very complex description of what you have produced. The PostScript printer has its own computer and memory on-board (this is why they are relatively expensive) and this converts the description of the page into an image that is stored in the printer's memory. This is, broadly speaking, turned into an image on the paper by using the laser in the printer to add and remove charges to the paper onto which toner particles become bonded and then sealed.

Normal printing operations don't use PostScript to anywhere near its full extent. It comes into its own when used by applications for desktop publishing and complex drawing.

If professional printing is required, typically for flyers, newsletters, brochures etc created in a desktop publishing program, then imagesetting is the intermediate stage. Instead of printing to your own printer you can either send the original file on disk to the repro house or print the file to disk as a special PostScript file. This is then run through a typesetter which is a very high resolution output device, typically 2000-3000 dpi compared to many laserprinters 300-600 dpi.

The typesetter usually outputs either a positive or negative image onto transparent film or just a positive image onto photographic paper (bromide) depending on what your printer requires. If colour is involved then the bureau will separate the colours and output four films. The bromide or film is then used to create the plates which go onto the printing machinery.

Printing from Programs

Most of your printing will be done from within a program which will present you with certain options, such as turning the print sideways so that it fits better along the paper. You'll have noticed that, although the computer screen is usually wider than it is deep, printer paper is usually deeper than it is wide! Most programs however will pass the printer job, and your selections, onto the Windows Print Manager program before it gets to the printer. This means that you don't have to set up every program for your printer.

Paper Chase

Tractor paper handling is best for fanfold continuous paper (for listings), labels on carrier paper, and for multi-part forms. However, only an impact (ie dot matrix or daisywheel) printer can print all parts of multi-part forms.

Cut sheet feeders holding 50 or more sheets are available as optional extras for most dot matrix and inkjet printers. This is particularly appropriate for office use, where cut sheets do not require that tractor margins be removed and look better than fanfold. Some printers can print on Overhead Projector (OHP) film, though each type may require an appropriate (eg coated) grade of film for best results. There are merchants who specialise in appropriate coated paper for, especially, inkjet and laser printing when quality really matters. Some colour inkjet printers demand the use of a special paper provided by the manufacturer.

For printing wide tables and spreadsheets with a dot matrix printer, you can print sideways in graphics mode on a standard (8") model, or choose a wide (13") model. With the other printer types, it is usual to print sideways (landscape) in character or graphics mode since – even if available – models which can handle A3 paper are much more expensive.

For dot matrix printers the so-called true A4 size (ie 8.25" x 11.66") is the closest possible to 210 x 297mm, while having a whole number of print lines spaced at one-sixth of an inch. You'll find that 70 gsm (grams per square metre) is a good weight as a compromise for both draft and correspondence use. It may be obtained with tractor margins that are micro-perforated which leave a reasonably clean edge when they are removed.

As for labels, you get them on fanfold carrier paper for use with a variety of software, such as a database printing out from a name and address list. If you buy them Indian file, one after the other, it's easier to set up the software! If your database can print onto two, or more, labels across the sheet then you will find you can get through your printing more quickly.

For page printers copier paper is quite acceptable and 80 gsm a good weight. The same paper may also be used (preferably with a cut sheet feeder) with dot matrix and inkjet printers. On occasion I have noticed that the extra ink applied when printing graphically can spread and slightly distort the curves of the characters, so if this happens, try a coated paper of some kind.

The ribbons for dot-matrix printers are relatively low in cost, whereas the cartridges for inkjet printers can be quite a bit more expensive and give you a higher cost per page. In the case of the page (eg laser) printers, the consumables include the toner and the development unit, which can be expensive. If you anticipate doing a lot of printing then the cost of doing it should be investigated thoroughly.

Background and Buffers

Windows treats printing as a separate task and can do it at the same time as running a program. Further speed gains can be made by sending the data quickly to a temporary storage area in the computer's RAM memory (called a *buffer*). Getting back control of the keyboard and mouse doesn't mean that printing has stopped, only that it is going on in the background as data is sent from the temporary store to the printer unseen.

The memory buffer can also be in the printer but the bigger the memory capacity of the printer, the more expensive it will be. Some laser printers have enough memory to form up complete pages in their own memory and can therefore be asked to print multiple copies without troubling the computer again.

Inking Up

Ink cartridges are an important part of the inkjet printing process and there are some companies who specialise in supplying inks, both standard cartridges and sets of ink which can, for instance, turn an ordinary black and white printer into a colour printer by changing inks and overprinting. To do this you need a program which will control the process, separating the colours out from the screen picture and printing them one at a time.

For instance, any colour/shade which contains blue (cyan ink) will be printed on the first pass with a cyan cartridge fitted, any colour containing yellow will be printed on the second pass, and so on. For the Deskjets, Paintjets and Bubblejets you can get full colour printing systems which provide ink refills for the multipass process together with the software.

Laser printers take toner cartridges. Many companies offer a refill service allowing you to re-use your current cartridge. This is commendable and very Earth friendly which is to be applauded – but the results simply aren't as good in my opinion. This often manifests itself in poor quality that sees you having to reprint pages and also it isn't the best method of looking after your printer as rollers and the other moving parts can get easily damaged. This all adds up to a situation which can cost more in both money and the environment.

So much for some theory about using and abusing a printer – the real crux of the matter is getting it to work. The next chapter looks at how to connect it up and getting Print Manager to do its business.

16

Print Manager

If you have your printer attached, inked up and ready to go – stop!

There's a few more things to do so visit the Print Manager first.

```
                    Print Manager
 View    Options   Help
 [Pause]  [Resume]  [Delete]   The Epson
                               (Local) is I
 Epson FX-85 on LPT1 [Idle]
```

*T*he advantage of having a working environment such as Windows is that all the things which are common to all applications that are used as part of the Windows world can be controlled from one point. This is particularly true of printing. In the years BW – that's Before Windows – and for programs that are not run under Windows all had to supply their own interface with the printer. This meant installing special printer driver software for each and every one. Not only that, you also had to fiddle to ensure you got things hunky-dory. Now under Windows you still have to fiddle to get things working occasionally but because printing is handled by Windows itself, once one application is working correctly the rest should toe the line. As you use File Manager to control and manipulate your files you use Print Manager to control and manipulate your printing requirements.

Connecting Up

Before you plough ahead with Print Manager you need to ensure that your printer is correctly set up and plugged in.

Although we have negotiated the various types of printer in the last chapter we didn't look into the way the data from the computer is moved to them. This is done in one of two ways – either using a parallel connection or a serial connection. As a rule of thumb dot-matrix and inkjet printers are normally of the parallel type and lasers are of the serial type.

However, the sure-fire way to determine what you have, in case you didn't already know, is in the type of lead that plugs into the back of your PC. A serial printer will almost nearly always have a nine pin plug which is in a D-shaped container. A parallel printer will have a much bigger and differently-shaped plug.

There are four steps to setting up a printer. One, ensure that the printing medium is in place. This would be a ribbon for a dot-matrix, and ink cartridge for an inkjet and a toner cartridge for a laser printer. Two, ensure that the paper is in place. Three, connect the lead between the printer and the PC and four, ensure the power lead is in place and plugged in. Now, unfortunately all four of the above might need you to move and consult your printer's manual, as I have no idea what you have in that respect. However, these are such basic everyday functions that should be relatively straightforward and hopefully the dealer where your purchased your printer showed you how!

While you have your manual to hand look up how to conduct a self test of the printer. Most printers have a test function that you can initiate as you turn them on – this means that they will print out a page containing, for example, a list of fonts or examples that they can produce. Doing this also confirms that the printing medium and paper are all installed and working correctly.

When you have done that, the key button and light on the printer is the one called *On-line*. A printer can be either on-line or off-line. When the printer is on-line it is ready and able to receive information from the computer. When it is off-line is is internally disconnected and anything you try to print from the computer simply won't happen, or at least it won't happen until the printer is back on-line. So check the on-line light to ensure it is on and if you have an on-line button (printers such as laser printers often don't) press it until the On-line button is illuminated.

PC Beginners First Steps

> ### Insider Guide #29 – Print Manager anatomy
>
> The Print Manager window is dominated by the print queue area. Here all current print jobs are listed along with their status.
>
> Because print jobs may go to various printers that might be connected – jobs are listed under their destination printer.
>
>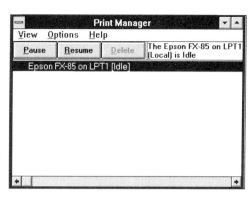
>
>
>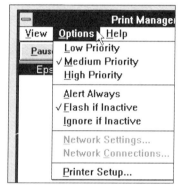
>
> In addition to the standard Help menu Print Manager has two other menus – the View Menu (above left) and the Options Menu (above right). The Options menu is the most interesting of the two and allows you to directly control your printer or printers.
>
> There are three buttons at the top of the Print Manager window. Pause and Resume allow you to stop and start printing while delete allows you to delete a file from the print queue.

Inner Workings

Here, briefly, is how Print Manager works. When you issue a print instruction from within any Windows application, Windows launches Print Manager itself. Print Manager copies the file you want printed, and then proceeds to print this in the background. There is a small delay while it processes the file, but once this is complete Print Manager hands control of Windows back to you and works unobtrusively (well largely) in the wings.

That's the theory. Actually, Print Manager hardly ever goes wrong. When it does, however, it's useful to know how to correct things. However, there are good reasons for starting Print Manger yourself if you know you are going to be doing some printing. These centre around the fact that it works by organising print tasks into 'jobs'. You can:

- Suspend/resume print jobs
- Delete print jobs
- Reassign print job priorities
- Change print emphasis
- Access your printer's specific settings

The third option – reassigning print job priorities – is particularly interesting. Normally, Print Manger prints jobs sequentially. In other words, the order in which you issue print instructions determines the order in which printed documents emerge from your printer. You can change the queue sequence, if you want.

The fourth option is perhaps less useful. When Print Manager has processed its copy file and started printing in the background, you should bear in mind that, although you can work on other tasks while printing is underway, your computer has only one internal processor. This means that your machine's processing power is being divided between both tasks. The result is that both are rather slower than they would otherwise have been. Normally, this causes no problems – in fact, it's a very convenient trade-off. Print Manager, however, lets you determine what emphasis to allocate to printing itself, within broad limits.

Working with PM

If a print job is currently in progress, Print Manager will already be operating; you don't need to launch it yourself in order to work with it. Simply do either of the following:

- Press CTRL-ESC to produce the Windows Task List. Highlight Print Manager and click on Switch To.
- Press ALT-TAB as often as necessary, until the Print Manager window appears.

Insider Guide #30 – Print Manager Setup

Print Manager allows you to change printers and to determine what sort of output you get from Windows on your selected printer. To do any of the above first select the Printers Setup option from the Options menu. This produces the Printers dialogue box.

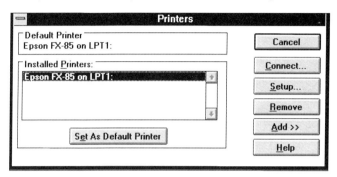

In here will be a list of installed printers – this may be just one printer or it may be several. Where there is a selection to choose from simply click on the name of the printer you wish to use.

To select or define further options click on the Setup button – this produces a dialogue box which will have the name of the selected printer.

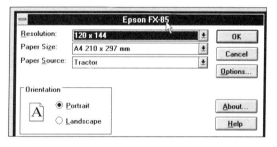

From here you can select your requirements for Resolution, Paper Size and Paper Source – as described in Chapter 15. You can also define if the output is Portrait or Landscape, while clicking the Options button will produce a further Options dialogue box from which other aspects of the printer can be defined. This includes Print Quality and Margins to name but two. Note that the options available may and will vary between printers.

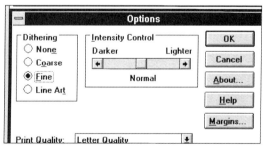

If Print Manager isn't already operative then simply double click on its icon in the Main program group window to set it going.

From within Print Manager, highlight the currently active printer. Click on the Pause button to suspend printing – you may want to do this for instance, if your printer is about to run out of paper, or if you want to change the ribbon/cartridge – but it is a good idea to do this before you start printing.

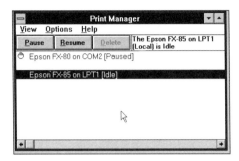

You can then set about sending your print jobs to the printer – remembering to select between printers if you have more than one installed.

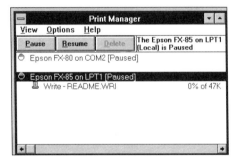

If you go back to Print Manager you should see your print job or jobs listed. When you are satisfied that your printer is ready you can click on the Resume button to commence printing on the highlighted printer.

Insider Guide #31 – Adding new printers

Adding a new printer to the list of those installed is easily done and there is no real limit – other than a practical one – to the number you can install. Display the Printers dialogue box by going through the Printer Setup option on the Options menu.

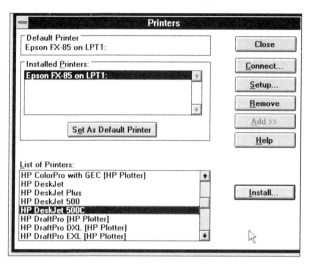

Then click on the Add button – this expands the window to include a list of printers that you have available to install. Scroll through this list until you locate the printer you require and double click on its name. At this point you may get a dialogue box asking for you to insert the printer drivers disk (this is part of your Windows set). Do this and then once the driver software has been read from the disk, follow the setup options described earlier.

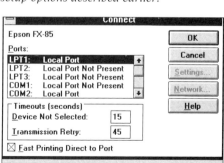

If the new printer is to be installed on a different port (for example it is a serial printer rather than a parallel one) you can define where Print Manager should look for the printer through the Connect dialogue box.
First ensure you have selected the required printer in the Installed Printers list, then click on the Connect button. This displays the Connect dialogue from where you can select the appropriate port.

PC Beginners First Steps

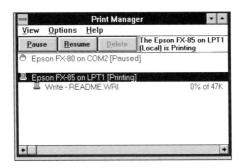

Job Priorities

As mentioned towards the start of this chapter, one of the reasons for printing with Print Manager in an active window is that you can re-order print jobs on the fly. To move one of the pending jobs higher up the queue, simply highlight it. Click and hold down the left mouse button; drag the job to the new level in the queue. You can also use the keyboard to reassign queue levels. Highlight the print job. Then hold down the CTRL key; use the up or down arrow keys to drag the job to its new level.

You can also use the print queue to delete a print job if you realise you gave the original instruction in error. This is readily done simply by highlighting the file name in the job window and clicking on the Delete button.

Print Emphasis

Print Manager has three broad settings listed in the Options menu:

   Low Priority
   Medium Priority
   High Priority

Medium Priority is the default. This means that when you engage in printing and other tasks simultaneously, they share processor time equally. If you don't want this, do the following. Pull down the Options menu and choose either Low Priority (other tasks take precedence) or High Priority (printing takes the lion's share of processor time).

Notepad

As promised in the chapter on Notepad – here's a step-by-step guide to printing from Notepad which you might like to try. This example assumes you are going to print from within Notepad itself. This is different from what we have discussed above – however, you might like to try the Print Manager direct route for yourself afterwards.

Print Setup

The first thing to do is to ensure that your printer setup is correct. To do this select Print Setup from Notepad's File Menu. Once you are happy with this you can proceed to the next stage.

Page Setup

The next thing to do is to ensure your margin setups are correct. Pull down the File menu and click on Page Setup. In the Page Setup dialogue, type in revised margin settings, if necessary. If you need guidance then left and right page margins of 0.75 inches and top and bottom page margins of 1 inch are good numbers to start with.

You can then set the header and footer details if you need them. By default Notepad will give you a header which contains the file name, centred between the margins and a footer which contains the page number and the text 'Page', all centred between the margins.

For instance, if you want your Notepad document to carry the following as a header:

```
Jottings for 18/12/94
```

simply type this into the Header Field. Don't be put off by the smallness of the box: Notepad scrolls the text to the left if you exceed the box capacity.

In addition to header and footer text, you can also insert codes which define the text alignment, and also to some extent the contents. These codes are:

&c Centres the header/footer between the margins
&l Aligns the header/footer on the left margin
&r Aligns the header/footer on the right margin
&p Inserts consecutive page numbers
&f Inserts the document title
&d Inserts the current date
&t Inserts the current time

Another example. If you wanted to create a footer which contained:

>your name
>the page number (but without the word 'page')
>the current date and time

all flush with the right margin, you might type:

>**F. Bloggs &r&d &t &p**

in the Footer field. Don't forget to insert spaces between the text codes to make the result more easily readable.

Printing

With the document you want to print currently open, pull down the File menu and choose Print. Printing should begin almost immediately.

Wordprocessing is the most popular use for a PC. Write is the perfect introduction to the subject for novices and ye olde fashioned typists alike.

*W*hereas Notepad is intended to serve as an electronic jotting pad, Write is a wordprocessor *per se*. It is not and does not pretend to be the be all and end all and certainly lacks features which are present in modern, commercial products. However, as a means to get you going it will meet your every need and in this respect it is surprisingly useful as an introduction to wordprocessing.

You can use Write to create, edit and print documents. These can include letters, memos, even reports. Unlike Notepad, you can apply special formatting to text within Write. You can:

- Insert tabs
- Specify which font text should have
- Change the size of the text
- Apply indents to text
- Embolden, italicise and underline text
- Align text appropriately
- Determine the line spacing within certain bounds
- Apply headers and footers

Equally there are some things you can't do with Write. A few of these are listed below just in case you have used a wordprocessor before and are wondering if they are included.

- Apply colours to text
- Spell- or grammar-check text
- Apply automatic text hyphenation
- Insert pictures or tables created in other software
- Look up synonyms in an in-built thesaurus
- Apply columns to text
- Apply text borders or fills

We have already used Write in a very simple form in earlier chapters to demonstrate the use of the keyboard and file creation, so you should be familiar with its screen. As always double click on the Write icon in the Accessories group to fire it into life.

Like Notepad's, Write's opening screen is deliberately understated. This means that you can begin entering text immediately. Incidentally, you don't have to tell Write to 'wrap' text (ie, move it onto the next line when it encounters the end of a line): it does it automatically.

The Letter

If you have followed all the examples herein you will know that we started the famous letter file some time ago and saved it as ADDRESS.WRI and it seems simple to stick with this to sort out some of the other facilities that Write provides. Just to remind you of a few things that you may not have remembered from those earlier chapters that seem a long way away now.

To tell Write that you want to insert text on the next line, press the RETURN key. Then type it in. Repeat this as often as necessary. Note that you can't see the carriage return that Write inserts at the end of each line; you can in more expensive wordprocessors, but Write is too minimalist for this.

And that's just about all there is to basic text entry in Write. Our letter now looks something like this:

PC Beginners First Steps

Insider Guide #32 – Write anatomy

The Write window has a few additional refinements that are not found in other windows. It has a second scroll bar that allows you to scroll left and right across a page, as well as up and down through a document. It also has a page indicator to display the current page number.

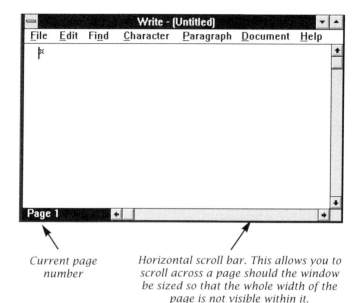

Current page number

Horizontal scroll bar. This allows you to scroll across a page should the window be sized so that the whole width of the page is not visible within it.

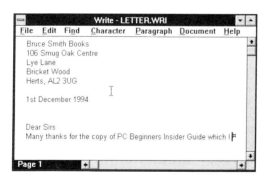

Of course, there are refinements. We'll look at some of these in later sections.

PC Beginners First Steps

Working with Text

The basis for most work in Write is text selection. In this respect, Write functions identically to Notepad. If you need help with how to select text using either the keyboard or mouse, refer to Text Selection in the chapter covering Notepad.

Sometimes, when you've entered text you need to correct it. Look at the next illustration.

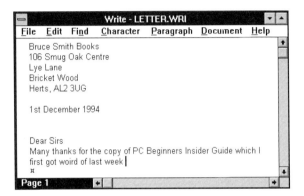

Although Write has no spell checker, it's obvious here that a typographical error has been made in the spelling of word. How do you correct it? There are various methods. Firstly you could use the keyboard or mouse to select the 'i' in 'woird' and then press either the BACKSPACE or DELETE keys.

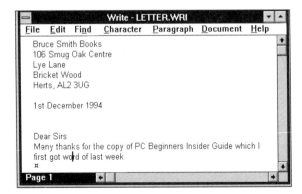

Alternatively you could position the cursor immediately after the letter 'i' in 'woird' and press the BACKSPACE key once.

PC Beginners First Steps

Finally, you could position the editing cursor immediately before the 'i' in 'woird' before pressing the DELETE key once. More sophisticated editing operations are possible in Write. See the next chapter for more information.

Write Moves

Like Notepad, Write lets you use keystroke combinations to move around in its editing screen. Those available are listed in the following table.

Keypress	Action
HOME	Moves the insertion point to the start of the current line.
END	Moves the insertion point to the end of the current line.
CTRL-HOME	Moves the insertion point to the start of the document.
CTRL-END	Moves the insertion point to the end of the document.
PAGE UP	Moves the insertion point up by one screen.
PAGE DOWN	Moves the insertion point down by one screen.
CTRL-PAGE UP	Moves the insertion point to the top of the window.
CTRL-PAGE DOWN	Moves the insertion point to the bottom of the window.
Right arrow	Moves the insertion point one character to the right.
Left arrow	Moves the insertion point one character to the left.
Up arrow	Moves the insertion point one line up.
Down arrow	Moves the insertion point one line down.
CTRL-right arrow	Moves the insertion point one word to the right.
CTRL-left arrow	Moves the insertion point one word to the left.

Saving Write

Saving again shouldn't present too much of a problem to you – not just because we have done it before but also because the layout of the various Windows dialogue boxes should now be rather familiar to you. Select the Save option from the File menu, enter a name – try LETTER.WRI this time – and click on OK having ensured first that it is going to be saved to the directory of your choice – again perhaps one of those we created in an earlier chapter.

When you tell Write to save its files, it does so in its own proprietary format. It also applies the WRI extension. Note that, if you don't include it as part of your filename, Write will automatically assign it for you. So if we had just entered LETTER in the filename box, the file would still have been saved as LETTER.WRI. However, you can also save Write files in two other principal formats. These are:

> Word for DOS   suffix: .DOC
> Text only (ASCII)   suffix: .TXT

ASCII is an acronym which stands for 'American Standard Codes for Information Interchange'. But why would you want to save Write files in these formats? If you use the Word for DOS file type, most other wordprocessors will be able to import (load) the resultant file without any loss of formatting information. For instance, if you save a Write file which has italicised text to this format and then open it into another wordprocessor, the text would still be italicised. If you save a Write file to its ASCII format, though, all formatting will be lost. However, you can then import it into just about every other wordprocessor and even into Notepad.

To save a Write file in Word for DOS format, click on the arrow to the right of the Save Files As Type field in the [Save As] dialogue before you select the drive and directory and allocate the file name. Choose Word for DOS in the drop-down list. To save a Write file in ASCII, choose Text Files from the list. Now complete the Save As dialogue as above. Another use of the Save As option is to make a copy or rename a file as you are saving it to avoid overwriting the original.

Opening Write files

Again, we have already seen how to open Write files in earlier chapters but the Open option can present a few other alternatives. First, to open a plain vanilla Write, pull down the File menu and choose Open. The Open dialogue launches.

Write is set up to recognise files which end in .WRI (its own format) automatically. If you want to open files in other formats, click on the arrow next to the List Files of Type field and make the appropriate choice from the drop-down list. Choose Word for DOS to load up files created by the DOS version of Microsoft Word, or Text Files to import ASCII files. When it encounters files in formats which aren't its own, Word produces the next message.

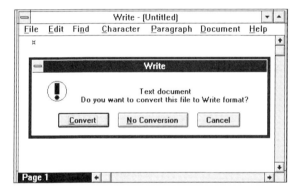

Click on Convert to have Write translate the file into its own format. This means that when you come to save it later, it will be saved in Write format rather than the original. If you click on No Conversion, however, the file isn't converted. You'll often need to select No Conversion. For instance, if you load up one of the essential DOS text configuration files that require editing (CONFIG.SYS or AUTOEXEC.BAT for example which we'll look at in a later chapter) for editing, it's vital not to save the result in Write's format (your computer can't understand this!)

If the file you want to open isn't on the drive shown in the Drive field, click on the arrow to the right and select the correct drive from the list. Select the correct directory in the Directories field. Finally, highlight the appropriate file in the list below the Filename field. Click on OK to open the file.

18 Write On

Now you've started Write why not write on!

With Write you can create anything from a letter to a multiple page report. Why – even a novel – and that's not a story!

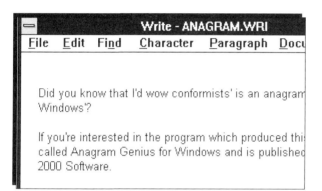

The basic aspects of Write were dealt with in the last chapter. In this chapter we'll start to look at the more advanced features on offer and how to use them to best effect – and get some printed hardcopy using them. Because there are a good number of features the temptation is to go overboard using them. Don't! Wordprocessing is about effective presentation to get a message across. You may want to make it look good but over-use of effects can have a negative effect, making your document look untidy and overbearing. They also take time away from your writing which should be the main function of Write. Using Write you can:

- Specify an alternative font
- Increase or decrease the type size
- Specify the font style
- Superscript or Subscript text
- Underline text

You carry out each of these by first selecting the text that you want to apply them to.

Face and Size

You can change the look of your text on screen – and on the printed output – by specifying a particular font. Now fonts are a subject in themselves and one that is dealt with in the next chapter. To that end I'm not going to delve into the topic too much here so please have a little bit of blind faith which will come good in the next chapter. To distinguish one font from another they are given names. If you pull down the Character menu and select the Fonts option the Font dialogue launches.

The font used by Write by default is called Arial and this is highlighted in the list of fonts. To change the font from Arial to another select one from the list, for example, Times New Roman. Whichever font you click on a sample of it is displayed in the Sample box. The illustration below shows the highlighted text along with the Fonts dialogue box.

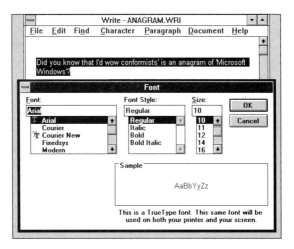

You can also alter the size or height of a font. This is also done from the Fonts dialogue box by typing the size into the Size field. Into this you can enter sizes in a numeric range of 4-127 where 72 is roughly an inch. The text that you are reading is about 10 in this range.

Using the Fonts dialogue box you can also select the style of the font and there are four options available in the Font Style; choose from:

> Regular (standard formatting)
> *Italic*
> **Bold**
> *Bold Italic*

Note that not all of these choices are available for every typeface, but once you have made all your selections from the dialogue box click on OK to apply them to the selected text. The next illustration shows what the text looks like after it has been set to Times New Roman 12 point italic:

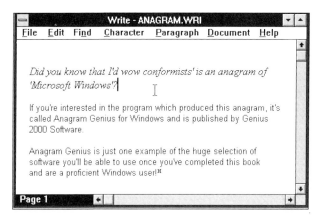

The type effects outlined above are the most common but there are a few others which are available directly from the Characters menu. Selecting underline will underline all the highlighted text including spaces. Underline is a feature that has been left over from the days before wordprocessors when the most effective, and really only way, to emphasise text was to type a _ character under each letter. The best way to emphasise text really is to italicise it.

Another option is to make text Superscript or Subscript. This involves shifting the line on which text is normally printed either up or down. The best way to see this is to look at the next illustration. Here the typeface for the first paragraph has been changed to Times New Roman, a variant on probably the most popular typeface. Additionally, the type size has been changed to 16 points, 'Microsoft' has been placed in superscript and 'Windows' in subscript. As before to use either of these select the text and then choose the effect from the Characters menu.

PC Beginners First Steps

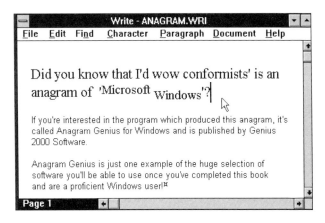

Having applied any of these effects you can remove them again simply by selecting the relevant text and choosing the option again.

Tabbing Text

Tabs are fixed numbers of blank characters, specifically (though not exclusively) at the start of paragraphs. Look at the first illustration in this chapter again. The layout is rather flat and unappealing. It helps the eye (and makes the text much more readable) if the first line of each paragraph is moved in from the left text margin. Write lets you achieve this in three ways:

- Using spaces
- Using tabs
- Using indents

You should never use spaces as tabs. The simple reason is that spaces take their size from the specific typeface/type size combination currently in force for a particular paragraph. If you apply different typefaces or type sizes to different paragraphs within a Write document, the effect is very uneven. Always use either tabs or indents.

By default, Write applies tabs every half inch. To apply specific tabs to text, do the following. Pull down the Document menu and choose Tabs. In the Tabs dialogue, click on Clear All to remove any pre-set positions.

Then enter tab measurements in the Positions line. Each measurement is the distance between the tab and the left margin. If you want to set a decimal tab, select the appropriate Decimal check box. Decimal tabs are specially configured tabs where the values align at the decimal point (useful for tables of figures). Click on OK when you've finished. The illustration below shows the Tabs dialogue box.

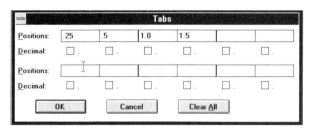

A more practical way of setting tabs is to use the Ruler and this is discussed a little later in this chapter.

Although using tabs to move the first line of a paragraph inwards is perfectly acceptable, you can also do this by using indents. Indenting paragraphs is easier and more convenient for specific paragraphs, because the effect is more localised, whereas tabs apply to the entire document. Another advantage is that you can also indent the whole paragraph, and/or the right paragraph margin.

To indent a paragraph, click in it. Or select the entire paragraph. Pull down the Paragraph menu and choose Indents. The Indents dialogue appears.

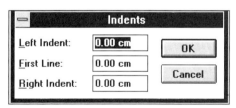

To amend the first line indent, enter a value in the First Line field (this is the distance between the left text margin and the start of the line). If you want to move the entire paragraph in from the left margin, enter the appropriate value in the Left Indent field. To apply a right indent, type in the required value in the Right Indent field. Click on OK when you've finished. The next illustration shows the entire first paragraph in our sample text indented from the left and right margins by .5 inch. In addition, a first line indent of .5 inch has been applied.

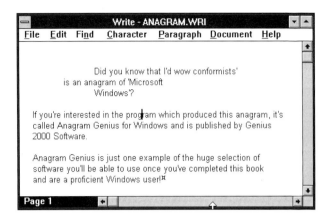

Aligning Text

Using tabs and/or indents gives you precise control over textual alignment. However, you won't always need this. It can often be more useful to align in more general terms. Write has four commands you can apply:

Left	Text is flush with the left margin
Centred	Text is aligned equidistantly between the left and right margins
Right	Text is flush with the right margin
Justified	Text is flush with the left and right margins

You may not wish to use the Justified option. When text is 'justified', Write inserts spaces between words to make the left and right edges meet the margins. More sophisticated wordprocessors have an automatic hyphenation feature which inserts hyphens to break up words and reduce the number of spaces required. Write lacks automatic hyphenation, and as a result its justified text is often unsightly.

To apply any of these options, first select the relevant paragraph(s). Then pull down the Paragraph menu and make the appropriate selection. See the illustration for a demonstration of alignment options.

PC Beginners First Steps

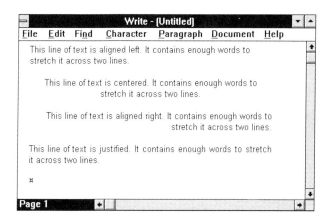

Line Spacing

You can choose to amend the line spacing for selected paragraphs. Write provides three choices:

        Single
        1_ Space
        Double Space

Examples of each of these are shown in the screen shot below:

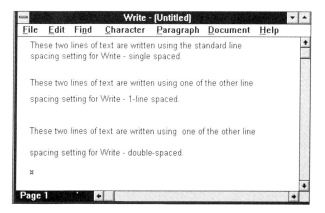

Double line spacing is a frequent requirement for all kinds of fiction and non-fiction manuscripts. To apply one of these options, select the relevant paragraph(s). Then pull down the Paragraph menu and make the appropriate choice. The illustration shows the effects of the various line spacing options. The first paragraph is single spaced (the default). The second has 1_ line spacing. The third is double-spaced.

Using the Ruler

Write provides a very useful shortcut for imposing tabs and amending line spacing and paragraph alignment: the Ruler. To make the Ruler visible, pull down the Document menu and click on Ruler On. This is the result.

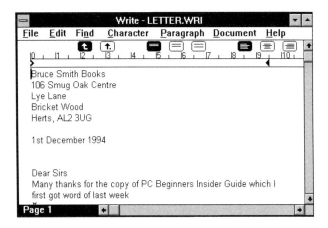

As you can see the Ruler has been positioned across the top of the page and this will show the margin edges, any set tabs and the text alignment in use. To use the Ruler, click within the paragraph whose attributes you want to change. Then:

1. To insert a new tab, click on the Standard tabs or Decimal tabs icons, as appropriate. Click in the Ruler where you want to set the tab; Write inserts a tab symbol in the lower section of the Ruler. The paragraph is realigned accordingly.

2. To amend the paragraph alignment or line spacing, click on the appropriate icon.

Insider Guide #33 – Using the Ruler

The Ruler allows you to format and align text directly from the screen without having to resort to use of menus and options. It also allows you to do it visually so that you are able to see the effects immediately. To switch the ruler on use the Ruler On option in the Document menu.

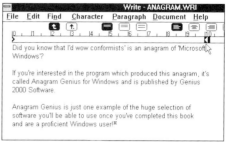

You can set the margin on your text by dragging the diamond left of right in the Ruler bar. This enables you to set the width of the text to suit the window you want to work in. Note that when you do this you should already have text in the document and you should select it all first. As in the illustration you may need to maximize the Write window first to do this.

The Ruler is shown in isolation below. With it you can – from left to right – set tab stops, set line spacing and define how text is aligned. To use any of the icons on the Ruler – select the text and then the icon depicting the required function.

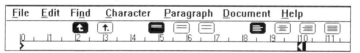

Setting tabs using the Ruler is far easier than using the dialogue box. However, unlike other paragraph effects tabs are always applied globally – therefore you cannot have a series of tab settings. To set a tab first select the type by clicking on the appropriate icon. Then click in the

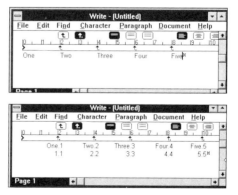

Ruler at the position required. Tabs may be repositioned by dragging and removed by dragging them down and out of the Ruler. The above two illustrations show normal tabs (upper) and decimal tabs (lower) which are aligned on the full-stop.

Find and Replace

Like Notepad, Write lets you search for specified text but unlike Notepad, Write lets you perform Replace operations on it, too.

To locate text, first position the editing cursor at the point within your document from which you want Write to begin searching (Write's search operation will only operate in one direction: towards the end) at the very start is normally the best option. Pull down the Find menu and click on Find. The Find dialogue launches.

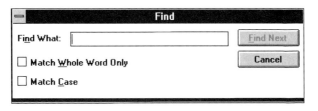

Enter the text you want Write to flag in the Find What field. If you want the search to be case specific, click on Match Case. This means that, if you enter 'anagram' as the search text and select Match Case, Write won't find:

ANAGRAM

Anagram

or any other permutation.

If you want to locate whole words, click on Match Whole Word Only. In this instance, doing so would mean that Write would omit 'anagrams'. Click on Find Next to initiate the search.

To find and then replace text, first position the editing cursor at the point within your document from which you want Write to begin searching (Write will only search in one direction: towards the end). Pull down the Find menu and click on Replace. The Replace dialogue appears.

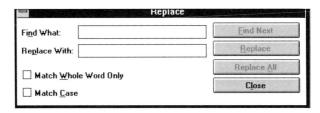

Insider Guide #34 – Headers and Footers

When you implement headers or footers in Write, they are not normally visible. Instead, Write has a special Header/Footer window which only displays when you create them.
To create a header or footer, do the following:

1. Pull down the Document menu and choose Header or Footer. Choosing Header will show the Header window and the Header Page dialogue box. If you choose Footer instead, the Page Footer dialogue appears instead of the Page Header dialogue. This is almost identical.

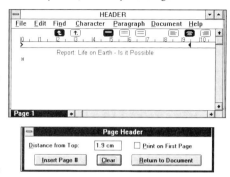

Any header or footer text you've previously allocated appears in the Header or Footer window. If you want to delete this, click on Clear.

2. Select the Header window and type in the header or footer text – note that the Ruler will not appear in the window unless it has been switched on through the Document menu. You can apply styles and fonts in the normal fashion should you wish.

3. If you want to amend the distance between the header/footer and the top and bottom of the page respectively, enter a revised measurement in the Distance from Top or Distance from Bottom fields. The default is 0.75 inches.

4. It's common not to require headers or footers to print on the first page of a document. For example, if you set up a header which contains the document title, you clearly won't want this to display on the first (title) page – Write assumes this is what you want. If you do want your header or footer to print, click on Print on First Page.

5. If you want Write to insert automatic page numbers in your header or footer, click on Insert Page #. Write inserts a special formatting code.

By default, Write aligns this on the left of your header or footer. If you want to centre or right align the page numbers, select the code in the normal way. Pull down the Paragraph menu and click on Right or Centered.

6. When you've completed your header or footer, click on Return To Document.

Enter the text you want Write to replace in the Find What field. Enter the text you want substituted for the original in the Replace With field. Select Match Case and/or Match Whole Word Only, as appropriate. Click on Replace All to have Write find and replace all instances of the original text, automatically. If you want to vet the substitutions yourself, click on Find Next instead. Write finds and highlights the next instance of the search text, and pauses. Choose Replace to have the text replaced, if appropriate; if not, click on Find Next again. Write resumes the search. Continue until Write tells you it can't find any further instances of the search text. When you've finished, click on Close to close the dialogue. Note that this can sometimes have unexpected side effects so always save your file before you run a Find and Replace action. This way, if the result isn't what you expected you can close without saving and re-open the file to start again!

Cut and Paste

The process of Cut/Copy and Paste was introduced in the chapter on Notepad. Write supports this as well and a full discussion of how useful this can be is provided in Chapter 20 which introduces the Clipboard.

To copy text, select it. Then pull down the Edit menu and choose Copy. Or press CTRL-C. To cut text, select it. Choose Cut from the Edit menu (or press CTRL-X). To insert the copied or cut text into your Write document, position the insertion point at the correct location. Pull down the Edit menu and click on Paste. Or press SHIFT-INSERT.

Headers and Footers

The final advanced Write feature is its implementation of headers and footers. Headers are specified text repeated at the top of every printed page; footers are text repeated at the foot of each page. For example, look at the page you are reading – the header of the page is 'PC Beginners First Steps' and the footer is the page number. These are not hard and fast rules for headers and footers – just what is implemented in the production of the book. You can have text in both or neither, and while you probably wouldn't want them in letters you almost certainly would in some sort of document.

Printing Write Documents

So long as your printer is working well with Print Manager you really should find printing from Write a piece of cake. There are three stages:

- Setting the page margins
- Making sure your printer's proprietary settings are correct
- Issuing the print instruction

You can set the page margins at any time. To do so, pull down the Document menu and click on Page Layout. In the Page Layout dialogue, enter revised top, bottom, left and right margin settings, if required. For basic stuff you'll keep these as they are but as with most things in Write it is a good idea to experiment and try things out. Most of the options in this dialogue box will be familiar as they are consistent for Windows and first encountered in the Print Manager chapter.

After setting the print margins – or confirming they are what you want – you can perform the remaining two tasks from the Print dialogue box which is displayed by selecting Print from the File menu.

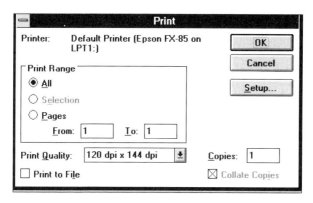

The precise form of this dialogue depends on the printer being used. However, certain components are standard to every Write print job:

The Print Range Section

Select All to print the entire document. Click on Selection (if this option is available) to print text sections selected before launching the Print dialogue. If you want to print a page range (e.g. 3-6, 5-12), enter the starting page number in the From field and the final page number in the To field.

The Copies Field

If you want to print more than one copy of a document, enter the number of copies required here.

Print to File

Click on this if you want to send the printed document to a disk file, rather than a printer. You might do this if you need to print out your Write document on a computer on which Write isn't installed (although this is rather unlikely). The print file produced using this method can even be printed on computers which don't have Microsoft Windows. See your DOS manual for how to do this.

The Setup Button

Click on this to access and reset your printer's own proprietary settings. See your printer's manual for how to do this.

When you've finished with the Print dialogue, click on OK; Write begins printing. Note, however, that if you selected Print to File, Write launches a further dialogue before starting to print.

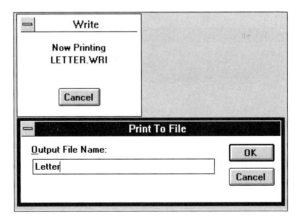

Write's print files have a .PRN suffix.

Use the Print File dialogue to select the drive and directory to which you want the file saved (or accept the defaults). Type a file name in the File Name field. Click on OK to have Write save the file.

First impressions last.

And nothing creates a greater impression, nor decides how ledgeable your documents are, then the type style you choose to present them in.

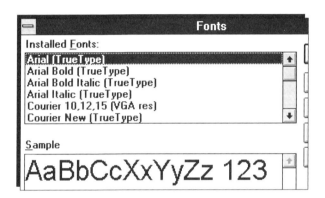

*O*ne of the major reasons that has allowed the PC to develop into a sophisticated work tool is its ability to display and print text in different styles or *fonts*. This is a vast and complicated subject and an important one. But I can only begin to touch the surface of this topic here.

The study of fonts is a science in itself and comes under the heading of *typography*. With the increasing use of computers such as the PC in publishing, especially in the application of programs such as desktop publishing (DTP), typographical terms have wormed their way into the ever expanding world of computer jargon. More terms for you to learn!

Unless you are into typography you have probably never paid much attention to the style of the text (type) that you read. In fact, there are many hundreds (and probably thousands) of styles of type and these are called fonts. For instance, the very text you are reading now is typeset in a font called New Aster. For shorthand we might normally say: the text is set in New Aster. The two most common fonts in use are called Times and Helvetica and these are often seen in newspapers. Check out your daily!

One thing you will have noticed is that the printed word comes in many sizes – type sizes are normally measured in their own system called *points*. A point is very fractionally over $^{1}/_{72}$nd of an inch, although it is normally referred to as being $^{1}/_{72}$nd of an inch. Therefore a font that is one inch high is said to be 72 points high. Samples of various point sizes are shown in the example below.

Fonts also come in type styles and the three most common styles are Roman (normal), Italic and Bold. Although there are many different fonts to choose from they can all be divided into two basic categories which are called *serif* and *sans serif* fonts and these are illustrated in the Insider Guide.

A serif font is one that is adorned with fancy edges, the most famous of which is Times. Helvetica does not have these extra bits and is an example of a sans (without) serif font. Although there are no hard and fast rules, by convention sans serif fonts are used for headlines and serif fonts for main text because they are easier on the eye. So, how do you know what fonts are serif and which are sans serif? Look at them!

The appearance of a font on your PC screen might well look very different to that which you get when you print out hard copy containing the same fonts. This is especially the case when printing from DTP style programs which have specialist printer drivers rather than those that simply dump the screen. The printed font looks infinitely better. Bear these points in mind when you use fonts initially, with some experience you will get used to this.

Window Fonts

Fonts and the ability to display them relies on having a graphical interface and this is why Windows works well with them. Indeed you already have several different fonts installed on your PC which happened when Windows was originally installed for you. These fonts are handled by the Fonts control panel and we'll have a look at this shortly, first though it is important to realise that there are two types of font for use in Windows – screen fonts and TrueType fonts.

Screen fonts are designed to look good on the screen and are not really best for use with printers other than dot-matrix printers. They come in predefined sizes but despite their limitations they are there because they can be displayed very quickly on the screen and for this reason

PC Beginners First Steps

Insider Guide #35 – Font types and font sizes

There are many types and styles of fonts. The way in which a font looks is called its typeface and there are many hundreds of different styles.

This font is New Aster
This font is Lucida
This font is Palatino
`This font is Monospace`

This is 12 point

This is 18 point

24 point

36 point

The size of text is defined by a unit called the Point. A point is, for arguments sake, $1/72$ nd of an inch. Therefore text that is 72 points high is 1 inch high.

The 36 point text on the right is half an inch high.

Generally text is set in either 10 point or 12 point.

Times is a serif font
Helvetica is a sans serif font

Fonts can be broadly categorised as serif or sans serif. Serif fonts such as Times have ornate edges while sans serif ones do not.

Sans serif means without serifs.

they are normally used by Windows to display information in dialogue boxes.

TrueType fonts are in fact mathematical representations of the characters. From what is essentially a list of co-ordinates any size character can be produced – this makes them resolution independent. This is different from screen fonts which are stored as the physical patterns of each character. This means in theory that they will look as good on the screen as they do on the printer – although laser printed True – Type fonts look better in general than dot-matrix printed ones.

There are other types of fonts and the most common group of these is Printer fonts. These are fonts that can be either built into the printer (by placing them in a ROM chip) or can be stored on your hard disk and sent to the printer when they are required by downloading them into the printer's RAM. When you install a printer and select it through the Print Manager the printer fonts will appear in the Fonts list of the application you are using – for instance the Font list of the Fonts dialogue box in Write.

I'm not trying to get out of this – honest – but the combination and how to handle fonts will depend largely on what applications you have installed and what printer you are using. This provides a plethora of combinations that it would be virtually impossible to cover in the space available – so please do consult your printer's handbook. Look for a chapter covering Fonts or look Fonts up in the index.

Fonts CP

Windows already comes with a number of fonts installed and you can see these by opening the Control Panel and running the Fonts applet.

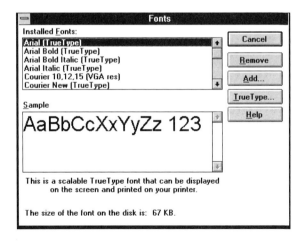

The type of font is normally listed within brackets after the font's name. Screen fonts are indicated by the name of the monitor type you have. For instance a True Type will have :

(TrueType)

listed whereas a screen font for a VGA monitor will have:

PC Beginners First Steps

(VGA res) after its name.

You can see how each of the fonts look just by clicking on them and looking at the sample text that's displayed. The Fonts control panel provides buttons that let you add or remove fonts. In the case of the latter, the selected font will be removed from the list (after a suitable safety warning) whereas the Add button provides you with a dialogue box similar to an Open dialogue box. As stated before, if you are installing fonts refer to the documentation that comes with them for full detail.

The TrueType button will display the following dialogue box when clicked:

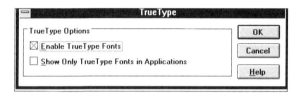

This allows you to decide if you want to use TrueType fonts exclusively or just in applications. If you need to use this option then the effects of it will not start until you have relaunched Windows – in other words after saving the change you need to exit Windows and then restart.

Character Map

In the Accessories program group you will find the Character Map applet. From this you can select, copy and obtain the key strokes required to generate a particular character from any of the fonts you have installed on your PC. The Character Map window is shown below.

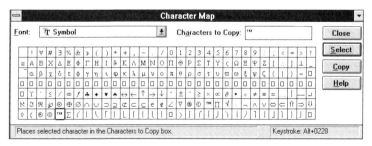

The window consists of a block of 256 squares each of which may contain a character, although some fonts may not have a full character set in this way and the characters available from font to font will vary. The base set of alphanumeric characters will always remain, but those in the bottom set of blocks will invariably change.

Character Map allows you to get at characters you may not be able to normally insert from the keyboard. The first thing you need to do is to select the font you require – this will normally be the font you are working in. This can be done by picking the font from the drop-down menu in the right of the window. Once this is selected the character map will change to reflect the characters available.

Now you can select the character you are after by clicking on its square. To copy this to the clipboard click on the Copy key. The character you are about to copy will be shown in the Characters to Copy box. You can then insert the character or characters you have copied by returning to the applications (such as Write) and selecting Paste from the Edit menu.

20

The Clipboard

Move text, pictures and numbers between applications in Windows is a breeze. If fact just about the only thing you can't transfer is the kitchen sink – but I suppose they're working on that one. Even if you know it or not you're using the Clipboard.

```
┌─────────────────────────────────────┐
│ ▬            Clipboard Viewer       │
│ File   Edit   Display   Help        │
├─────────────────────────────────────┤
│ The CD-ROM needs the following      │
│ drivers to make sure it works       │
│ with Delta-Zed:                     │
│     Hobart                          │
│     Sydney                          │
└─────────────────────────────────────┘
```

*O*ne of the main tasks of Microsoft Windows is to enable other Windows-based programs to work well together. One of the ways in which it does this is to facilitate the transfer of information between programs as diverse as wordprocessors, spreadsheets, databases, and drawing applications – in fact, the whole gamut of Windows programs. Windows will even let you transfer information between Windows programs and DOS programs running in a dedicated window. This allows programs in Windows to be fully integrated in a way that the more recent products can share data between and across them.

When Windows starts it sets aside an area of your computer's internal memory for the temporary storage of data. This data can be in the form of text, formatted text and/or graphics – in fact anything that can be highlighted or selected. The location in which the information is stored is known as the *Clipboard*. The clipboard can only handle on item at once – the item being defined as the last thing that you either cut or copied their using an applications Cut or Copy options from the Edit menu.

Cut and Paste

I'm not going to dwell too long here because this is topic covered in the preceding few chapters. In essence, you can use the Clipboard for transferring information between Windows applications. It consists of the following steps:

1. Open two or more Windows programs.
2. Verify that the programs have Copy, Cut and Paste commands.
3. Highlight the text (or select the graphic) you want to transfer.
4. Choose Copy or Cut.
5. Move to the second program's window.
6. Position the cursor where you want to insert the text or graphic.
7. Choose Paste.

Just about every Windows application has Copy, Cut and Paste commands (usually in the Edit menu). Let's examine these steps in more detail.

The difference between Cut and Copy is that the former deletes the original text whereas the latter keeps it intact. You should also bear in mind that once graphics or text have been copied to the Clipboard, paste operations don't remove them. This means that you can perform multiple pastes. Only when you when you copy something else to the Clipboard, or close down Windows are the Clipboard contents erased.

Transferring Text

Text can be transferred very simply not least because highlighting text is a very simple process. To do this you place the insertion point at the start of the text you want to highlight. Then depress the left mouse button, and while keeping it depressed move the pointer to the end of the text you are looking to transfer. Once here you can release the mouse button at which point the text will be highlighted in a coloured block. Any Cut or Copy operation will now work on this text.

The keyboard can also be used to highlight text. Again, place the insertion point at the start of the text and then hold down one SHIFT key. Use the cursor keys to move the cursor to the end of the text before releasing the SHIFT key.

Insider Guide #36 – Text Cut and Paste

Working within Windows' Cut and Paste soon becomes second nature. Not only because it is so easy to do but because it it is often the most efficient way to transfer text either from one application to another or even within the same application, particularly when using a wordprocessor.

In this example, some notes that were first made in Notepad are transferred into Write.

1. First open both applications and the relevant documents and position them side by side. Although this isn't vital it does make the process easier to follow. You could for example have the windows over lapping.

2. Next highlight the text you want to move. Position the insertion point at the start of the text and then, hold down the left mouse button, and drag out the 'block' until you reach the end of the text to be copied. When you release the mouse button the block will remained highlighted.

3. Now go to the Edit menu and select Cut (or Copy). Cut removes the block from the original source, Copy leaves it intact.

4. Move to the destination – in this case Write – select the window, move the cursor to where you want the text inserted and then select Paste from the Edit menu.

The Cut or Copied text remains in the Clipboard until something else is Cut or Copy(ied).

Transferring Graphics

We haven't looked into the subject of graphics yet – but it is up and coming in the chapter dealing with Paintbrush. Essentially a graphic is a picture and just like text, pictures can be cut and pasted.

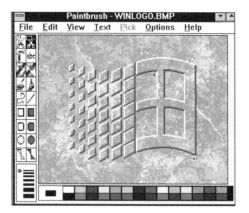

The illustration above shows the Windows logo loaded into Paintbrush. The object of the exercise is to insert a copy of this in Write. This is easily done using the Clipboard. The illustration below shows this having been done:

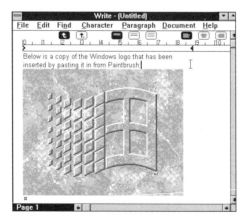

This was done in an almost identical fashion to the pasting of text. In this instance the image in Paintbrush was first selected (I'll show how to do this in Chapter 24) and then copied using the Copy option in the Edit menu – this effectively transferred a copy of the selected area into the Clipboard. At this point the Write window was selected and the

PC Beginners First Steps

Past option from its Edit menu selected. The image was then pasted at the point of the insertion point.

In the Family

It's not as spectacular, but you can use the Clipboard to copy data within the same document, or between documents within the same program (if the program lets you open more than one document at a time; most do). The procedures are identical. Here are some tips:

- If you're working with more than one document within the one program, you don't need to have the windows displayed side by side. Simply press CTRL-F6 to move between documents, as necessary.

- If you do elect to have document windows displayed side by side (after all, this is what Microsoft Windows was designed for), you can use copy and paste and cut and paste shortcuts. To copy text or graphics from one window another, select them. Hold down one CTRL key. Click and hold down the left mouse button. Drag the graphics or text to the second window. Release the mouse button. For cut and paste, omit the CTRL button component. This tip also applies to data transfers between differing programs. Actually, when you use this technique, Windows doesn't use the Clipboard, but it's very useful nonetheless.

Viewing Clipboard Contents

Although in reality the Clipboard is merely a transient storage area, Windows lets you treat it as though it were a program in its own right. You can look at the Clipboard using the Clipboard Viewer which can be kicked into life by clicking on its icon in the Main program group. The Clipboard Viewer launches, displaying whatever happens to be in the Clipboard at the time.

PC Beginners First Steps

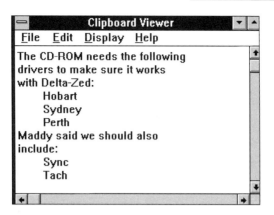

Load and Save

The Clipboard has its own file format to which you can save graphics or text to disk. To do this, pull down the File menu and choose Save As. In the Save As dialogue, select the drive and directory to which you want to save the Clipboard file. Then type in a file name in the File Name field. Note that Clipboard files end in .CLP. Click on OK to save the file.

To reinsert Clipboard files into the Clipboard, pull down the File menu and choose Open. Select the appropriate drive, directory and Clipboard file. Click on OK.

Clipping DOS Data

You can transfer data between DOS and Windows programs by performing copy and paste operations between DOS programs running under Windows and Windows programs themselves, but the process can be tricky and there are technical difficulties. You should note the following:

1. If possible, run DOS programs in a window, rather than full-screen (this facilitates access to the Control button – see below).

2. Not all DOS programs will run in a window. If you can't run a DOS program in a window, however, the plus side is that you do have access to a shortcut. With the DOS program displaying full-screen, press the PrintScreen key on your keyboard to capture all text within the program to the Clipboard.

PC Beginners First Steps

3. If you have a 386 machine (or better), run Windows in 386 Enhanced Mode (this can be done through the Control Panel).

4. You can't carry out cut and paste operations from DOS programs running under Windows to Windows programs.

5. In theory, it is possible to transfer graphics (pictures) from DOS programs running in a window to a Windows program. However, since few DOS programs display graphics, anyway, and since even fewer let you paste in graphics from a Windows program, it's best to use the 'file' method. In other words, in whichever direction you want the transfer to take place, save the graphic as a bitmap file and then re-import it into the destination program (see this program's manual for how to do this).

DOS-Windows Text Transfers

Here's a simple example of a text transfer from a DOS window into Write which you can do for yourself. The technique is the same if you are using other DOS based programs. In this example though some the text from a DIR listing is copied into Write. First open Write and then open a DOS window (see Chapter 13 on how to do this if you need a reminder). Then:

1. Click on the Control button in the top left hand corner of the window.

2. In the Control menu, choose Edit.

3. Choose Mark in the sub-menu.

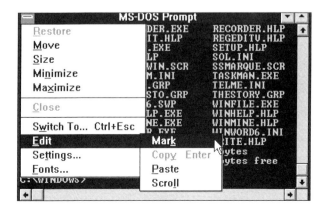

Now click and hold the left mouse button; drag with the mouse to select the text you want to transfer. Or hold down one SHIFT key and use the cursor keys to highlight the text.

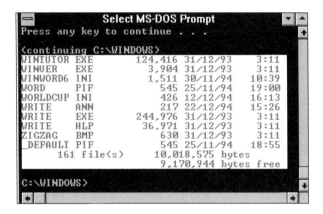

Press Enter. The text is inserted in the Clipboard. Now switch to the Write and select Paste from the Edit menu.

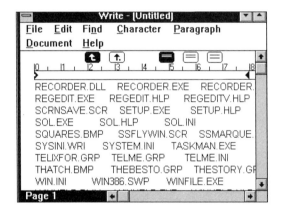

Windows-DOS Text Transfers

In the Windows program, use standard Windows techniques to highlight the text you want to transfer. Press CTRL-C to copy it to the Clipboard. Now switch to the DOS program running in a window. Pull down the Control menu and choose Edit, Paste. The text should be inserted.

**Games, games keep work at bay,
the more you play the better your day!**

**Don't say I didn't warn you –
the two games supplied with
Windows are just the start!**

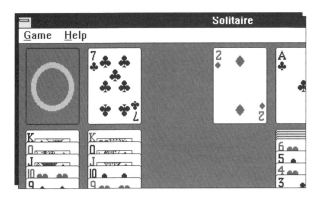

*A*ll work and no play ain't good for yer! And one thing that your PC is very good at is playing games. You can pick up games from just about anywhere now and the rules are the same here as for purchasing other software. Make sure you know the specification of your computer – that's its type, processor, speed, how much memory you have and what sort of monitor display. Armed with this you should be able to ensure you get a product that works properly on your particular machine by looking on the pack which will give a minimum specification. Like 'This game requires a PC with blah blah'. As long as you have this as a minimum you'll have no problems. Avoid getting games for which your PC doesn't fulfil the minimum spec otherwise they either won't load or run like frozen treacle. The other thing to bear in mind is whether you will need a joystick to play the game or whether the mouse and/or keyboard are good enough.

But before you rush out and get the latest chart blockbuster hold on because Windows comes with two games which you can use when you need a break from serious work. Solitaire and Minesweeper are both fairly unadventurous as games go,

PC Beginners First Steps

but they do provide some therapeutic light relief. Solitaire is also excellent practice in using your mouse. You'll find both games located in the Games program group and double clicking on either of the icons will bring the game to life.

Solitaire

Solitaire provides an effective implementation of the popular card game. If you need help with the rules pull down the windows Help menu, select Contents and then move the pointer over Rules of the Game (where it changes to a hand) and click once. Essentially, the game involves moving cards around, using the traditional mouse, select and drag technique, to create a complete set of all four suits starting from the Ace upwards. This is done by placing cards on top of those you all ready have dealt, in descending numbers and in alternating colour suits. Solitaire doesn't like cheats so if you try to make an illegal move – intentional or otherwise – the program won't let you!

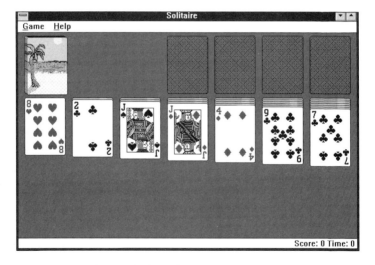

The Solitaire window includes a few menus which allows you to set up certain aspects of its play – however, as soon as you are up and running a fresh deal has been made and you can set off if you know how to play. If you pull down the Game menu and click on Deck you can select an alternative design for the back of the cards. Note that once you have done this a new deal is made – so don't do this once you have started a game – unless you know you're onto a loser of course! As always, clicking on OK will implement the change.

Insider Guide #37 – Scoring at Solitaire

You can play Solitaire using two different scoring systems. These are known as Standard and Vegas.

Standard is the default way of playing. You can change from one system to the other by setting the appropriate option in the Options dialogue box which is available through Solitaire's Game menu.

Under the Standard system the moves and the time taken to make them are taken into account. When you are playing a timed game, the shorter the game the bigger the bonus awarded.

You earn – or lose – points as follows:

Each card moved to a suit stack: 10 points.

Each card moved from the deck to a row stack: 5 points.

Each card moved from a suit stack to a row stack: -15 points.

Each pass through the deck after three passes
(Draw Three option): -20 points.

Each pass through the deck after one pass
(Draw One option): -100 points.

In the Vegas system you play for money and your ante is $52 and your aim is to earn more than you wager. Unlike Standard, there are no time penalties or bonuses awarded. You earn $5 for each card you move to a suit stack.

If you try to change from one scoring system to another, Solitaire will end the current game and start a new one.

You can keep a running total of your score from game to game by selecting the Keep Score option in the Options dialog box.

To return your score to -$52 select the None or Standard option in the Options dialogue box, and then press ENTER. Then reselect the Vegas option, and press ENTER.

PC Beginners First Steps

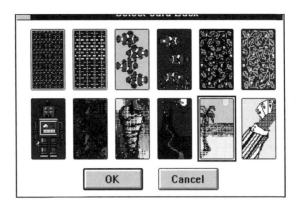

Using the One- or Three-Card Draw option from the Game menu you can define which card off the pack that Solitaire turns over the next. One-Card Draw will make it turn each card in turn while the Third Card will make it turn every third card from the pack. One-card draw increases your chances of winning (ie using all the cards in the deck to build the four suit stacks from Ace to King).

The Options dialogue allows you to select whether you want the elapsed time to be displayed. This can be done by selecting the Timed Game option to display the elapsed time in the status bar at the base of the Solitaire screen. The status bar needs to be visible for the game time to be displayed and this option is enabled by clicking on the Status Bar option in the Option dialogue box.

Another option available in the Options dialogue box is Display Card Outlines. If this is enabled then as you use the pointer to drag a card from one point to another the card's outline is displayed as you make the move. Aside from providing outlines, Outline Dragging changes the colour of the space or card you are moving to if the move is valid.

Scoring and Options

Solitaire has three scoring options: None, Standard and Vegas. To select the scoring method, make the appropriate choice from the Options dialogue. If you use the Vegas scoring method, the Keep Score field in the Options dialogue becomes available. Click on this to have Solitaire display the updated score in the status bar.

The Game menu provides the following additional options:

PC Beginners First Steps

Deal   Click on this to have the cards re-dealt

Undo   Click on this to take back the last card move

Exit   Click on this to close down Solitaire when you've finished playing it. Alternatively, choose ALT-F4.

Minesweeper

Minesweeper is a game of strategy but is an essentially simple game with some refinements which make it appear complex. The Minesweeper window depicts a mine field consisting of squares – the harder the level set the more squares there are. At first, all of the squares are covered. Some cover mines, some don't. The object of the game is to uncover all the squares which don't conceal mines without uncovering those which do. If you stumble on one square which contains a mine, you've lost: the rest of the mines are revealed, and the game is over.

There is another aspect to Minesweeper: you play against the clock. The faster you play, the lower your score. Minesweeper displays a timer in the upper right-hand corner of the window (it doesn't begin counting until you select a square); this shows your playing time in seconds. The timer in the upper left-hand corner of the windows displays the number of hidden mines. Every time you mark a square as a mine, this number decreases by one, even if you incorrectly mark a square.

PC Beginners First Steps

Starting to Play

There are four levels of play – Beginner, Intermediate, Expert and Custom. To set a level use the Game menu and make the appropriate choice. The strategy of the game involves you trying deduce where the mines are. To help you do this, the following actions are necessary – the Left and Right click refer to the mouse button you press:

To uncover a square	Left-click in it.
To mark a square as a mine	Right-click on it once
To change a square marked as a mine	Right-click on it once into a question mark
To mark a square as a question mark	Right-click on it twice
To clear a square marked as a mine	Right-click on it twice

When you believe you've worked out where a mine is, you have to 'mark' the square. Minesweeper provides hints to help you find mines. If the square isn't a mine, it either contains a number or is blank. The number, if any, represents the number of mines in the surrounding eight squares.

If the uncovered square is blank, there are no mines in the surrounding eight squares, and Minesweeper makes this clear.

If you're not sure about a square, you can play it safe and mark it with question marks. Later, you can either mark the square as a mine, or uncover it.

To initiate a new game, do either of the following:

1. Pull down the Game menu and choose New.
2. Press F2.
3. Click on the face at the top of Minesweeper's window.

When you've finished playing, pull down the Game menu and click on Exit. Or press ALT-F4.

22 Cardfile

Now's the time to get yourself fully computerised. If you don't at least get your address book on to Windows then you are a sorry sight indeed!

```
┌─────────────────────────────────────────┐
│         Cardfile - [Untitled]           │
│  File  Edit  View  Card  Search  Help   │
│         Card View        ← →        2 ( │
│                                         │
│                                         │
│   ROB, Roy              0101 112 9      │
│   EAGLE, Eddie      0202 111 8888       │
│   32 Skyview Avenue,                    │
│   Downhill                              │
│   Herts                                 │
└─────────────────────────────────────────┘
```

*C*ardfile is a simple database. A database is an application into which you can not only just store information but also extract information, sort information and even produce output (either to a file or printer) that is formatted according to the information stored or sought! If that all sounds a bit confusing don't worry, you see I'm quite sure that you have already been using databases for years. If you have an address book or one of those fancy personal organisers you have a database. Indeed you will almost certainly have it sorted and arranged as well – alphabetically of course.

Although it's simple, Cardfile may do all you require of a database. It uses a card metaphor, so that it closely resembles the standard office card file. Cards each relate to distinct pieces of information. Once you've created cards in Cardfile, you can organise the information in the way you want. Cards can contain text and/or pictures. And you can also elect to view cards as lists (see later). You could use Cardfile to store your address book electronically, perhaps catalogue your video or CD collection and even both! In fact you can create a database out of anything you might want to keep records of – because a database is just a collection of records.

Launching Cardfile

Cardfile can be found in the Accessories group window and when you run this it gives you the following window.

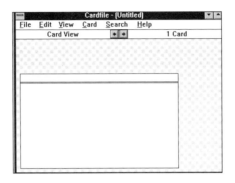

Cardfile is based on cards and when you launch it inserts a blank card automatically. The design of each card is very straightforward. The thin rectangle at the top is the Index bar; Cardfile organises the cards by reference to the information contained here (in terms of computer databases, this is known as the 'index'). The process of organising the information is known as 'sorting'. In other words, if you use Cardfile to create an address book, the Index bar will contain (as a minimum) the name of each entry. The larger rectangle below the Index bar is where you enter the data itself (or, to continue our example, the address) once the Index has been allocated. The Status bar tells you how many cards you've created in a particular database (it doesn't here because we haven't yet created any). The Status bar also tells you which view mode is operative. There are two choices. Card view displays the information displays as cards (as it is by default) whereas List view displays only the Index bar of each card, in alphabetical order. The advantage here is that you can see more than one entry at once.

Completing a Card

Let's look at a simple address book example using Cardfile. As we have already seen Cardfile will automatically have created the first

PC Beginners First Steps

card in the database and is ready to receive the relevant information. The first step is to create the index – this is the name or item by which Cardfile will organise and search for. The most obvious choice here in an address book is to use the Surname. Pull down the Edit menu and choose Index to display the Index dialogue window.

In the Index Line field, enter the information you want to serve as an index. You can enter as many as 39 characters, so you can have more than just the name if you want. In the illustration, I've entered a phone number, as well. Enter the surname first though, as this is how the file will be indexed.

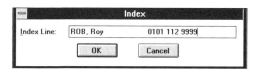

Click on OK to have Cardfile enter the information. Now for the address. Cardfile automatically places the insertion point in the information area, so you can begin typing immediately. Enter the address, together with any other information you need.

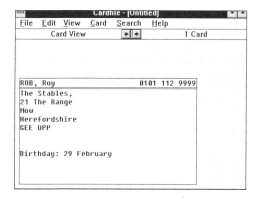

And that's all there is to filling out your first card.

Adding a New Card

Adding a second and additional cards is no trouble. Select Add from Card menu or press F7. In the in the Add field in the Add dialogue, enter the index for the new card.

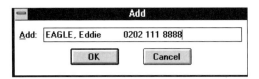

Click on OK when you've finished. Cardfile has added a new card. To add the address, simply type it in.

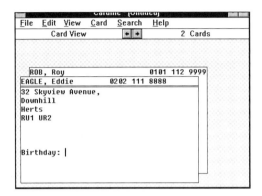

You can carry on adding cards and entering data in this way until you have completed your electronic computerised address book.

Saving Your Database

As always, it's important to save your Cardfile database to disk. You should do this frequently, so that in the even of a mishap (for instance, a power or hardware failure), you lose the minimum of work. To save your work, pull down the File menu and choose Save; Cardfile saves your work. If this is the first time you've saved your database, however, the Save As dialogue launches.

By default, Cardfile saves its files to your \WINDOWS directory. If you want your database saved to a different drive and/or directory, use the Drives and Directories field to select them. Enter a file name in the File Name field; note that Cardfile saves its files with a .CRD extension. Click on OK.

To open a database you've already saved, pull down the File menu and choose Open, highlight the database you want to open in the File Name box. Click on OK to open it.

PC Beginners First Steps

Insider Guide #38 – Using Find

Cardfile also lets you search for text within the Information area. This is a very useful device. Let's say you've set up a sizeable Cardfile database as an address book. If you know that one of the cards contains someone who lives in Nottingham, but can't remember his or her name, you could browse through each record individually until you find it. But this is likely to take a long time. A much quicker method is to use Find.

Pull down the Search menu and choose Find. In the Find What field in the Find dialogue, type in the Information area text you want Cardfile to locate.

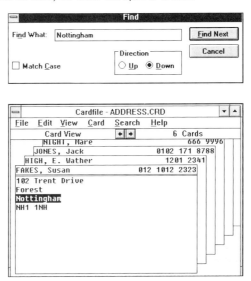

Click on Match Case if you want Cardfile's search to be case-specific. In other words, if you search for 'Nottingham' with Match Case selected, Cardfile won't flag 'nottingham', or 'NOTTINGHAM', or any other permutation . . . Click on Up or Down to control the search direction. Click on Find Next to initiate the search.

Editing and Deleting

To amend cards you've already created, simply click on the card; Cardfile brings it to the front of the pile. Now amend either the index or the contents as required. It's as simple as that.

You can erase any cards which aren't required. You should do this periodically, to ensure that your Cardfile databases are easy to manage. To do this, click on the unwanted card to select it. Then pull down the Card menu and choose Delete. Cardfile produces a message requesting permission to delete the card; click on OK to proceed.

Moving Stuff

You can use a variety of methods to move through Cardfile databases. Perhaps the most intuitive, and therefore the easiest, technique is simply to click with the mouse in the card you want to inspect. However, this doesn't work so well with large databases which have a lot of cards. There are other methods you can use here.

Using the Mouse

Click on either of the arrows in the Status bar; this cycles through cards – in other words steps through them one by one.

Using the Keyboard

Use any of the following key combinations:

> PAGE UP   moves to the previous card
> PAGE DOWN moves to the next card
> CTRL-HOME moves to the first card in the database
> CTRL-END   moves to the final card in the database

There's a further keyboard technique you can use. Pressing CTRL-SHIFT followed by the first letter of an index entry takes you to the first entry which corresponds to the letter. For instance, if you have a database with cards for Turner and Turnbull, CTRL-SHIFT-T takes you to the Turnbull card. If you need more precision, see 'Using Go To' below.

Using Go To

The CTRL-SHIFT... technique mentioned earlier works up to a point. However, if you have numerous cards which start with the same letter, moving to the first may not be much use. Much more helpful is Go To. Pull down the Search menu and choose Go To. Or press F4.

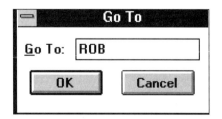

PC Beginners First Steps

The Go To dialogue searches for text on the Index bars of all cards within the current database. Enter the text you want to search for in the Go To field and click on OK to start the search.

Here, entering 'Turn' in the Go To field would find the card for Turnbull (this is the first card whose Index begins with 'Turn'). 'Turne', on the other hand, would only find the card for Turner. Cardfile continues this process until it encounters a search combination it can't find. For example, entering 'Turner, Z.' wouldn't locate the card for 'Turner, Zachary' because it isn't an exact match. You need to make sure the text you enter is precise enough to ensure Cardfile interprets it correctly.

Card and List View

It can sometimes be helpful to view your Cardfile database as an alphabetical list. This sort of overview is particularly useful if it contains a lot of cards. In List view, only the indices are visible, and these are arranged in alphabetical order.

To switch to List view, pull down the View menu and choose List. The List view presents a scrolling list of the Index entries:

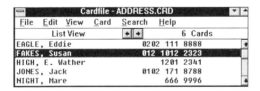

You can use List view – because it displays more cards – as a means of navigating through large databases.

Adding Pictures

You can pictures to your database, if you want. However, there are two restrictions:

- You can only have one picture per card
- Cardfile has no Insert Picture command

The latter restriction means that inserting pictures is a two-stage process. First, you have to copy the picture you want to insert to the

Windows Clipboard. You can do this with Paintbrush (see Chapter 23), or with many other programs capable of working with graphics. Then you paste the image copy into your card. This is what you have to do once you've copied the image to the Clipboard:

1. Click in the card in which you want the picture inserted.
2. Pull down the Edit menu and choose Picture.
3. Pull down the Edit menu again and choose Paste.
4. If the picture isn't correctly positioned, move the mouse pointer over it. Click and hold with the left button. Drag the picture to its new location. Release the mouse button to confirm the move.
5. To return to Text mode (in order to work with your cards as a database), pull down the Edit menu and click on Text.

Merging Databases

You can merge two Cardfile databases. When you do this, Cardfile consolidates the two into one single collection of cards.

To merge the current database with a second, pull down the File menu and click on Merge. In the File Merge dialogue, highlight the second database in the File Name box. Click on OK.

Don't forget to save the joint file under a new name – this will keep your two original Cardfiles intact and unaffected by the merge.

Paintbrush

Even if you're not a budding Picasso, you'll find that Paintbrush can help you realise that creative artistic bent you've always had.

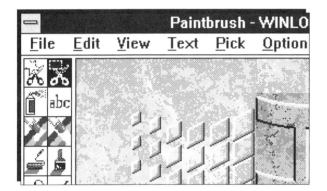

We've looked at a wordprocessor and in the last chapter, a database. The final application in the quartet that are supplied with Windows is a paint program that goes by the simple name of Paintbrush. With this you can create simple drawings and illustrations which you can use to combine with Write or Cardfile. As with Write and Cardfile, Paintbrush is a relatively basic implementation of the more commercial offerings now available, however, with it you can learn the basic techniques which will serve you well in future.

Paintbrush has limitations as a drawing/paint program. For instance, once you've added lines and/or text to a picture, they become an ineradicable part of it. You can't treat them as separate objects (you need to do this in order to edit them). In spite of its limitations, however, Paintbrush is a useful introduction to more sophisticated paint programs. And you can, if you want, buy the up-to-date version of Paintbrush, now sold not by Microsoft but by Softkey – see the end of this chapter for contact details.

As with the other applets you'll find the Paintbrush icon in the Accessories group window.

Let's look at Paintbrush's screen components in more detail. There is no better way to learn Paintbrush than to try it out – what follows then is more a description of the tools and their use rather than how to create a Rembrandt.

You can access some – but not all – of Paintbrush's commands by pulling down menus. However, you can also do so by using the Toolbox, Line Area and Palette. Using these is much more convenient.

The Palettes

The Toolbox is one of the easiest ways to access many of Paintbrushes features. You use these tools, as appropriate, to create or edit Paintbrush drawings. For instance, if you want to draw a line, you'd left-click on the Line Tool. We'll look at the tools available in more detail later.

The Linesize palette offers several pre-set line thicknesses which you can apply to various tools. These include:

- Airbrush
- The Box Tools
- The Circle Tools
- The Polygon Tools
- The Colour Palette

You use the Colour Palette to select and apply colours to objects you create or import into Paintbrush. You can apply colours to borders, or to object fills. A fill being just that – filling a complete, normally enclosed, area. For example, you can create coloured lines, or you can create a box, circle or polygon and fill them with colour. Colours can also be divided into *foreground* and *background*. Paintbrush tells you which colours are currently allocated to which in the Foreground Fill and Background Fill sections. To allocate a new colour as the Foreground Fill, left-click on one of the colours in the Palette. To allocate a new Background Fill, right-click on one of the colours.

You create and paint object in the *Drawing Area*. Look on it as your canvas.

Insider Guide #39 – Paintbrush anatomy

Paintbrush has a very busy window by default so for the best results it is wise to use it in its maximized form. It consists of five main areas. The menu bar, the drawing area, the toolbox palette, the lines palette and the colour palette.

All the palettes can be turned on and off by selecting them from the Options menu.

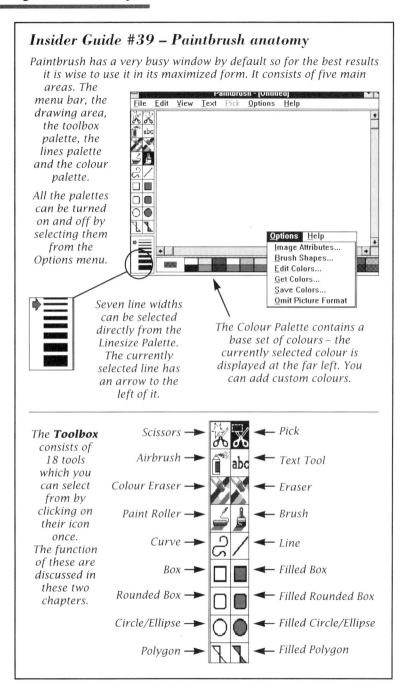

Seven line widths can be selected directly from the Linesize Palette. The currently selected line has an arrow to the left of it.

The Colour Palette contains a base set of colours – the currently selected colour is displayed at the far left. You can add custom colours.

The **Toolbox** consists of 18 tools which you can select from by clicking on their icon once. The function of these are discussed in these two chapters.

Scissors → ← Pick
Airbrush → ← Text Tool
Colour Eraser → ← Eraser
Paint Roller → ← Brush
Curve → ← Line
Box → ← Filled Box
Rounded Box → ← Filled Rounded Box
Circle/Ellipse → ← Filled Circle/Ellipse
Polygon → ← Filled Polygon

Keyboard Routes

Before we explore the Toolbox in more detail, here are some tips for Paintbrush users who may prefer to use the keyboard. The following keyboard routes are available:

Tab Press Tab to move between screen components. For instance, if one of the tools is currently selected, pressing Tab moves the mouse pointer to the Line Area. As you'd expect, Shift-Tab reverses the direction of movement.

The left, right, up and down cursor keys
Use these to move between choices in sections. For example, if the mouse pointer is over the Red colour in the Palette, pressing the right cursor key moves to Yellow.

Insert Press Insert over a tool, line size or foreground colour to select it.

Delete Press Delete over a background colour to select it.

Using Paintbrush

More so than most applications supplied with Windows, the best way to get to grips with Paintbrush is to sit down and experiment with it. Start with simple line drawings and progress from there.

First, let's look at Paintbrush drawing operations. The basic methodology is identical for all three object types whether they are lines, circles or squares:

1. If you want to apply a foreground colour, select it from the Colour Palette by clicking on the appropriate colour.
2. If you want to specify a line thickness for object borders or lines, select the thickness you need from the Linesize palette.
3. Click on the appropriate tool in the Toolbox.
4. Position the pointer in the Drawing Area, at the location from which you want the object to start. The mouse pointer changes to a cross.

PC Beginners First Steps

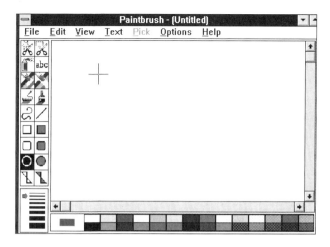

5. Press and hold down the left mouse button. Drag the pointer until the object is the size/shape you want.

6. If you decide the object isn't what you require, and want to start again, right-click once without releasing the left mouse button (this works with most of the tools).

7. If the object is OK, release the left mouse button to confirm object creation.

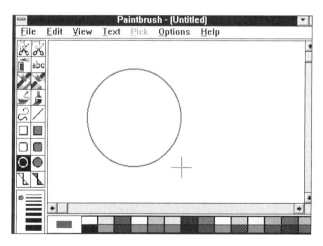

Holding down one SHIFT key while you create lines, circles or squares has interesting results:

lines	constrains lines to 45° increments. One advantage is that this makes it easy to draw perfectly horizontal and vertical lines.
circles	forces Paintbrush to create a circle rather than an ellipse.
squares	forces Paintbrush to create a square rather than a rectangle.

Curves and Polygons

At first, you may find the Curve Tool rather clumsy. However, it's easy to use once you're had some practice at it. As before choose a colour and line thickness as appropriate then:

1. Click on the Curve Tool icon in the Toolbox.

2. Position the pointer in the Drawing Area, at the location from which you want the curve to start. The mouse pointer changes to a cross.

3. Press and hold down the left mouse button. Drag the pointer until the line is the correct length. Release the mouse button.

4. To turn the line into a curve, click and hold the mouse button again. Drag away from the line. The further you drag, the more pronounced the curve. Release the button.

6. If you don't want to add any additional curves, left-click again without moving the mouse pointer; this inserts the curve.

If you do want to add another curve, move the mouse pointer to the other side of the existing curve and repeat step four.

A *polygon* is a closed object consisting of any number of lines. To draw a polygon, having selected colour and line thickness:

1. Click on the Polygon Tool icon in the Toolbox. Alternatively, if you want to create a filled polygon, click on the Filled Polygon Tool icon.

2. Position the pointer in the Drawing Area, at the location from which you want the polygon to start. The mouse pointer changes to a cross.

3. Press and hold down the left mouse button. Drag the pointer until the first line is the correct length and has the correct angle. Release the mouse button.
4. Click with the mouse where you want the next line to end. Paintbrush joins the lines.
5. Repeat step four as often as necessary. To complete the polygon, make sure the final line connects with the beginning of the initial line.

Freehand Lines

Paintbrush lets you draw lines entirely by hand. This is probably for the really artistic, but it can create some interesting effects. Besides, it's fun. Again select your colour and line thickness then:

1. Click on the Brush Tool icon in the Toolbox.
2. Position the mouse pointer in the Drawing Area, at the location from which you want the line to start. The mouse pointer changes to a square.
3. Click and hold the left mouse button. Drag to create the line.
4. Release the mouse button to confirm line creation.

Undo

Immediately after you've created an object, you can 'undo' it if it isn't what you want. To do this, pull down the Edit menu and choose Undo. Or press CTRL-Z.

Saving Your Work

It's important to save your work at regular intervals. To do this, pull down the File menu and choose Save. Paintbrush saves your work. If you haven't saved your work before, Paintbrush produces the Save As dialogue.

Note that Paintbrush doesn't save its files into a proprietary format. Instead, you have the following choices:

16 Colour .BMP
256 Colour .BMP
24-Bit .BMP
Monochrome .BMP
.PCX

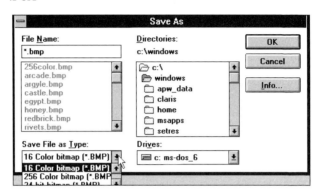

Paintbrush shows its age here by not supporting the numerous additional graphics formats which are now available. However, the vast majority of Windows programs will convert .BMP and .PCX files successfully, so you should have no difficulty in using the files you create with Paintbrush elsewhere.

By default, Paintbrush saves its files to your \WINDOWS directory. If you want your drawings saved to a different drive and/or directory, use the Drives and Directories field to select them. Enter a file name in the File Name field. Click on OK.

In the next chapter we'll look at how to use the other Paintbrush tools to achieve advanced effects. In the meantime, this is the address if you want to buy the latest version of Paintbrush (it has a lot of additional features). Contact:

Softkey International (UK) Ltd.
Heritage House
21 Inner Park Rd.
Wimbledon Common
London SW19 6ED
Tel: 0181 789 2000

If you've had enough drawing lines, squares and circles why not start to get to grips with the more advanced aspects of Paintbrush. Then you'll even be able to do your own wallpapering!

24

More Paint

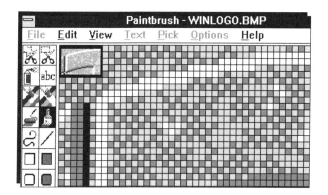

*I*f you have mastered the basic concepts of the various Paintbrush tools and how to use them to some effect you're ready to look at some of the more advanced features of software. These techniques will allow you to create cutouts (crop areas from pictures) and perform a variety of actions on the cutouts; spray colours onto the screen; repair drawings by editing pixels; fill shapes; transform colours and add text to pictures to annotate them. Once again, I would stress that the best way to get to grips with these is to try them for yourself. I'm no artist but it's surprising what even some basic skills can lead you onto.

Before we go on it is worth making a distinction here between the two major types of paint/graphics creation programs. They are bitmap and object. *Bitmap* programs work by allowing you to build up drawings and designs in individual pixels. A pixel is a picture element and is best thought of as a tiny square of colour on the screen. If you want you can think of a bitmap picture of being a mosaic of different colour blocks. If you've ever seen the opening ceremony at events like the Olympics or the Word Cup – or even those great British Airways adverts – you'll be familiar with this effect.

An *object* orientated program is one where the lines and curves which construct the drawing are just that – in fact they are derived by mathematical expressions. This makes them resolution-independent and generally give a more professional result. This doesn't make the bitmap approach obsolete – far from it. They are two totally different approaches and you could think of bitmap and object pictures as comparable to an oil painting and a photograph.

Paintbrush is a bitmap orientated program and with it you can create a variety of effects to bitmaps. Everything Paintbrush produces is a bitmap, so in a sense it's wrong to discuss its tools separately. However, this is functionally useful. There are both advantages and disadvantages to working with bitmaps, but the principal benefit is the wealth of special effects you can apply.

The Paintbrush tools which are related to painting are:

- Pick and Scissors Tools
- Airbrush Tool
- The Roller
- The Erasers
- Text Tool

We'll discuss these individually.

Pick and Scissors

These perform a related function (you can use them with drawings, too) in that they both allow you to select an area of a drawing. You do this by creating a path which is an outline of an area. This path encloses a section of the picture which you can then do a number of things with – for instance cut or copy it to the clipboard or change its orientation.

The Pick tool creates a simple cutout area for you by allowing you to drag out a rectangle – this is often called a marquee. The Scissors tool has the same end effect but allows you to trace a path around an object which can be of just about any shape.

Once you have defined your cutout you can then:

- Copy or cut cutouts
- Flip cutouts horizontally or vertically
- Invert cutouts
- Tilt cutouts
- Sweep cutouts

Whichever action you perform, the initial procedure is the same.

1. Click on the Scissors Tool (if you want to define an irregular cutout) or the Pick Tool (if you want to create a rectangular or square cutout).

2. Move the mouse pointer to the point in the Drawing Area where you want the cutout to start.

3. Click and hold the left mouse button. Drag round the area you want to define as a cutout.

4. Release the button; Paintbrush surrounds the cutout with dotted lines.

5. Initiate the operation you require on the cutout (see 'Cutout Operations' next for more information).

Cutout Operations

To copy the cutout, pull down the Edit menu and choose Copy. This inserts a copy of the cutout into the Clipboard. To cut the cutout, choose Cut from the Edit menu. This inserts a copy of the cutout into the Windows Clipboard while at the same time deleting the original. The next illustrations shows the original image minus the cutout.

To flip the cutout, pull down the Pick menu and choose either Flip Horizontal or Flip Vertical. The illustration is an example of a horizontal flip on the Windows logo:

PC Beginners First Steps

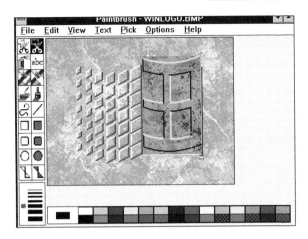

To invert the cutout colours, choose Inverse in the Pick menu.

To produce a tilted copy of a cutout, choose Tilt from the Pick menu. Then place the cursor where you want to begin to draw a flexible box (you do so to define the tilt angle). Press and hold down the mouse button; the box appears. Move the mouse to the left or right (the bottom of the flexible box shifts with the mouse) until the angle is correct. Release the button. To confirm the tilt operation, click anywhere outside the cutout.

To sweep cutouts, place the cursor inside the cutout. Hold down one SHIFT key. Click and hold the left mouse button to sweep the cutout transparently, or the right button to sweep opaquely. Drag the cutout across the drawing area. Release the mouse button and SHIFT key when you've finished.

The Airbrush Tool

The Airbrush Tool can be a lot of fun and in its more sophisticated form in more major paint packages it can be used to create some stunning effects. Here's how to use it:

1. Select the appropriate foreground colour.
2. Select the appropriate line thickness.
3. Click on the Airbrush tool icon in the Toolbox.
4. Position the mouse cursor where you want to start drawing with Airbrush.

5. Click and hold the left mouse button. Drag across the Drawing Area.

Bear in mind that the quicker you drag, the finer and lighter Airbrush's output.

The Roller

Use the Roller to fill shapes with selected colours. For example, to fill a circle or polygon that you have already created with a colour:

1. Select a foreground colour – this is the fill colour.
2. Click on the Roller icon in the Toolbox
3. Move the cursor into the polygon.
4. Left-click once.

If you click outside the polygon instead, Paintbrush fills the Drawing Area itself, excluding the polygon.

Here are some points to bear in mind. When you fill drawings with the Roller, make sure there are no breaks in their borders. If there are, the colour leaks through and fills the entire Drawing Area. In the next illustration, we clicked with the Roller inside the drawing. Incidentally, Paintbrush doesn't let you create incomplete polygons like this with the Polygon tool.

If you experience this unwanted bleed, simply press CTRL-Z immediately to 'undo' the fill. Then repair the gap in the drawing (see 'Pixel Editing' for how to do this) and re-fill it.

Pixel Editing

Images on computer screens consist of a myriad of pixels ('picture elements'). Paintbrush lets you edit individual pixels. Apart from being fun, this is also useful. You can go in, so to speak and refine detail at the smallest level. To select the edit option select Zoom In from the View menu. The illustration below shows a typical screen appearance at this time:

PC Beginners First Steps

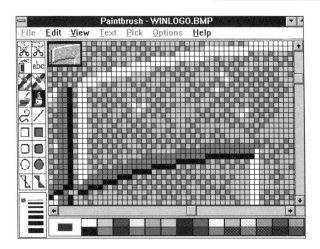

The mouse pointer changes to a rectangle. You can see the separate pixels which go to make up the screen display. To draw at this level select the foreground colour you want from the Colour Palette. Click on the Brush tool. Move the mouse pointer over the squares and click to set the points. If you click and hold down the left mouse button you can fill a stream of pixels in your wake as you drag with the mouse.

Note that the top left-hand corner of the Drawing Area provides an overall view of your progress.

If you make a mistake (i.e. if you've filled in the wrong pixels), don't press CTRL-Z to 'undo' the error; this reverses every change you've made. Instead, select White as your foreground colour and use the Brush tool to blank out the incorrectly filled pixels. When you've finished, choose Zoom Out from the View menu.

This pixel editing approach is a good way to repair any breaches in a border that might have caused a fill action with the Roller to leak.

The Erasers

The function of the Eraser is to change the area under the mouse pointer to the same colour as the background colour specified in the Colour Palette. The Colour Eraser, on the other hand, goes at least one step further. It has two functions. You can use it to change portions of the foreground colour to the background colour, or every occurrence of one colour to another colour.

To use the Eraser first select a background colour in the Colour Palette which matches the colour of the region of the Drawing Area you want to erase. This often means selecting White. Then:

1. Select the appropriate line size.
2. Click on the Eraser tool icon in the Toolbox.
3. Position the pointer at the correct location in the Drawing Area.
4. Click and hold down the left mouse button. Drag the cursor.
5. When you've finished erasing, release the mouse button.

The Colour Eraser can be used in much the same way. For example, to change a foreground colour into a specified background colour:

1. In the Palette, make sure the foreground colour is the colour you want to change.
2. Select a background colour which is the same as the new colour you need.
3. Choose the appropriate line size
4. Click on the Colour Eraser icon in the Toolbox.
5. Position the mouse pointer (now a small box) in the Drawing Area over the colour you want to transform.
6. Click and hold down the left mouse button. Drag the pointer to replace the colour.
7. Release the mouse button when you've finished.

To erase a horizontal or vertical line, press and hold down **SHIFT** as you drag the cursor. This applies to both the Eraser and the Colour Eraser tools.

To have Paintbrush replace every instance of one colour with another, first display the whole of the relevant section(s) of the drawing/picture on screen. Then follow steps 1-2 earlier. Finally, double-click on the Colour Eraser icon in the Toolbox.

PC Beginners First Steps

The Text Tool

The Text tool lets you annotate pictures by adding text to them. While you are able to specify the font and some of the effects, the Text Tool does not provide anything other than the most basic of editing functions.

To add text to a Paintbrush screen:

1. Select the foreground colour in the Colour Palette; this will be the colour of the text.

2. Pull down the Text menu and choose Fonts.

Use the Fonts dialogue to see all the standard requirements such as the typeface you want to use and the style you want it in. When you've finished setting your text parameters, click on OK.

3. Click on the Text tool icon in the Toolbox.

4. Position the mouse pointer (it turns into a capital I) where you want the text to begin. Left-click once.

5. Begin typing.

To start a new line, press Enter. If you don't do this, Paintbrush stops registering text when you reach the right edge of the Drawing Area. When you've finished typing, click elsewhere within the Drawing Area. Note that once you've done this, the text becomes an integral part of the remainder of the drawing/picture. This means that it can no longer be edited as text.

The illustration below shows the Windows logo with some appropriate text:

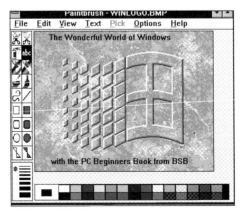

Wallpaper

We have already looked at the use of Wallpapers in conjunction with the Desktop control panel to enable you to customise your own desktop patterns. Using Paintbrush you can use your own designs as wallpaper designs.

When you create them remember that they must be saved in the .BMP format and they must be in your main \WINDOWS directory. When you save your finished picture to its '256 Colour bitmap (.BMP)' format (select this from the Save Files as Type field in either the Save or Save As dialogue, as appropriate). Then select your BMP file as your Desktop background using the techniques discussed in Chapter Eight.

Not so much a horse with no name as a chapter. These pages contain details on a number of useful topics that are small in themselves but can have a big impact on your use of the PC.

25

This and That

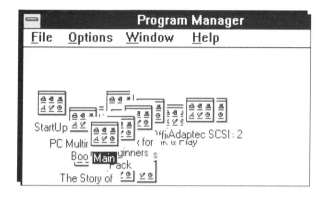

*T*his chapter is the one with no title. That's because it covers a wide range of subjects that are important and well worth knowing. Because the coverage of these is quite short they might get lost in other sections dealing with more specific topics.

Desktop Housekeeping

Windows lets you perform basic housekeeping on your Desktop. What is basic Desktop housekeeping? Part of it is controlling the way windows displays (tile or cascade) on screen; we looked at this in Chapter 11. Sometimes, however, program groups – and program icons within groups – become duplicated; you can delete superfluous examples. Often, the icons in Program Manager lose their pristine order and need rearranging. Sometimes, you need to copy or move program icons from one group to another.

Icon Tact

To delete a program group icon, click on it. Press Delete. Choose Yes in the message which launches, requesting your confirmation that the icon should be deleted. The same procedure also works for program icons within groups.

We have touched on the subject of copying and moving icons in previous chapters. There are two ways to copy and move icons. You can use the mouse, or you can use a menu route.

Using the Mouse

To move a group or program icon, simply position the mouse pointer over it. Click the left button and hold it down. Drag the icon to the new location. Release the button to confirm the operation. To copy a program icon (you can't copy group icons), hold down one CTRL key as you drag.

Using the Menu Route

This only applies to program icons. With the program icon selected, pull down the File menu and choose Copy or Move. The Copy Program Item or Move Program Item dialogues launch, depending on your choice. The illustration shows the Copy Program Item dialogue, but the Move Program Item dialogue is identical except for the name.

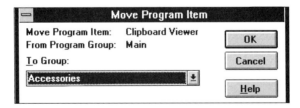

Click on the arrow to the right of the To Group field. Select the group in which you want the copy icon placed from the list which appears. Click on OK to proceed.

Automation

Microsoft Windows provides several methods for automating the way you work with it. You can make programs start automatically, or you can launch them at the same time as you start Windows. You can also record actions you initiate frequently and 'play them back' later . . .

PC Beginners First Steps

Insider Guide #40 – Icon tidy

As you develop and add more applications and projects to your Program Manager desktop you'll find that it will start to get very cluttered with program group icons.

You can, if you want, rearrange icons on your Desktop manually by dragging them with the mouse. If you have a lot of icons, however, this can be a tedious process. And it's difficult to arrange them with any precision. Fortunately, there are two ways to automate this process.

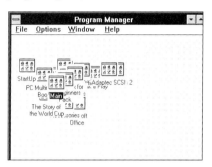

To have Windows rearrange icons automatically, use the mouse first to arrange the icons in the general order you want. Then pull down the Windows menu in Program Manager and choose Arrange. Windows orders the icons neatly. Repeat this whenever your Desktop layout is untidy.

To have Windows maintain this order each time you resize your Program Manager window, pull down the Options menu and choose Auto Arrange; a tick appears against this option to show it's selected.

If you want, you can have Windows start up programs automatically each time you turn on and enter Windows. This is very useful with certain applications which you're likely to use frequently, or all the time. For instance, many Windows users run File Manager as a minimized icon; in this way, you can invoke it whenever needed. Rather than load up File Manager (by double-clicking on its program icon) each time you initiate a Windows session, have Windows start it for you. Another common program to run each time you start-up is the Clock. To do this, you copy the relevant program icons into a special program group called Startup. Here's how to do this. From within Program Manager, double-click on the Startup icon.

Ensure the icon of the program that you want to run every time is also readily available. This is best done by opening the group window that contains it and then tiling the two windows.

Click on the title bar for the program group to make it active. Hold down one CTRL key and click on the icon which represents the program you want to copy to Startup. Hold down the left mouse button and drag the icon to the Startup group. This is the result.

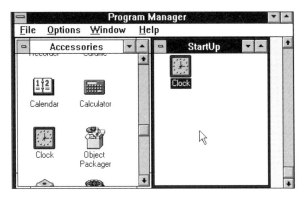

Repeat this as often as necessary to copy any other applications you want to launch. Close the Startup group window and next time you start Windows the programs will start after windows. If for some reason you don't want Windows to run any programs whose icons have been copied to Startup, hold down one SHIFT key while Windows is loading.

Another really useful thing to do is to copy what ever file you are working into the Startup group before you finish your current session. In this way it will be opened for you when you next turn on. (See Chapter 11 for details on how to assign an application icon to a file)

There is another way to run a program automatically, as a one-off when you start Windows from the DOS prompt. Let's say you're about to start Microsoft Windows. You know you'll want to run Write. If you don't want to run Write every Windows session, but you do want to save yourself the trouble of having to find the program group and start it, you can simply type the program name after the command which launches Windows. For instance, to launch Word at the same time as Windows you'd normally type:

WIN C:\WINDOWS\WRITE.EXE

since the Write program file is WRITE.EXE.

Recorder

Windows comes with a macro recorder. A *macro* is a recorded list of program commands or actions which can be replayed at will. The Windows Recorder will record keyboard and mouse actions. Its approach is very basic. For instance, it records mouse actions extremely literally. Probably the best (and least error prone) use for Recorder is to save menu/dialogue selections so that they can be invoked with a single key combination. You can specify whether Recorder's macros should apply to the program from which they were created, or globally to all Windows applications.

For example, users of any Windows wordprocessor have something of a problem if they need to insert characters which aren't on the standard PC keyboard. A frequent case in point is '_'. Word 6.0 for Windows works round this problem by providing a special Symbol dialogue from which specific symbols can be inserted. You reach this by pulling down a menu. You then select the font you want to use in the dialogue and highlight the special character. Then you have to tell Word to insert it into your document, and close the dialogue. Something such as this would be an ideal candidate for macroing and recalling at a single keystroke combination.

Let's look at how Recorder works by using a simple example which you can then build on yourself. This macro starts the three main Accessories Write, Cardfile and Paintbrush and shrinks them to an icon ready to use. Before you do anything ensure that you Accessories screen is open and occupies a good open area of the Program Manager screen.

Next, start Recorder whose icon is located in the Accessories program group to display the Recorder screen which isn't too explosive at the moment:

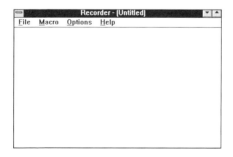

Pull down the Macro menu and choose Record. The Record Macro dialogue appears.

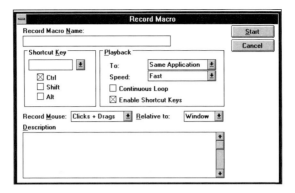

In the Record Macro Name field, type in name for the new macro (up to a maximum of 40 characters). To enable the completed macro to be run when you press a specific key combination, you have to complete the Shortcut Key section. Shortcut key combinations in Microsoft Windows generally involve two keys: usually, ALT and a letter of the alphabet. This means that it's not a good idea to have a macro invoked by ALT without SHIFT and/or CTRL (you can have all three if you want). Recorder pre-selects CTRL for you, which you can take as a hint that the best combination initiator is CTRL-SHIFT since few Windows programs use this for anything else. When you've decided on the CTRL, SHIFT and ALT permutation you want, click on the arrow to the right of the Shortcut Key field and select the key you want from the drop down list. A good key combination to use is ALT-SHIFT-ENTER.

Next, set the playback options. You can have the macro available from within any Windows program, or just from within Program manager. In this instance, since the macro will be Program manager specific, choose Same Application in the To field in the Playback section. Make sure the Speed field shows Fast (the other option, Recorded Speed, is for demonstrations). Ensure that the Enable Shortcut Keys option is selected (has a cross against it) and the Continuous Loop option is de-selected (no cross)

Continuous Loop makes the macro repeat itself indefinitely (until your PC is switched off), which is clearly undesirable here. Recorder will record three categories of action:

Clicks and Drags

Records every key combination you press, and mouse movements when the mouse button is held down.

Everything

Records everything. This option isn't recommended: it makes it almost impossible to stop recording your macro when you've finished.

Ignore Mouse

Records key combinations only.

I suggest using Ignore Mouse for most purposes wherever you can. This is a good idea because Recorder interprets and records mouse movements very literally. If you're creating a macro which records interactions between several icons and/or windows, their relative positions will have changed by the time you run the macro again. This means that Recorder won't be able to find them, and the macro will abort. But! There's always a but – in this example it isn't possible to igore the movement of the mouse unless you are very proficient in the use of the keyboard to get around Windows. For now don't use the Ignore Mouse option!

Click on the arrow to the right of the Record Mouse field and choose the option you want from the list which appears. Choose Window in the Relative To field. The other option – Screen – is unavailable if Ignore Mouse is selected (see earlier). Enter descriptive text in the Description field; this is optional. Click on Start to have Recorder begin recording your macro. As you do this the Recorder will minimize itself and start flashing at the bottom of the screen to remind you it is running. Now in turn move to the Write, Paintbrush and Cardfile icons and:

- Double click on the icon to open it
- Select Minimize from the Control menu

When you have launched and minimized all three double click on the Recorder icon at the bottom of the screen to stop recording. This should leave the screen looking a bit like this:

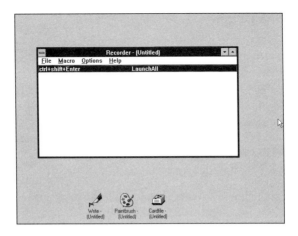

Next close each of the three programs that have been minimized. When you have done this you can run your macro either by double clicking on the name in the Recorder list or by pressing the specific hot key combinations, here ALT-SHIFT-ENTER.

When you have created a macro you can save it using the Save option in the File menu. In fact you are not saving the macro but the macro sheet because you can continue recording and saving macros to this particular list. In this way you can create files of specific macros which you can open and load through Recorder.

Software Versions

One of the most confusing and often infuriating aspects of software is the numbers. Just like any other aspect of life in the technological fast lane, software is undergoing a continual process of research and development. Windows in the mid-Nineties for example, is a much changed beast from the infant it was at the turn of the decade.

To distinguish these implementations from one another, a version numbering system has developed. The version of Windows that is illustrated in this book is Windows version 3.1 (three point one).

As a rule of thumb when software is first released it is called version one (1.0). When a minor change in the software takes place then the decimal portion of the version number is incremented. Thus a minor change to version 1.0 of a piece of software might make the new version 1.1. More significant changes are normally signified by a change in the main version number, version 1.1 might therefore jump to version 2.0.

These changes can affect you in different ways. Let's first take the example of a wordprocessor that is launched as version 1.0. Lets call this WP 1.0. This might be a very basic wordprocessor. The manufacturers decide that the software contains a number of things that need changing because they don't work properly and so these changes are produced and WP 1.1 is released. This might be a free upgrade to registered users. Certainly if you contact your dealer and say you are having problems – he will ask you what version of the software you have and that can help him sort things out.

The manufacturers now decide that because of the success of the first version of WP they will continue and a year later they release WP 2.0. This contains many new features and because of this it costs registered users of WP 1.x (the x is used to signify both versions 1.0 and 1.1) to upgrade. This upgrade charge is normally a good deal less than the cost of the full package when brought for the first time but often still substantial.

This may at first sight seem a bit of a rip-off; however you should bear in mind that there is normally a good deal of development work gone into the new product and this has to be recouped. It is not unlike buying a new VCR only to find out a newer model has been released a few weeks later. Unlike this scenario though, most software houses allow a period of grace as such that if you purchased your software in a certain period before the new release, they will upgrade you free of charge. This is normally to help sales continue once news of a new release has broken in the computer press.

The question for you though, then to answer is if the new features offered by WP2.0 are worth the additional cost and whether you need them. If you are happy with your current version 1.x then you may decide to stick with it. This comes down to research on your behalf and then a decision based on money. The research is best done by reading magazine reviews, speaking to people in the know and trying the software out for yourself in your dealer's.

AUTOEXEC

There is one file on your hard disk that you will hear referred to an awful lot, called:

AUTOEXEC.BAT

You pronounce this as it looks:

> Auto
> Exec (as in Executive)
> Bat

This file plays a very big part in your PCs startup process. A file that has the extension .BAT is normally a file that is executed because it contains a list of commands for the computer to perform. In many respects it is like the macro files we saw earlier in the chapter when looking at the Recorder.

The commands in the AUTOEXEC file are lists of DOS commands. Generally you shouldn't touch this file unless you are proficient in DOS itself. However, sometimes when you install software on your machine it will tell you that your AUTOEXEC.BAT file needs to be updated. Generally, though it will do this for you and as such will provide you with that option.

Goodbye

Although this isn't the final chapter in this book – it is the final chapter that deals specifically with Windows. The remaining chapters deal with software and other aspects of computing which you should be aware of. What we have touched on in looking at Windows is a little bit more than scratching the surface – it's difficult to gauge how much we've covered but it probably approached about half of what you might want to learn to be considered a serious Windows user.

If you want to delve further look towards the Windows User Guide as you should have enough basic information to hand now to allow you to interrogate what was seemingly a daunting volume with a degree of optimism! Then there is the Help files – these contain tons of material and useful information – spend some time using it.

26 Free Software

With commercial software costing hundreds of pounds per product a suite of software can set you back close on £500.

But there are cheaper routes that you can go down with nearly as good results for a fraction of the cost.

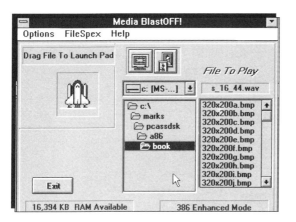

*E*veryone reacts positively when they see FREE displayed in a shop window or in a magazine advert. But there's always a sneaking suspicion that nothing in life is free! This applies to the world of public domain and shareware on the PC.

Public domain (PD) programs are made freely available to all PC owners by their authors. They are passed on through personal contact and through PD libraries. Shareware programs are more common but are not free. However they are supplied on a try-before-you-buy basis and are normally a fraction of the cost of commercial software and many of them are as good and sometimes even better.

There are many programs swimming about in the PD and Shareware software ocean, just waiting to be fished out. But what are the costs involved in sourcing the software? Essentially there are two: firstly you have to pay a Shareware/PD library to duplicate the programs onto a disk and to send it out properly packaged and with the correct postage – this charge might be based on a per disk basis or on a megabyte basis; there is normally a minimum charge; secondly there is the indirect cost of the magazines you will need to buy to help you track down the software.

But this would seem to be a small price to pay – probably under £10 to let you sample a wide range of software – and it is an excellent way to start your interest in computing. You will be receiving programs submitted to the PD/Shareware libraries by programmers who have created an application or a utility which they feel is good enough for public exposure.

The PD/Shareware librarian plays an important role in sieving the material available and it is common for a library to specialise in a particular type of software, music files for instance, and a library will have a demonstration disk to give a flavour of what it offers.

Another excellent source of software if you are on a budget is the magazine cover disk. Although much of the material on these disks is designed to advertise products to you, there are some which contain useful PD and Shareware as well as original programs and programs which, although a few years old, still stand up very well and are worth having.

Definitions

There are two fundamental types of free software available for the PC. These are the definitions so you know what you are dealing with when ordering and it is important, especially when purchasing Shareware, to follow the etiquette.

Public Domain/Freeware

This software carries the copyright of the author. The author has given their permission for you to freely copy the software and pass it on to other users as long as:

- No files that it contains are deleted or changed.
- No files are added.

Further wishes of the author may be contained in a text file and these should be adhered to. If you wish to use or change any part of a public domain program it best to write to the author and ask for permission. If no address is contained within the program, make sure that you give the original author credit.

Shareware

The standard rules of Shareware are:

- You may freely distribute copies of the software to other users.
- You have a 30 day trial period to evaluate the software.
- If, after this time limit, you are still using the software or intend to use it in the future then you must register with the author and pay any registration fee due. You are breaking the law if you fail to do so.
- If you do not intend registering the software then you must delete it from your floppy/hard disk.

So now you know where you stand. You may well find more conditions within the program itself or in a help/text file. This is increasingly the case as Shareware is more and more used as a legitimate method of software distribution. I haven't heard of any Shareware millionaires yet but you never know, the time may come.

There are other wares in the market, such as Licenceware, but these don't come free or on trial but rather you have to pay up front as with any other commercial product.

How to Get Shareware

From this point on I'm going to concentrate on Shareware. However, the rules here apply equally the same for PD software although it is not as readily available as Shareware.

There are a number of easy ways of getting hold of Shareware software:

- By copying colleagues' disks.
- By sending off to a Shareware distributor or library.
- From magazine disks.
- From a bulletin board via the telephone.
- At PC exhibitions and shows.

Copying from friends and colleagues is the quickest and cheapest way of obtaining material. Unlike normal commercial software, for which passing between parties is illegal, you are positively encouraged to copy them. Shareware authors desire the widest possible distribution, as this increases the number of people who may possibly register.

Choosing Shareware is a matter of scouring the magazine adverts or sending off to the libraries for their sampler or library disk, possibly for a nominal fee. Many magazines have Shareware columns where current and updated material is reviewed to help you make your choice – these are worth watching out for. This disk you get may contain some actual Shareware programs or it may be packed with lists of programs. The more ambitious catalogue disks have quite sophisticated presentations and the most useful have full descriptions of the programs. Your aim, as far as possible, is to find out what you are buying – for instance is it a program that works under Windows? Does it work under my version of Windows? Does it need special hardware? Does it run under MS-DOS? Each disk in the catalogue (or advert) has an identification number which you use when ordering so note down the numbers of any disks that interest you.

Watch out for duplication of material because some libraries compile their own collections of utilities, pictures etc, which are taken from existing disks in the catalogue. If you are dealing with more than one library then this becomes more difficult to check. Most libraries don't do a pick and mix service so you have to buy the disk with 20 printer programs on it because it's got the one you want even though you will immediately delete the other 19 because you've already got them.

A lot of Shareware comes from the USA and Europe as well as the UK but nearly all of it is available though UK libraries. Disk magazines – magazines which come on floppy disk or CD quite often carry Shareware items but be careful because it is often mixed in with copyright material which you cannot copy.

Shareware distributors come in all shapes and sizes, from hobbyists doing it for fun, to professional firms with large and detailed catalogues. Naturally, a professional firm employing staff and printing catalogues will have more overheads, so you might expect to pay a little more per disk for the material. Costs range from about £1.50 to £10 per disk, although virtually all the distributors at the higher price bracket reduce the unit price if you order several disks at once. In practice, the cost of blank media plus duplication is usually the smaller part of the distributors' overheads, the larger part being staff to fulfil orders and answer telephone calls, handle enquiries and advertising and printing.

PC Beginners First Steps

There is, incidentally, no law preventing anyone actually making a profit from Shareware distribution, but natural competition has brought the charges to a very fair level. Some distributors have a club system, whereby as a member, you obtain better prices.

Demos and Free Applications

Another large and popular past-time is looking at Demo Disks. The most popular forms are PD and include pictures, music and sampled sounds. The demo is a completely new art form unique to computers and is the creation of an individual programmer or group of programmers to show off their skills through pushing the PC's sound and graphics to their limits. A basic demo involves a long text message moving across the screen with multicolored effects, Star Trek type backgrounds and loud music.

A different type of demo is the commercial demo which is often distributed on the cover disk of a national magazine. This will normally take one of two forms. The first provides you with what is virtually all the program bar a few fundamental features – for example, the ability to Save or Print. These are also normally time limited to 30 days. At the end of this you can, if you so wish, apply to purchase the full product and sometimes at a special discount as part of a reader offer negotiated by the magazine.

The second type of freebie is that you get the whole full-blooded program. You can then send off for the manual for a nominal charge – perhaps £15. This still normally represents very good value as the original product might have cost £100 or more. However, this type of promotion normally happens at about the time the company is bringing out a new version of the software – they then have your name and address and they can offer you the upgrade at a charge. If you want it you take it and both parties are happy – otherwise you still have the earlier version.

Using It

Shareware and PD software is often distributed in a compressed format so you may have to run a decompressor utility before you can use it. This is especially the case if you are buying on floppy disk – if you have a CD-ROM drive then you might find this a more convenient medium and a much better value one.

Although it's cheap, it's still annoying if a floppy disk corrupts during this process, so take a copy beforehand. When decompressed you can take the programs that you really need and put them onto your working disks by copying them your hard disk. If there's an option to decompress onto another disk then choose this. Copying the compressed program to another disk and then trying to decompress it may not work because the distribution disk contains the decompression utility required.

Registration

Once you have ploughed through and tried and tested the Shareware you will probably have decided to purchase some of it. This is done by registering the software. Details of how to do this will normally be supplied with the product as a text file on the disk which you can either read on screen or print out. However, it normally involves you either paying the fee to the Shareware house who distributed the software (who then pass it onto the author) or sending it direct to the author. Costs here vary but whatever it is it won't hurt your pocket and will be a fraction of similar commercial products (perhaps £10-£50).

Once you have registered there are often many extras – for instance you will often get a new update of the program if one is available and in many cases a printed manual. You will also be in direct contact with the author who might also be able to offer a help service should you experience problems. All-in-all it's very worthwhile registering and remember Shareware is a software distribution system which works on a principle of honour. As such registration is a matter of trust – no-one is going to know if you don't register. However, if you are serious about a particular shareware program, you are likely to want the full documentation and extras that are available, so there is a natural incentive to register. Indeed the products are often so good that you want to register to receive future updates.

Payment is not the problem. Most of the authors will accept Access and Visa card payments, or have European agents. International Money Orders and Eurocheques are readily available for a small charge at your local bank.

If you think that putting some new software on your PC is simply a matter of handing over the credit card you're wrong. You need time and space as you'll find out here!

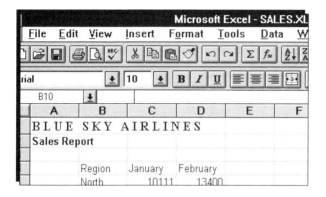

There comes a time in every PC user's career when he or she decides to buy new software. We'll examine the types of software you might require in Chapter 28. However, in this chapter we'll take a brief look at some factors you need to take into account before you take the plunge. This is important because software can cost and cost big – so you'll want to spend your money wisely.

In addition to this we'll also look at the thorny question of removing existing software from your hard disk. Windows software tends to be very large and occupy copious amounts of hard disk space. Removing what you don't need or don't use can increase the performance of your PC and has the advantage of giving you more space to use.

Installing Windows Programs

The vast majority of Windows programs now require to be installed onto your hard disk before you can run them and they are supplied on a floppy disks or, more increasingly now, a CD.

You can't just copy the files across from the master disks or CD. For one thing, it's common for the original installation files to be compressed. Software developers use special software to shrink files to the (more or less) irreducible minimum – this is called *compression*. This allows much more data to be written to the disks, thereby saving on production costs and – to some extent – installation time, but it also means that you need to run a separate installation routine to decompress the files onto your hard disk. The installation routine for Microsoft Windows itself does this. Installation programs tend to have a lot of additional functions, too. For instance, the installation routines for some programs actually construct the main program file on-the-fly, during installation.

Additionally, most also examine your hard disk setup to determine whether, or on what basis, installation can proceed. A (very) few installers amend your computer setup invisibly by writing a distinctive code into the boot track (the section of your hard disk which initiates loading of the operating system, normally DOS); this rather sneaky tactic is designed to prevent illicit copying. This used to be fairly common but is now, thankfully, rare.

Planning

So you must install programs before you can use them (the only exceptions to this are a small but steadily diminishing number of DOS programs which you can run from the original floppy). In view of this, a certain amount of planning is essential before you install Windows applications. The first, and obvious, step is to examine the floppy disks or CD from which the program is to be installed. Many Windows programs come on several floppy disks (and therefore take up a lot of hard disk space when installed).

For instance, Microsoft's Word 6 for Windows comes on nine 1.4 Mb floppy disks. Given that the files on the disk are highly compressed, this means that a full Word installation can occupy in excess of 24 Mb of hard disk space!

Some programs have explanatory files on the original master disks, often called README.TXT or README.1ST. A specific example: CorelDRAW! 5, has README.WRI, in Windows Write format, on its installation CD. Before you run the installation program itself (see 'Starting Installation' later), run Notepad or Windows Write and load up any available explanatory file. Search for a section on installation (for how to do this, see the chapters on Notepad and Write).

PC Beginners First Steps

README files on master disks are put there after (sometimes, long after) the manual(s) were produced, which means that they're your best source of up to date installation information. If there aren't any, however, refer to the installation section of the main manual, or to the separate installation booklet. Often, it will be called 'Getting Started', or something similar. Read the relevant section before you begin installation. In particular, you should look for:

1. Details of any external programs with which there are known incompatibilities (most often found in the README file)

2. A statement of how much hard disk space is required for the installed program

3. Details of how much RAM (Random Access Memory) is required to run the program acceptably, and how much is needed to run it well (there will be a surprising gap)

4. Details of the minimum display or monitor required (usually EGA)

Once you've verified that your PC meets the minimum requirements, you're almost ready to proceed with the installation. Before you do so, a few general tips:

1. Ensure that no other programs are currently running. Many installation routines have a tendency to balk if other programs are operational in the background during installation – usually the problem is specific to particular programs. As a safeguard, most modern installation programs are set up to detect incompatible programs automatically before installation begins. They will then advise you to close down installation, close the offending program and re-start installation.

2. If you're installing from floppy disks, use File Manager to copy them before you begin installing. Install from the copies. There's nothing more annoying than finding that one of your master disks has become unusable and not having a working duplicate.

3. Read the details about installation options in the README file or manual. This will give you a good idea of the decisions you'll have to take once installation is under way. See 'Installation Options' later.

Installation Options

The number of Windows programs available is now vast and increasing all the time. It's therefore impossible to provide guidelines which are more than generalised. However, the following should be useful.

Most Windows programs of any size now offer at least three installation options:

- Typical installation
- Complete/Custom installation
- Laptop/Minimum installation

The wording, of course, varies. The essence, however, is fundamentally similar. Choose Typical Installation if you want to be faced with the fewest decisions; what you get is an installation which, though entirely adequate, is geared to the relative novice. A Typical Installation installs the most common program components you need to use the product effectively and for the purpose it was designed. It would probably leave out the more advanced features and those that have a very specialist nature. This is quite a good option to choose because you can always come back and install any other items you need later on without too much trouble.

Complete/Custom Installation installs everything unless you manually deselect components which aren't required (for example, you can opt to install a Spelling Checker but not the Thesaurus). Laptop/Minimum Installation installs the absolute minimum. Choose this option if hard disk space is very limited.

Modern installation routines warn you if you attempt to install a program to a hard disk which has insufficient space.

Starting Installation

Having made sure that no other programs are currently running, pull down the File menu in Program Manager and choose Run. Or pull down the File menu within File Manager and click on Run. Either method produces the Run dialogue.

PC Beginners First Steps

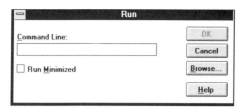

In many cases, the installation program is SETUP.EXE. Sometimes, it's INSTALL.EXE. Occasionally, there will be other variants – this is especially the case now with larger applications that are designed to run from CDs. In these cases you'll need to refer to the documentation as already mentioned. The advantage of running an application from CD is that the installation doesn't have to copy so many files onto your hard disk. The disadvantages are that there is a reduction in operating speed because CD drives have slower access times than hard disks and you have to keep the CD in the CD disk drive while you run the installed program

More and more programs, especially the more unusual examples, provide this CD-based option. Many companies now specialise in putting out programs which are based entirely on CD.

If more than one likely installation file is present on the floppy disk or CD, you need to find out which option is valid for a given program. Normally, this is easy. Often, the disk label itself will tell you (Microsoft's often do). If not, the README file or Installation booklet will. If all else fails, click on Browse in the Run dialogue.

The Browse dialogue searches for program files on the specified drive. Click on the arrow to the right of the Drive field and select the appropriate floppy drive (usually A: or B:). Highlight the relevant program file in the File Name list and click on OK. Back in the Run dialogue, click on OK to begin installation.

From now on, follow the instructions offered by the installation screens. Most have HELP buttons you can click on for context-sensitive assistance. If not, try pressing F1 anyway: often help will be available even if the designers haven't included a specific route to it.

Duration

How long will installation take? There's a lot of diversity. Some Windows programs install in a minute or two. Others can take at least an hour of your time. Most programs fall somewhere in between these two extremes. A factor in this is the speed of your PC's internal chip. Faster machines process information more rapidly. A reasonable average would be in the region of 20-30 minutes for a sizeable program.

If you install programs from CD, however, expect the above times to be drastically reduced.

There is a growing trend for software manufacturers to set their price structures so that versions of their programs which are supplied on CD are cheaper. Corel Corporation are a prime example: CorelDRAW! 5's CD version is less than the floppy disk version by roughly the cost of an acceptable CD-ROM drive. The reason? To encourage you to buy a CD drive with the money you save.

It is well worth buying and installing a CD drive if you can: for one thing, it makes it so much easier and quicker to install programs. See the chapter on Multimedia in this book and also the sister publication to this title *PC Multimedia First Steps*.

What if it Goes Wrong?

What happens and what do you do if your installation of a program goes wrong? Thankfully, this happens a lot less than it used to. It shouldn't happen at all if you've closed down all other programs before beginning the installation process. If something does go wrong, the most likely result is that Windows will 'crash' (ie, freeze and accept no more instructions). Usually if this happens pressing keys has no effect. The exception is the following combination:

CTRL-ALT-DELETE

Use this now; it produces a special message. There are two options. You can press any key to return to Windows, in the (unlikely) hope that whatever is wrong will resolve itself, or you can press the combination again to restart your computer. When your PC has restarted successfully *(rebooted)*, load Windows in the normal way but don't re-run the installation process which caused the problem in the first place.

You need to consult any README file and/or the manual to determine what caused the crash. Usually, there will be suggested 'work-rounds'. For example, you may be instructed to re-run SETUP.EXE, or whatever the installation program is called, with a specific 'switch' (a switch is just a special command after the main instruction). An example of this is Windows itself. Some hardware configurations can cause spurious installation difficulties. As a result, you're advised to try starting installation with:

```
SETUP.EXE /I
```

which turns off Setup's automatic hardware detection, if you experience any problems.

Causes of installation difficulties? Excluding an incompatibility with another program, which you should have avoided, probably the most likely cause is a conflict with your video card. Or there may be a conflict with a third-party desktop or program manager (such as Norton Desktop).

Whatever the cause, the README file or installation booklet should help you resolve it. Failing this, you can only contact the software manufacturer for more up to date assistance.

Installing DOS Programs

One major advantage of Microsoft Windows is that software developers have a common standard to meet. The result is that installation programs are fairly uniform. This isn't the case with DOS installation programs, where pretty much anything goes. This makes it especially difficult to provide guidelines which are consistent and comprehensive. However, in a general sense many of the points made in the 'Installing Windows Programs' section will also apply. The following more specific notes should help, too.

Some DOS applications can, even nowadays, be run from the original floppy disk (to some extent, at least) without any need to expand the program files, still less copy files to the hard disk. However, there are normally limitations if you run these programs fully from the master disk, and they are, in any case, becoming fewer all the time.

Another difference between DOS and Windows installations is the fact that, since DOS programs occupy much less space on disk (typically, 2-4 Mb. as opposed to 30-40), their installation routines often make provision for installation to several floppy disks. This means that users on relatively low-powered machines can run the program by inserting floppy disks in sequence.

In general though, unless you have a very specific reason for doing so you should try to stick with Windows based applications as DOS is becoming less common and will be dropped by Microsoft altogether.

Removing Software

It's sometimes necessary to uninstall Windows software. Often, this isn't as simple as it sounds. There are a variety of reasons for this. Aside from creating a dedicated directory complete with optional sub-directories, the installation routines for Windows programs may also:

1. Amend your DOS configuration files, CONFIG.SYS and AUTOEXEC.BAT
2. Amend your Windows configuration files – WIN.INI and SYSTEM.INI – and specialist application INI files.
3. Create program group and program icons
4. Copy program files (often with a .DLL extension) to your /WINDOWS and/or /WINDOWS/SYSTEM directories

The first of these options only happens occasionally. An example. Some programs, if it isn't already operational, will amend your AUTOEXEC.BAT file so that a special DOS program called SHARE.EXE runs automatically each time you start your PC. The remaining three options however, are pretty standard.

Deleting the dedicated directory and any associated sub-directories is easy and simply performed using File Manager). For instance, if you wanted to uninstall Word 6 for Windows, you'd delete the WINWORD directory (together with 7 sub-directories) on your hard disk. SHARE.EXE can normally be left running with impunity. And deleting superfluous program group and program icons is straightforward – see Chapter 25 for how to do this.

So far, so good. The problem comes in in detecting which of the many program files in your /WINDOWS or /WINDOWS/SYSTEM directories relate to the program you want to uninstall. Their titles tend to be helpful only to the original programmers.

Often, it's impossible to say with any certainty to which programs the .DLL files relate. Deleting them is therefore a kind of Russian Roulette. The result is that, as you become more experienced with

Microsoft Windows and buy and use more and more programs, your /WINDOWS and /WINDOWS/SYSTEM directories become the repository for increasing number of program files, some of which will be superfluous.

What can you do about this? There are four potential solutions:

1. Some programs have separate Uninstall options which you can access by running the original installation program again. This Uninstaller knows where all the relevant files are located, and can therefore delete them with impunity.

2. Some programs, while lacking (presumably out of reluctance to admit that anyone could want to delete them) a distinct Uninstall icon, do have uninstall options hidden within the basic Setup routine.

   During installation, many programs place a special copy of the original SETUP.EXE (or whatever) file on your hard disk which you can run by double-clicking appropriate SETUP icon within the applications program group.

3. Some programs provide lists of associated files. You can use these as signposts when you come to manually delete the files. These are often detailed are often in associated README.TXT files.

4. Finally, there are now some commercial programs available which are written for the job of uninstalling programs.

If options 1-3 are inapplicable, and you don't have an Uninstaller, you can only delete the dedicated directory and sub-directories. You could, additionally, delete the references to the relevant program in your WIN.INI and SYSTEM.INI files, but this would have virtually no effect on available hard disk space or system performance.

28 The Home Office

No this isn't about some Government department, it's about what you can do in the privacy of your own house to run your business. Oh, and that business may just be your own household – let's face it there's enough paperwork!

*O*ne of the most popular uses of the PC is as the basis of an office at home. Now this doesn't mean that you're going to bring work home all the time if at all – but you run your home as a going concern and your family is your main business. You fund it by providing sales and those sales (your job or jobs) provide the income you need. Of course it may also be that you are self employed or run a business from your home. In all these cases you will find the use of the PC an invaluable aid to write letters, produce budgets and keep track of materials and sources etc.

This chapter deals with the type of software you might need – it isn't a review or a guide to a particular suite of software but it poses all the questions you need to ask yourself before parting with your cash. Your requirements will be different from those of other users.

Software is like your video recorder. If you are like me then you have a video machine that does everything and includes a place for the kitchen sink. However, most of the time you will use it for playing hired tapes or for time shifting a programme. Software is like that – you use 10% of the features 99% of the time. Is it worth paying the extra cash for the bells and whistles? Your decision and it might be the difference between a £500 commercial offering and a £50 shareware registration fee.

But a home office isn't just about software it's also about the hardware you have – is it up to the job? Only you can decide that and you should refer back to the chapters covering hardware and also printers to help you decide. This chapter concentrates on the software.

The Big Three

What are the software tools which you will need to enable your PC to deliver productivity? The big three applications on any computer are wordprocessor, spreadsheet and database. The wordprocessor and database are often linked through the merging of name and address data and form letters. Writing to your MP has never been easier. The spreadsheet is a less well-understood tool but is becoming equally significant, linking its numerical data with graphics presentation software so that the less numerate can also understand what's going on. In addition to these other important software includes accounting and desktop publishing (DTP).

One important thing to remember – and it's so obvious you might forget it – is to ensure your program is written to run under Windows and the version of Windows you are using.

Wordprocessing

More than any other application software, the wordprocessor has to be the most versatile of all programs. On the PC a wordprocessor can be expected to perform the main tasks of editing text but also to spell check it, incorporate graphics and produce an attractive layout on the available printer.

Hopefully a wordprocessor will take advantage of the advanced features of Windows such as mouse click control, different fonts and printing via the available drivers. It should also conform to the standard methods laid down for working with applications, such as mouse clicking and dialogue boxes.

PC Beginners First Steps

What's in a Word?

Wordprocessing means different things to different people. You could use a wordprocessor for preparing an essay or article which needs to have page numbering and the same heading on all the pages. You could prepare a letter to customers telling them about a new product, ready for personalising by merging the letter with individual names and addresses from a database. You could have a picture and twenty carefully devised words to create an effective advert for your next rave! Different tasks, different requirements.

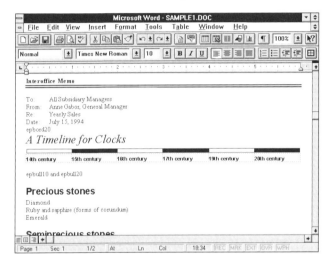

The way a page is printed from your wordprocessor is fundamental to how you go about any wordy job and you have two choices: character based printing and graphics printing.

Depending on your printer, graphics printing can be a joy or a liability. Graphics, including fancy fonts, take time to form up in memory ready for printing so a single page of text can take some considerable time and each page has to be formed in the same way. When a printer has no on-board memory to hold the page image, ie when it's not a laser printer, second and subsequent copies of a page also take the same long form-up times. A long document can take a very long time to print. A single A4 letter in 12 point can take up to five minutes on a modern dot-matrix.

If you are doing big mailmerges with hundreds of letters you aren't going to wait around for outline font printing unless you've got a laser printer. On the other hand, the combination of graphics fonts and the new bubblejet printers is very attractive. But if you are looking for a really professional result then the best software available with a PostScript laser is what you'll need.

Editing and Checking

Using a wordprocessor can be great fun. Whatever the standard of your typing, you can always get it right eventually! Firstly you can edit the text by selecting it and choosing to delete it, move it elsewhere in the document or copy it.

Moving text is also known as cut and paste. The cut action removes the text and stores it out of sight temporarily until you position the cursor where you want the text to go and paste it in. The term comes from the design industry where, before computers, the artist would use a knife to cut out the paper with the text on and glue it into position somewhere else.

To make sure everything is correct you can spell check your document. The spellchecker is a program which works together with a couple of dictionaries which are held on disk. It's pretty stupid really and only knows words which are in these dictionaries. Therefore the bigger the dictionary, generally the better at spelling it is. Each word in your document is checked to see if it is identical to a dictionary entry. If the word is not found, you are informed and you can change it if is obviously wrong, look up a similar word if it is an awkward spelling or teach the spellchecker the word because it is correct but not in the dictionary.

There are even grammar checkers which will analyse your sentence structures, word frequencies and style. These are fun but not much use unless you are a professional writer and then they just make you feel small! Search and replace is another useful standard tool on a wordprocessor. For instance I've just written this piece using "wp" to denote wordprocessor, that's two characters I had to type every time I wanted wordprocessor in my text, not 13. I've then chosen to search for "wp" and to replace it with "wordprocessor" and I chose to do so selectively so that I could keep the "wp"s above.

Search and replace can be used to do individual versions of a form letter. For instance you can send the same letter to all your relations at Christmas but search and replace their names! There is another way that wordprocessors let you do this and it is called merging. Merging involves writing just one letter and typing a special code into the letter where you want the merged data to appear. When you print, the data is imported automatically to where the code appears and the letter is printed. When finished, the next item of data is merged and another letter printed and so on. Very productive these wordprocessors!

Presentation

As well as the words themselves, a wordprocessor also handles the layout of your document. Presentation these days is very important and the wordprocessor takes care of your margins around the page, the number of lines and the text styles such as bold and italic. You can define a header and a footer which is text which appears above or below the main body of the document, sometimes a page number or heading which is required on every printed sheet. You can also set the justification of the text, which effects its appearance and readability.

Wordprocessors also handle the setting up of a document so that the printed version is correctly positioned and looks the part. The more up to date wordprocessors will show you what your document looks like while you are editing it but some have a print preview which displays a screen version of what will appear from your printer. This is especially useful for checking page breaks so that you don't find yourself printing over the perforations in the printer paper.

Databases

All applications handle data of some sort or another but databases have the job of organising it for a useful life in your computer. Useful is the operative word here. However much data you can collect, it's not much use if you can't access it in the way you wish. And so the first piece of advice when considering data handling on the PC is to think through how you will want to access any information you gather. The sort of questions that are relevant are: how quickly do I want the information? In what form do I want it, printed as a report, graphically on screen, ready for export to another application? How much data can I store on my system? Do I want to protect my data from inspection by others? Much of these will depend on your own requirements – your data might range from a simple electronic address book to a list of parts for an engineering job.

Make a checklist if you are at all serious about this operation and then check it against the available software. As an example consider the requirements of a picture editor/librarian on a football magazine. He or she gets in plenty of pictures, it's what to do with them that counts. A record card can be designed to hold information about each photograph, containing a field to indicate the type of photo – action shot, team photo, football ground, player portrait etc. A field is a box on a record card into which information can be typed or imported. Further details would include the name of the football club concerned and the league they play in. An important field would allow a flag to be set to indicate whether the photograph has been used and, if so, when. A flag is a computer term for a yes (the flag is set) or a no (the flag remains unset). The field containing the information about when the picture was used will be a date field and a field to show how much was paid for the photo will be a money field. These field types are used to make it possible for the database to calculate, for instance, money spent on photographs between one date and another.

Once the record card has been designed, information can be typed into many cards and all of them saved as part of a single data file. You might want to keep track of a collection, to keep club records, to track subscriptions or print name and address labels. All can be carried out by a database. Some other programs are specialist databases hiding behind another name, eg a family tree program.

What Do You Need?

Keep in mind that the first question to ask is: what do you need from a database?

As an absolute minimum every computer database needs a card index structure, which is the ability to store data in tabular form, with fields (possibly of different lengths and data types) representing columns in the table and each row in the table representing a separate record. Sound like Cardfile?

An important feature is the size of table that can be manipulated, how many fields, how big can they be and how many records can be contained in the data file before it becomes too large for the program to manipulate it. Also important is the number of data types available. Are you going to enter large numbers? Do you need precision mathematics? For historical or payroll purposes you may need a date type from which you can calculate periods of time.

To get information to and from the tabular file you need a form. Conventionally this is designed like an index card, with the various fields positioned conveniently and helpful text labels and headings added so that the information is meaningful. You should be able to design a form on screen without too much difficulty.

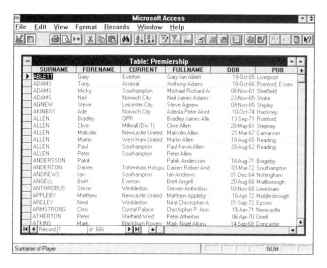

More important you should be able to flick from one record to another (often achieved with video style controls), scroll around the card form or move to second and subsequent pages if it is too large for the screen, edit and add data.

Searching and Reporting

A screen form usually displays only a single record although very sophisticated programs offer scroll zones in the form, which can display multiple values.

To examine several records or produce a selected set of records requires a report generator. This can select a specified subset of records, sort them into a given order and format the fields to suit a document across the page, in columns, in separate blocks for mailing labels or as continuous paragraphs. You should be able to add titles, subheadings, headers and footers and page numbers and to intersperse the records with text. You should be able to print reports out directly or to export them to another program such as a wordprocessor.

The available range of mathematical and allied functions (statistics, financial analysis, trigonometry, etc) determines whether or not you can perform more complex calculations. For answering immediate queries you'll need a quick search facility, preferably with wildcards for finding entries you are not quite sure of. Wildcards are characters which can represent any other character as far as the program is concerned and learning to use them is a skill in itself. For example you might use:

*burgh

for a town ending in burgh but you aren't sure which one, and:

Ma???

to find all the names starting with Ma

Logical operators, which are ways of comparing one item of data with another, are also useful to find entries based on other factors, for instance:

Martin AND designer

to find all the Martins who are designers and:

Martin AND (designer OR postman)

to find all the Martins who are designers or postmen. The above examples would have different information in different fields.

Relationships

You may also need to relate one file on your database to another: given three files: of video tape, shelf number and orders, can you look up a given order, find which video tape is required and which shelf it's on for picking?

If a customer rings with a complaint, can you find them in your database, extract all related orders, identify the goods they contained, then find who supplied you with them? At the very minimum you may want to have two database forms open at the same time so that you can compare and exchange data between them. The ability to relate one data table to another is what differentiates a relational database from a mere card index. Relational databases are more complex and more expensive by far.

One advantage of related data files is that, having created a database structure, you need not worry if it later proves inadequate. Instead of rebuilding the structure you simply create a secondary table which you join to the original one.

Collecting Data

What a database, however good, won't do for you is type in the data. But data is available in forms other than on paper. You can collect data from bulletin boards and from the TV teletext services via teletext adapters and there are even services that can sell you data pre-entered in a format for the PC.

There's a mass of data already around on disk too, from bits and pieces, such as UK telephone dialling codes, to massive files such as the complete Bible on PC format disks or CD disks.

Once you've got text then a database can import the files in various formats but it'll need to know what text should go into what field and when to stop filling one record and to begin filling the next. This it does by recognising markers in the text. A common file format is comma separated value (CSV) which marks fields with commas and the records with a return character. As it meets a comma, the importing utility moves to the next field and reads more text before encountering another comma. On encountering a return character it closes the record and moves onto the next, filling each field again in turn.

Spreadsheets

The third program in the holy trinity of computing is the spreadsheet. Because we've all only got quite small monitors or TV screens to view the data inside our computers, it is difficult to describe a spreadsheet. In the same way that a platform game has many different screens, above, below and side by side each other but only one screen is displayed at a time, so the spreadsheet is a large sheet of ruled paper which can only be viewed one screenful at a time.

The blank sheet can usually be as big as you'll ever need, certainly big enough for home accounts, a work schedule, even a small business accounts. The sheet is ruled vertically and horizontally. The squares enclosed by these lines are known as cells and it is in the cell that you place information, either text or numbers.

Manipulating Numbers

A spreadsheet is a program designed to manipulate numbers. You input a number by activating a cell and typing the number into it. Usually you type into a line editor at the top of the screen and then enter the number into the cell at the cursor by pressing Return. As well as a number, you can type in a formula for instance:

4+3

will appear in the cell as 7 and:

4*3

will appear in the cell as 12.

The * (asterisk) is usually used to mean multiply in spreadsheet formulae. The value in the cell is then available for use in another formula, for example:

C3-5

where C3 means the cell which appears three in from the left – A, B, C – and three down from the top. This is the grid reference method which is used to refer to any cell in the sheet. When a large sheet gets to Z, it continues with AA, AB, AC etc.

As well as numbers and formulae typed in by yourself, the spreadsheet program works with its own built-in functions. The number and type of functions depends on the program you are using. The simplest involve adding up columns and rows of cells. For instance:

sum(A1:A50)

might add all the values in the first 50 cells in column A. The way in which you enter these functions (the syntax) depends on the program but spreadsheets adopt broadly similar approaches. More complex functions might calculate the percentage APR on a loan, the depreciation of a piece of equipment or the time it will take for a chemical process to occur.

Typical categories of functions are time, trigonometry, maths, financial, database look-up, statistics and finally control functions which glue together the others with ifs, thens and gotos, just like a programming language.

Text Labels and Reports

Text entries are more important than you might think in a numbers program because they are needed to describe and document the numbers, whose meaning you would soon forget if they were left on their own, unlabelled. Imagine a colleague at work finding a sheet full of figures on your desk. The figures wouldn't mean much unless there were quite detailed descriptions. Text can also be used to present the numbers in the spreadsheet in the form of a report. Some spreadsheets are better at this than others and it may be that you will export (save in a standard format) the numbers for use in a wordprocessor.

Spreadsheets are also commonly used for project management and for testing out "what if" scenarios in business.

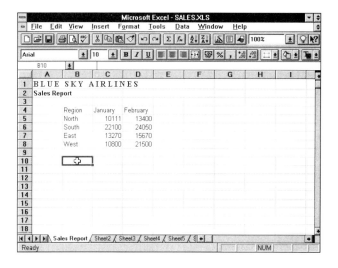

Integrated Software

If you are likely to require all three of the trio then it is well worth considering an integrated package. This basically means that the software has been written so that the three products can dovetail together and virtually act as one. This makes transferring and exchanging data between them simple and effective. Columns of data with results can be copied from the spreadsheet and added straight into the report in the wordprocessor. Information about a product can be taken from a database in similar fashion. What is more with the modern range of products it is also possible to create active links between the two so that as the data in one application changes the alterations are automatically reflected in the other. Microsoft Office is particularly useful in this respect.

Desktop Publishing

Desktop Publishing is included here because all businesses need to produce literature. If you produce office stationery, proposals and letters to clients then I refer you back to wordprocessors. The DTP programs for the PC are for real design and print purposes. Product catalogues, newsletters and advertisements are among the documents which can benefit from the typographical and design features offered by these programs.

One of the most important considerations when embarking on DTP on your PC is to match your hardware to the program you choose to use. There is no point using a fully featured program which redraws slowly on your screen or which doesn't support your printer. DTP involves working with page sizes that are bigger than your monitor can display so the program will need to redisplay the screen quickly to make it usable. Large or lengthy documents require extra hardware such as multisync monitors and hard drives so take it easy. For a modest newsletter you can get away with a basic hardware setup.

When using DTP you are creating a document which will have to be printed. Is it going to be in black and white (and grey) or in colour? How many copies are going to be printed and how? Is a colour print-out going to form an original for colour photocopying (hundreds) or are you going to use a typesetting bureau to prepare the document for commercial printing (thousands). If the answer to any of these questions is Yes then it must also support PostScript printing – does your printer?

More Figure Work

Accounts programs are naturally considered boring and unusable but they are sometimes a necessity. Not to take advantage of your PC if you are self-employed or run a small business is to waste an opportunity. An accounts program may be a daunting prospect but it is usually less so than a flexible tool such as a spreadsheet because the accounts program is set up ready to use, with forms on the screen to fill in and lists and categories already defined. You enter the data about your business and the program sorts out the figures. A printer is an important add-on for this kind of work because someone, eg your accountant or bank manager, will want to see the results and he may not have a PC!

Databases can also be used for running business affairs such as stock control, if they can handle the right type of data such as dates and money values. Home accounts is a different matter and can be handled by a simple spreadsheet model or check out the public domain libraries for a suitable program. Home banking is possible using your computer as a terminal but not all banks offer this. For a small business wishing to keep track of funds, it has considerable potential. For this reason programs such as Sage and Quicken have been in the best seller lists for a long time.

The fact of the matter is – any office function can now be performed on the PC and generally at a relatively low cost. Happy home computing!

29 Virus Menace

Computing can make you feel very tired – but don't feel the strain. That's a viral strain I'm on about – if you're tired (or even well awake) and things are going haywire for no apparent reason it might be that you've caught a virus.

With the computer has come the computer virus, and with the PC has come its own specific viruses. A virus is something that your PC can catch and, just like the multitude of viruses that you and I might fall foul of, their severity ranges from plain annoying to software lethal. They are a very real threat but provided you follow a set of basic principles you can avoid catching them. And if you do fall foul of one or more, you should be able to find a cure – which is more than can be said for the Common Cold!

The word virus derives from the 16th Century Latin for slime or a poisonous liquid. In modern terms, it belongs to any of a vast group of sub-microscopic DNA nuclei dressed in a protein coat (take my word for it!). These simple organisms are one of the most basic forms of life, only capable of living and reproducing within the cells of other animals and plants. Many are pathogenic, creating symptoms ranging from mild discomfort to death. Computer viruses ape their protein-coated namesakes very closely. So closely in fact, some pundits have speculated that they constitute a simple form of life. Indeed a recommended read is the Trojan by James Follett which exploits this topic in a thoroughly enjoyable novel. However, that is a philosophical avenue best explored during a late night discussion over several glasses of an intoxicating substance.

As I have already said computer viruses are like human viruses, in the sense that they infest the host and pass themselves on through a point of contact. On the computer the point of contact is disks, so when a disk comes from an external source (a friend, a magazine, a PD house, a software company), there is a risk that there will be a virus on that disk. Having said that, magazines, PD houses and software companies are very, very conscientious about their disk production and it is extremely unlikely that you will catch a virus in this way – though the possibility remains. Dodgy sources are the more likely culprits. A disk from a friend of a friend's brother's sister is a dodgy source!

What Is It?

A computer virus is nothing more than a computer program written by a devious mind. The problem is that the devious mind of the writer can be quite brilliant and you may not know you have a virus for some time. Some are time coded so that they openly appear at certain times or dates – Friday 13th for example – and some might only appear when you try to do a certain task – such as print a file or copy a file. Some are mega awful and go as far as erasing the contents of your disk. Some are simply mischievous and say they are wiping your hard disk only to return a few minutes later saying fooled you!

Of course this can all lead to an unmitigated state of paranoia. Your PC might well crash for a host of other reasons – out of memory, a poor piece of software, incompatibility – not for just playing host.

Once you put the infected disk into your computer, the virus spreads into the system, in other words the virus program jumps ship and copies itself into your machine and then will almost certainly infect any other disk you put into the computer by copying itself onto it. If you pass any disks onto your friends then they put the virus on their machine, and so it goes on. Do not underestimate the potential of viruses. Some can even survive soft-resets so that you need to turn your PC off before you can sort things out. So you need to be vigilant. Every time you get a disk, check it using one of the many virus detection programs available and detailed later on.

Viral Types

There are several distinct strains of computer virus – variants of the way the infection (replication) program is written and each has a name. As can be seen from this, viruses are ostensibly simple to write, which is why there are so many around:

Limpet

Often called the bootblock or boot sector virus. The term Limpet derives from the way the virus adheres to a certain part of infected disks. These are the simplest viruses of them all – and usually the easiest to catch.

Doppleganger

This works by replacing the code of an original program completely with its own. Next it moves the code of the original program somewhere else on the same disk and gives it a blank name. When the original program is called, the virus runs (doing its dirty work) then exits by launching the real program.

Trojan Horse

Sometimes just called a Trojan they get their name from the Greek fable of the Trojan (or wooden) horse. As the story goes, the Greeks bluffed the Trojans by leaving a wooden horse outside the gates of Troy. The Trojans dragged the horse inside, and at nightfall the Greeks hidden inside the beast crept in under cover of darkness and murdered the Trojans in their beds.

In the same way, a Trojan virus is a computer program, usually placed in the Public Domain (see Chapter 26) not by Greeks, but still with a very sharp sting in its belly. The reason why real Trojans are rare is because they take some skill to implement. The only way they will spread is if the program hiding the stinger is useful enough for lots of people to use. And once the Trojan is uncovered, everyone stops using it. For this reason Trojans use a time-bomb technique whereby they only activate after they have been used a set number of times or, sometimes, on a certain date.

Parasite or Linkvirus

Also called Worm, Zombie, Lycanthrope, and Vampire. These bloodsuckers are the scourge of utility software and generally a real pain in the AUTOEXEC.BAT. Like real vampires they duplicate by attaching

PC Beginners First Steps

> *Insider Guide #41 – Making a Canary System disk*
>
> A Canary disk is one that you can use to boot your PC knowing full well that it cannot be contaminated by a virus.
>
>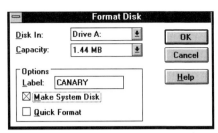
>
> To do this you must first format a new disk. When the Format dialogue box is displayed ensure that the Make System Disk option is checked. Name the disk Canary.
>
> You will also need to copy across onto the Canary disk a virus detection and disinfecting program. There are many of these available and many as Shareware.
>
> Once you have completed the disk run your anti-virus software to ensure that your Canary disk is free from infection.
>
> Remove the disk and write protect the disk using the Write Protect notch. Finally carefully label the disk and keep it handy but safe.

themselves to other programs. The problem with parasites is they turn genuine software into Trojans by locking onto their code and transferring across onto all and sundry. Like Trojans, Parasites are tricky to implement so there are less around. Unlike the Limpets, they multiply between disks and across directories at an alarming rate. Also they're very tricky to catch without software specifically designed for the purpose – Peter Cushing never had it this tough.

Prevention

It only takes one slip to catch a virus because once the little beggars get onto a disk, they spread very quickly. This checklist covers the most important points.

1. No known virus can get past the write protection notch on a floppy disk. Never insert a write enabled disk unless something has to write to it. Better still keep data disks separate from program disks.

2. Keep a Canary disk. This is a freshly formatted system disk that can be used to boot the PC. Ideally you should also have some form of disinfecting software on it as well.

3. Get protected. Either purchase one of the many anti-virus and backup devices available and check your hard disk regularly.
4. Never, ever, use pirated software. This includes games, utilities and applications – it's a sure-fire way to catch a virus.

Finally

If you currently swap files with other people and even if you move files between the home and office and vice versa always take precautions. What ever anti-virus software you obtain get to know how to use it probably and use it regularly.

30 Multimedia

Whether you are a seasoned computer user or not, you must have heard the term multimedia. It's many things to many people and seems to be the way ahead.

If you haven't heard about it – how was the trip to Mars?

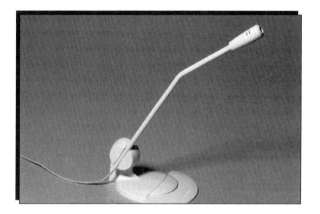

*M*ultimedia is being heralded as the means by which computers will lure the next generation of user by putting television like pictures on our screens, CD like sounds in our speakers and interactive control of masses of information in electronic books. If you have brought your PC system since the start of 1994 then you can't help to have been influenced in your purchase by this aspect of PC computing.

The theory is that the current systems are the early stages of this technology and that, like desktop publishing in the 1980s, multimedia will develop into a fully fledged industry that scarcely existed before the computer made it possible. Another theory says that multimedia is a nothing word, covering a host of possibilities but without real meaning or a real use.

Multimedia is indeed a coverall term which takes in the combined use of different media, usually delivered by different technologies, tied together by a computer. Resources, such as music, sound effects, speech, video footage, photographs, text and graphics are combined to deliver a message to the user. As the processing power, speed and storage capacity of the PC computers increases, the more these resources are turned into

PC Beginners First Steps

digital form, the less need there is for separate and specialist hardware to deliver them.

Thus we have a situation where software can playback a movie in a screen window with sound to match, with no hardware strings attached. Where hardware is playing a part is in the increasingly sophisticated way that we can capture the real world through digitisers, samplers and scanners. Perhaps one day all multimedia will be software based but for the moment even the PC needs the injection of specialised extras on add-on cards to capture and manipulate video footage. The combination of video and computer graphics – including text fonts – is one such area. Grabbing images into a framestore for digital processing is another. For a full and total description on how to upgrade and use these features on your PC see 'PC Multimedia Insider Guide' also published by Bruce Smith Books and of which details can be found in Appendix A.

Sometimes the forced combination of different technologies doesn't come off but the amalgam of PC and compact disc has resulted in a brand new home-entertainment medium called *Edutainment*. Indeed there is even specialist hardware being manufactured for just this purpose of which the Philips CD-I system is perhaps the best known.

The basis of this revolution is the CD-ROM and drive (shown above) as it alone can provide the storage capacity for all these media. In the development of the CD-ROM, developers have created a whole which is greater than the sum of its parts.

Books On CD

Undoubtedly the most common use of the CD on the PC is as a learning system. On one disk it is possible to have a shelf full of books, with its ability to combine text, pictures and even sound it has become the ideal basis for interactive encyclopedias and books on topic areas. With the ability to move almost instantly from one page to any other users can quickly look up and almost experience wherever their whim takes them.

For instance a CD on Space would allow the reader to find out about the Apollo moon landings, examine pictures taken on the surface, experience Neil Armstrong's first steps on the moon in video form and hear those famous words: "That's one small step for man, one giant leap for mankind."

PhotoCD

PhotoCD is a format that has been developed by Kodak in which you can have your own photographs transferred onto a CD disk which you can play back on your PC whenever you want. You take your film in as usual but, instead of prints or slides, you take home a CD with digital versions of your pictures ready to be played back on your television. There are programs to catalogue and manage your photo collections. You could create a complete CD on a particular person – a child perhaps that charts their life and loves – and then use this in combination with a database to provide a total experience.

Movies on CD

We're all familiar with the CD to play music and the use of video tapes to play film but now the two are being combined to put movies on CD. This normally needs the addition of a special bit of hardware called a MPEG card. Full motion video means digital video with each frame of the video being drawn on the screen in quick succession, resulting in something fast enough to fool the human eye, just like a real film or video. This is all supplied on a board which plugs into the back of your PC which can access and process the information from the movie CD at incredibly fast rates to allow you to see the film at full speed and full size. However, unlike a video tape which can hold the full film, movie CDs are normally supplied on two CDs.

Authoring Programs

With the PC's ability to handle and store pictures, sound and text a wide range of specialist applications – called authoring programs – have been developed that allow users to create their own multimedia presentations that can run from hard disk. Indeed if you are happy with your results you can have it written to a CD-ROM for a comparatively small charge.

What you need from a multimedia authoring program is the ability to use any of the standard resources of your PC, for instance pictures, sounds and fancy fonts, to create a presentation. A number of programs are now available that provide tools to present these resources in a controlled manner by positioning them, timing their use and the way that one screen moves on to another. It keeps track of the resources and can generate a stand-alone program to run the presentation.

Many of these programs control events through a script language which can be edited or written from scratch as well as being generated automatically by the program when you use its graphics tools. An authoring program like these requires absolutely no programming skills to use since the author interacts directly with the objects on screen. Therefore the emphasis is on design and planning rather than programming.

More!

Of course I have only just touched the surface of this wonderful topic. If you want to know more then I really do suggest that you get a copy of the book mentioned earlier and detailed in Appendix A.

If you have enjoyed your *PC Beginners Insider Guide* then you might like to delve into other books in the BSB library.

*B*ruce Smith Books have been producing quality personal computer publications which are both comprehensive and easy to read since the turn of the decade. Our PC titles are written by some of the best known names in the marvellous world of personal computing. Below you will find details of all our currently available books for the PC owner.

Brief details of these books are given below. If you would like a free copy of our catalogue and to be placed on our mailing list then 'phone or write to the address below. As a small, dedicated publisher, we are able to respond flexibly to customers' needs so if you would like to see a book from us on a subject that we don't cover then please call to let us know. Equally if you have an area of expertise in a personal computer related field and would like to produce a book then talk to us about becoming an author. Usually a letter of introduction with a brief synopsis of the book and the proposed contents list is enough.

Our mailing list is used exclusively to inform readers of forthcoming Bruce Smith Books publications along with special introductory offers.

**Bruce Smith Books,
PO Box 382, St. Albans, Herts, AL2 3JD
Telephone: (01923) 894355 – Fax: (01923) 894366**

Note that we offer a 24-hour telephone answer system so that you can place your order direct by 'phone at a time to suit yourself. When ordering by 'phone please:

- Speak clearly and slowly
- Leave your name and full address and contact phone number
- Give your credit card number and expiry date
- Spell out any unusual names

* Note that we do not charge for P&P in the UK and endeavour to dispatch all books within 24-hours.

PC Beginners First Steps

All our books can be obtained via your local bookshops – Dillons, Waterstones, Thins, Websters, etc, including WH Smith who keep a stock of some of our titles – just enquire at their counter. You'll also find appropriate titles in PC World, HMV, Virgin and other computer outlets. If you wish to order via your local High Street bookshop you will need to supply the book name, author, publisher, price, ISBN and the name of our distributors who are *Computer Bookshops Limited* of Birmingham, UK.

Bookshops and computer retail outlets can call Computer Bookshops Customer Services Department for advice and best terms on 0121-706-1188.

We endeavour to ensure that all our personal computer books are up to date and pertinent to all current releases of the relevant software.

Europe and Overseas Orders

Please add £3 per book (Europe) or £6 per book (outside Europe) to cover postage and packing. Pay by sterling cheque or by Access, Visa or Mastercard. Post, fax or 'phone your order to us.

QBASIC Beginners

QBASIC comes free with your computer so why not use it? QBASIC Beginners is a complete tutorial for novice users and will show you aspects of computing you'd normally need to leave to the experts.

The book contains carefully researched chapters on planning, structuring and entering QBASIC commands and programs, presenting information on screen, working with disks, handling data, creating graphics and sound and converting other programs to QBASIC.

QBASIC Beginners Tutorial by Ian Sinclair
ISBN: 1-873308-21-3, £17.95, 416 pages.

QBASIC A to Z Reference

QBASIC A to Z Reference is the companion volume to QBASIC Beginners. It complements the beginners tutorial and is designed to sit beside your PC to act as a reference and advisor while you are programming in QBASIC. Each command is given with a run-down on type, typical syntax, action, options, arguments and restrictions. Associated commands are given and QBASIC code examples listed with full explanation and ideas on further use.

Programmers converting from another version of BASIC will find QBASIC very accommodating and this guide advises on commands which are included for compatibility and for potentially useful alternatives which are available.

QBASIC A to Z Reference by Ian Sinclair
ISBN: 1-873308-22-1, price £17.95, 352 pages.

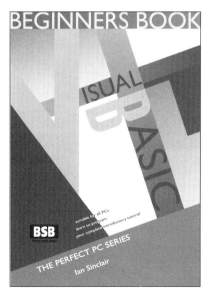

Visual Basic Beginners

Visual Basic has captured the imagination of programmers looking for an accessible and productive way to create their code. This tutorial guide starts from scratch with how to use the tools provided by Visual Basic with lots of shortcuts and hints, and a few warnings about limitations.

The advent of Windows 3.0 and 3.1 has made previous versions of BASIC look decidedly old-fashioned. By following this book step by step you will be able to create programs that make full use of all that is built into Windows, without the need to write vast numbers of lines of code.

You'll find plenty of help and lots of worked examples to practice with and use as the basis of your own programs. If you are starting out with Visual Basic or coming to it new from another version then this Beginners guide is an essential purchase. If you have some Visual Basic experience then you'll appreciate the hints and tips, advice on design and structure and the later chapters on more advanced programming.

Visual Basic Beginners by Ian Sinclair
ISBN: 1-873308-23-X, £17.95, 320 pages.

Secrets of Frontier Elite
Secrets of Sim City 2000

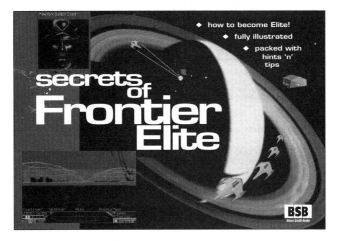

Secrets of Frontier Elite is the handbook for any budding pilot who wants to become Elite, or just incredibly rich! For Elite aficionados, this inspiring book is full of strategy and tactics, hints and secret tips.

Secrets of Frontier Elite by Tony Dillon
ISBN: 1-873308-39-6, £9.95, 128 pages.

Secrets of Sim City 2000 covers all eventualities in this classic city simulation game. From the smallest one-horse town to the largest megacity, it is packed with hints, tips and strategies.

Secrets of Sim City 2000 by Andrew Banner
ISBN: 1-873308-47-7, £9.95, 128 pages.

Quicken for Windows Insider Guide

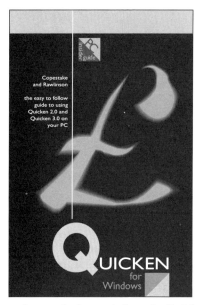

This Insider Guide teaches how to use Quicken and relates the features of the computer program to real-life financial scenarios which everyone will recognise. The book covers the UK software version of Quicken – versions 2.0 and 3.0 – and is written by PC journalist Stephen Copestake, well-known for his magazine columns on applications software.

The book's insider guides are step-by-step graphical guides to the essential actions which need to be regularly carried out in Quicken. They are the book equivalent of watching over someone's shoulder to see how it's done. The reader can go through the procedures again and again and refer back to them if they get stuck while using the software. These guides are clearly presented and separate from the main text.

The PC user of Quicken is also confronted by financial terminology and processes which are new. The book solves this problem through an introductory chapter on setting up computer-based accounts by Graham Rawlinson, a leading chartered accountant in this field. Graham also provides chapter by chapter recommendations and advice from the financial point of view, to balance the tutorial material on using the program.

All in all, this is a must have book for the Quicken user confronted with a powerful program but many question marks over its proper and effective use. The Quicken Insider Guide provides the answers.

Quicken for Windows Insider Guide
by Stephen Copestake and Graham Rawlinson
ISBN: 1-873308-32-9, 224 pages, £12.95

Books Available Early 1995

UK Comms

Two comms-hardened authors provide complete explanations of how to use national and international communication services with your PC from a totally UK point of view, using approved software and equipment available for the UK. They analyse common scenarios in the business and home use of PCs and provide solutions for a wide range of communications requirements – from looking up sports results and real-time updates on the stockmarket to gathering mail from a desktop computer when on the move.

All major computer platforms are covered with emphasis on IBM PC compatibles and popular software for Windows, including Windows for Workgroups remote networking, mail and fax, with many hints and tips for beginners and experienced users alike backed up by picture-based tutorials and handy script program examples.

UK Comms by John Kennedy and Darren Irvine
ISBN: 1-873308-40-X, £TBA, pages TBA.

Bruce Smith Books

Established in 1990 as a publisher dedicated to producing computer-related books in the UK, Bruce Smith Books has expanded its range at a steady pace, gaining a reputation for technical excellence in an easy to read style which makes learning a pleasure.

Our authors are experienced writers and journalists working full-time in the personal computer field, ensuring that they are in touch with you, the reader, and the requirements you have expressed. Our editors have long experience of designing and presenting technical material in an accessible manner. If you have any criticisms or suggestions, they will be very welcome.

Also available from Bruce Smith Books is a range of titles for the Amiga range of personal computers. If you use an Amiga for work or play then we have some interesting reading for you. We also publish for other formats. Please 'phone or send for a catalogue for your computer make.

New publications and their contents are subject to change without notice. E&OE.

.	140
.CRD	216
.DOC files	176
.TXT files	176
286	100
386	100
486	100
9-pin	105

A

A:	75
A: drive	75
A: window, File Manager	76
Accessories	121
Accessories window	31, 81
accounts programs	276
active window	30
adding a card, Cardfile	215
airbursh tool, Paintbrush	232
alarm, calendar	127
aligning text, Write	184
ALT key	44
Amiga	16
analogue clock	121
ANY key	44
applets	81
application	20
application icons	47
applications, running at startup	241
appointment, calendar	127
Arial font	180
arrow, up	34
association, file	65
authoring, CD programs	288
Autoexec.bat	248

B

backups	71
basic terms	16
bitmap graphics	229
board	18, 104
board, printed circuit	104
booting-up	21
box	16
box, dialogue	40
bubblejet printer	153
buffers, printer	159
buttons, mouse	30
byte	74

C

C:	54
C: drive	75
C: prompt	22
C: window	76
cache memory	104
Calculator	121
Calculator functions	124, 126
Calculator, scientific	122
Calculator, standard	122
Calendar	127
Calendar appointment	127
Calendar, alarm	127
Calendar, customisng	129
Calendar, day view	127
Calendar, month view	
Calendar, printing	130
canary disk	282
CAPS LOCK key	44
Card view, Cardfile	219
Cardfile, adding a new card	215
Cardfile, adding pictures	219
Cardfile, Card view	219
Cardfile, cards	214
Cardfile, deleting	217
Cardfile, editing	217
Cardfile, Find	217
Cardfile, Go To	218
Cardfile, index	215
Cardfile, Index Line	215
Cardfile, List view	219
Cardfile, merging	220
Cardfile, saving	216
Cardfile, status	214
Cascade, windows	116
CD	19, 107, 133
CD, authoring programs	288

CD, movies	287
CD, Photo	287
CD-ROM	107, 286
changing drives	136
chip	100
clicking	34
Clipboard DOS	204
Clipboard, cut and paste	200
Clipboard, load	204
Clipboard, save	204
Clipboard, viewing	203
clock	121
clock speed	100
Close function	46
Color Control Panel	88, 91
colour formats, Paintbrush	228
COM1:	105
compatible	15
computer components	16
computers, types	16
Confirm File Replace, dialogue box	77
Confirm Mouse, Operation dialogue box	66
Congtrol menu Restore	40
context sesnitive help	93
control blink rate	88
Control menu box	31
Control menus	39, 40
Control Panel	82
Control Panel icon	81
Control Panel, Color	88, 91
Control Panel, Date and Time	82
Control panel, Desktop	85
Control Panel, International	83
Control panel, Keyboard	90
Control Panel, Mouse	90
converting files, Write	177
COPY	138
Copy dialogue box	69
copy files	69
copying files, across disks	77
Country setting	83
creating directory	65, 67
CTRL key	42, 44
CTRL-ALT-DELETE	260
Currency format	83
current directory	56
cursor, Write	50
curves, Paintbrush	226
custom display	22
customisng calenader	128
cut and paste, clipboard	200
cut and paste, Notepad	147
Cut and Paste, Write	190
cutout operations, Paintbrush	231

D

daisywheel printer	153
database, Cardfile	213
databases	269
databases, collecting data	273
databases, relationships	272
databases, reporting	271
databases, searches	271
Date & Time	82
Date format	83
Date format	83
date, Notepad	148
decimal tabs	183
DEL	138
Delete dialogue box	69
deleting files	69
deleting, Cardfile	217
demos	253
design, desktop	81
desktop	29, 34
Desktop Control Panel	85
desktop design	81
desktop PC	101
desktop publishing	193
desktop publishing	276
desktop, housekeeping	239
Desktop, setting patterm	85
desktop, wallpapering	86
dialogue box\	40
dialogue box Write Font	180
dialogue box, Confirm File Replace	77
dialogue box, Confirm Mouse Operation	66
dialogue box, Copy	69

dialogue box, Delete 69
dialogue box,
   Error Selecting Drive..........64,65
dialogue box, Format 75
dialogue box, Formatting Disk ...75
dialogue box,
   New program Option 111
dialogue box,
   Program Group Properties....111
dialogue box,
   Program Item Properties.......112
dialogue box, Record Macro 244
dialogue box, Rename................68
dialogue box, Task List 115
dialogue box, TrueType 197
digital clock 121
DIR...132
DIR listing 135
directories..................................54
directories, changing 133
directories, nesting....................54
directories, renaming................68
directoriues, navigating 67
directory, creating.................65,67
directory, current 56
directory, listing 132
directory, parent........................56
directory, path...........................55
directory, root............................56
directory,
   selecting in File Manager 65
directory, sibling 56
directory, sub.............................55
disk drive icons..........................64
disk format 72
disk, canary 282
disk, double density 72
disk, formatted 72
disk, high density 72
disk, Label 75
disks 49
display adaptor card 104
DOS...131
DOS programs, installing 261
DOS, changing directories........133
DOS, changing drives 136

DOS, Clipboard 204
DOS, COPY...............................138
DOS, DEL 138
DOS, Font Selection.................142
DOS, Format 137
DOS, RENAME 138
DOS, wildcards.........................140
dot-matrix printer 153
double density disks..................72
double-clicking..........................30
drag and drop.............................66
dragging......................................30
drawing area, Paintbrush 222
drawing programs....................221
drawing, Paintbrush 225
drive A..75
drive C..75
drive, CD-ROM 286
driver, printers 152
drives, changing 136
DTP 193, 276

E

editing paterns...........................87
editing, Cardfile.......................217
edutainment 286
ENTER key................................24
erasers, Paintbrush 234
Error Selecting Drive
   dialogue box........................64,65
ESC keys 43
Exit, Windows 46
extension, filename 52

F

F keys 43
F1 94
features, in wordprocessors......267
file association...........................65
File Manager....................61, 62,63
File Manager, A: window............76
File Manager, C: window............76
File Manager,
   Create Directory.................66,67

File Manager, Format 75
File Manager,
　　selecting directory 65
File Manager, selections 64
File Manager, tiling 119
file moving 66
file naming 77,79
file, renaming 68
filename 52
filename extension 52
filename path 55
filename shortcuts.....................62
files 49
files, copy 69
files, deleting 69
files, incompatible 53
files, multiple copy 79
files, multiple move 79
files, orgainsing 65
files, README 257
files, replacing existing 77
filing cabinets 53
filing system, hierachical 57
Find and Replace, Write 188
Find, Cardfile...........................217
floppy disk 17,18, 71
floppy disk drives 106
floppy disk, storage space 72
floppy disk,
　　write protection notch..........71
flying windows 86
font, Arial 180
font, styles 180
fonts 193
fonts, adding 197
fonts, printer 195
fonts, resolution 194
fonts, screen 195
fonts, size 194
fonts, style 194
fonts, TrueType 194
fonts, type 194
fonts, VGA 196
Format dialogue box 75
format disk 72
FORMAT, command 137

Format, File Manager option 74
formatted disks..........................72
Formatting Disk, dialogue box ...75
free software 249
freehand lines, Paintbrush 227
freeware 250
function keys 43

G

game, Minesweeper 207, 211
game, Solitaire 207, 208
Games 207
Go To, Cardfile 218
graphical user interface 25
graphics, bitmaps 229
graphics, transfer 202
groups, switching 114
GUI 25

H

hard disk 18, 54, 101
hard disk drives 62, 106
hardware 16, 17, 99
headers and footers,
　　Write 189, 190
heat 16
Help 93
Help menu 94
Help, Search 96
hierachical filing system 57
high density disk 72
highlight....................................30
home office 265
hot key 42, 45
hourglass 46
housekeeping, desktop.............239

I

I/O card 104
IBM 15
icon tidy 241
icon types 47
icon, Accessories 31

icon, Control Panel 81
icon, File Manager 62
icon, hourglass 46
icon, Main 28,29
icon, minimized 33
icon, MS-DOS Prompt 47
icon, programs 47
icon, Startup 241
icons 26, 39
icons, applications 47
icons, desktop 29
icons, disk drive 64
icons, opening 30
icons, rearranging 239
incompatible 16
incompatible file 53
indents 183
initialisation 21
ink catridges 159
inkjet printer 153
installation, options 258
installing DOS programs 261
instillation, planning 256
integrated software 275
internal fan 18
International 83
items, menu 32

J

jargon 14
job priorities, Print Manager 168

K

k 74
key functions, Notepad 144
key functions, Write 175
key, ALT 44
key, ANY 44
key, CAPS LOCK 44
key, CTRL 44
key, ENTER 24
key, ESC 43
key, Function 43
key, hot 42, 45

key, RETURN 24
key, RETURN 44
key, SHIFT 44
keyboard 16,17, 43, 97
Keyboard Control Panel 90
Keyboard layout 83
keyboard, Paintbrush 224
keyboard, special keys 43
kilobyte 74

L

Label disk 75
laser printers 154
library, PD 249
library, shareware 249
line spacing, Write 185
Linesize, Paintbrush 222
List Seperator option 83
List view, Cardfile 219
LPT1: 106
LQ printers 156

M

Macintosh 16
macro recorder 243
Main 28,29
main computer 16
make, directory 138
mat, mouse 27
Maximized multiple windows 41
Maximizing 33
Mb 74
Measurment setting 83
megabyte 74
memory, cache 104
memory, Clipboard 199
memory, Random Access 101
memory, Read Only 101
memory, video 105
menu items 32
menu, Control 31, 39, 40
menu, Help 94
menu, Window 114
menus 26, 39

menus, Program Manager 32
merging databases 220
Mhz 100
micro chip 100
microprocessor..........................100
Minesweeper 207, 211
Minesweeper, rules 212
minimized icon 33
Minimizing 33
MKDIR..138
monitor 17
motherboard..............................104
mouse...........................16,17,18, 26
mouse buttons 30
Mouse Control Panel...................90
mouse mat 27
mouse, double-clicking 30
Move window 41
movies on CD 287
moving, files 66
MS-DOS......................................131
MS-DOS Prompt 141
MS-DOS Prompt icon 47
multimedia 285
multiple file copy 79
multiple file move 78
multitasking...............................109

N

nesting directories.......................54
New Program Option
  dialogue box...........................111
new software, adding................255
Next function..............................45
NLQ printers 156
Notepad 143
Notepad, cut and paste 147
Notepad, inserting date 148
Notepad, key functions 144
Notepad, opening files 149
Notepad, printing......................169
Notepad, printing from.............150
Notepad, saving files.................150
Notepad, text search 148
Notepad, text selection 145

Notepad, word wrap 146
number base conversion,
  calculator 125
Numbers format.........................83
numeric keypad..........................43

O

object orientated programs 230
office, at home..........................265
Online Help 93
online, printer...........................162
opening files, Write 177
options, Solitaire......................210
order, selcting tile 117
overhead projection film 158

P

page description language 157
paint programs 221
Paintbrush 202, 221
Paintbrush, airbrush tool 232
Paintbrush, colour formats 228
Paintbrush, curves 226
Paintbrush, cutout operations..231
Paintbrush, drawing 225
Paintbrush, drawing area 222
Paintbrush, erasers 234
Paintbrush, freehand lines 227
Paintbrush, keyboard................224
Paintbrush, palettes 221
Paintbrush, pick and scissors ...230
Paintbrush, pixel editing...........233
Paintbrush, polygons 226
Paintbrush, roller tool...............233
Paintbrush, saving....................227
Paintbrush, text tools................236
Paintbrush, Undo 227
Paintbrush, using 224
Paintbrush, wallpaper...............237
palettes, Paintbrush 221
paper types 158
parallel socket...........................105
parent directory..........................56
password.....................................89

path 55
patterns, editing 87
PC 15
PC speed 100
PC, desktop 101
PC, portable 17
PC, switching on 21
PC, tower 101
PCB 104
PD library 249
Pentium 101
peripheral 19
Personal Computer 15
PhotoCD....................................287
pick and scissors, Paintbrush ...230
pictures, Cardfile......................219
piracy, software 20
pixel editing, Paintbrush...........233
point sizes 180
pointer 26
pointer, clicking 34
points 194
polygons, Paintbrush 226
port, parallel 105
port, serial.................................105
portable PC 17
PostScript 156, 157
prevention, virus 282
print emphasis,
   Print Manager........................168
Print Manager 156, 161
Print Manager operations.........164
Print Manager setup 165
Print Manager,
   adding printers 167
Print Manager, job priorities....168
Print Manager
   print emphasis 168
print tasks 164
printed circuit board.................104
printer..16
printer buffers 159
printer driver 152
printer fonts..............................195
printer ribbons 158
printer types 153

printer, bubblejet 153
printer, dasiywheel...................153
printer, dot-matrix 153
printer, inkjet............................153
printer, laser 154
printer, online...........................162
printer, paper 158
Printers 151
printers, adding new 167
printing documents, Write 191
printing, Notepad 150
processor chip 100
program 19
Program Group Properties
   dialogue box..........................111
program group, deleting...........240
program groups........................110
program groups, switching.......114
program icons 47
Program Item Properties
   dialogue box..........................112
Program Manager 22,28,29, 109
Program Manager menus 32
programs, accounts...................276
programs, DOS installing 261
programs, object orientated 230
programs, running at startup ...241
prompt 22
prompt, DOS 132
Prompt, MS-DOS 141
public domain 249, 250

R

RAM 101
RAM, video 105
Random Access Memory 101
re-booting 260
Read Only Memory 101
README files 257
rearrnaging icons 239
Record Macro dialogue box 244
recorder, macro........................243
registration, shareware.............254
removing software 262
RENAME 138

Rename dialogue box 68
renaming directories 68
renaming files 68
resizing 35
resolution, fonts 194
Restore, Control menu 40
RETURN key 24, 44
ribbons, printer 158
roller tool, Paintbrush 233
ROM 101
ROM, CD 107
root directory 56
Ruler, Write 186
rules, Minesweeper 212

S

safety net 46
Save As, Write 56, 59
Save Settings on Exit 82
Save, Write 52, 56, 59
saving files, Write 176
saving work 52
saving, Paintbrush 227
scientific calculator 122
scoring, Solitaire 209
screen 16, 17
screen blanking 28
screen burn in 28
screen fonts 195
screen savers 28, 86
scroll bars 35, 36
scrolling 35, 36
Search, Help 96
search, Notepad 148
select 30
selecting windows 42
serial socket 105
Setting pattern, desktop 85
settings, Clock 121
setup, Print Manager 165
shareware 249
shareware, how to get it 251
shareware, registration 254
SHIFT key 44
shortcuts, filename 62

sibling directory 56
Size 41
slider 37
software 19, 22, 249
software installtion, time 259
software license 20
software versions 246
software, accounts 276
software, adding new 255
software, free 249
software, inetgrated 275
software, plainng 256
software, removing 262
Solitaire 207, 208
Solitaire options 210
Solitaire, scoring 209
speed, PC 100
spreadsheets 273
spreadsheets, numbers 274
spreadsheets, text labels 275
Startup icon 241
storage space, floppy disk 72
sub directories 64
sub-directory 55
switching groups 114

T

tabs, decimal 183
Task List 115
text search, Notepad 148
text selection, Notepad 145
text tool, Paintbrush 236
text, DOS-Windows transfer 205
text, highlight 200
text, transfer 200
text, Windows-DOS transfer 205
tidy, icons 241
tile order 117
Tile, windows 116
tiling, File Manager 119
Time format 83
time, installing software 259
time, Notepad 148
tittel bar 30
toner caridges 160

PC Beginners First Steps

Toolbox, Paintbrush..................222
tower PC 100
transferring text 200, 202
TrueType dialogue box 197
TrueType fonts 194
types, printer 153

U

Undo, Paintbrush 227
up arrow 34

V

Vegas, scoring 209
venting slots................................18
versions, software 246
VGA fonts 196
video RAM 105
viewing the clipboard...............203
virus, prevention 282
viruses..279

W

wallpaper, Paintbrush...............237
wallpaper, tiling 86
walppapering, desktop...............86
wildcards 139
WIMP..26
Window menu 114
window, Accessories 31, 81
window, active............................30
window, dialogue box 40
window, File Manager 62,63
window, highlight 30
window, Main......................28,29
window, move 41
window, multiple maximized.....41
window, resizing 35, 36
window, scroll bars 35, 36
window, Size 41
window, slider 37
window, title bar 30
window, Write 51, 173
Windows.....................................22

Windows 25,26
Windows, through keyboard 97
windows, Cascade 116
windows, dragging 30
Windows, Exit 46
windows, flying! 86
Windows, from DOS 46
windows, Maximizing 33
windows, Minimizing 33
windows, program groups 110
windows, select 30
windows, selecting 42
windows, Tile 116
word wrap, Notepad 146
wordprocessor 19
wordprocessor, simple 143
wordprocessor, Write.................49
wordprocessors, features 267
WRI 53
Write 49
Write Font dialogue box 180
Write functions.........................171
write protection notch, disks......71
Write, aligning text 184
Write, converting files..............177
Write, Cut and Paste 190
Write, deleting characters...........51
Write, editing text 174
Write, Find and Replace 188
Write, fonts 180
Write,
  headers and footers 189, 190
Write, key functions 175
Write, line spacing 185
Write, opening files 177
Write, printing documents 191
Write, Ruler 186
Write, Save 52, 56, 59
Write, Save As 56, 59
Write, saving files.....................176
Write, tabbing text 182
Write, use of text 174
Write, window 51, 173

Don't miss out on these other great titles from *Bruce Smith Books*.

PC Multimedia Insider Guide

Your multimedia PC can work with CD-ROM, soundcard and fax. This *Insider Guide* is the key to getting the full value from your multimedia investment with the beginner in mind.

In manageable chapters, with useful illustrations and photographs, learn how to:

- Choose the appropriate equipment for your multimedia PC.
- Safely install CD-ROM, soundcard and fax.
- Record and play music, video and sound effects in Windows.
- Connect to telephone-based services around the world.
- Send and receive faxes and mail.

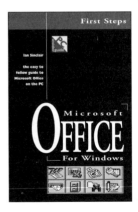

Microsoft Office First Steps Insider Guide

The best introduction available on the best selling software package. As with all our *Insider Guides*, this book assumes no prior knowledge of the software and shows you how to get going without simply regurgitating the manuals.

In manageable chapters you'll be shown how to quickly and easily:

- Identify and install the features you really need.
- Customise the suite of programs to your own personal taste.
- Create simple documents and templates in all applications.
- Use MSOffice programs together for maximum effect.